3000 800028 71839
St. Louis Community College

F.V.

D1319842

 St. Louis Community College

Forest Park
Florissant Valley
Meramec

Instructional Resources
St. Louis, Missouri

GAYLORD

SPEECHES

THE OXFORD MARK TWAIN

Shelley Fisher Fishkin, Editor

The Celebrated Jumping Frog of Calaveras County, and Other Sketches
Introduction: Roy Blount Jr.
Afterword: Richard Bucci

The Innocents Abroad
Introduction: Mordecai Richler
Afterword: David E. E. Sloane

Roughing It
Introduction: George Plimpton
Afterword: Henry B. Wonham

The Gilded Age
Introduction: Ward Just
Afterword: Gregg Camfield

Sketches, New and Old
Introduction: Lee Smith
Afterword: Sherwood Cummings

The Adventures of Tom Sawyer
Introduction: E. L. Doctorow
Afterword: Albert E. Stone

A Tramp Abroad
Introduction: Russell Banks
Afterword: James S. Leonard

The Prince and the Pauper
> *Introduction: Judith Martin*
> *Afterword: Everett Emerson*

Life on the Mississippi
> *Introduction: Willie Morris*
> *Afterword: Lawrence Howe*

Adventures of Huckleberry Finn
> *Introduction: Toni Morrison*
> *Afterword: Victor A. Doyno*

A Connecticut Yankee in King Arthur's Court
> *Introduction: Kurt Vonnegut, Jr.*
> *Afterword: Louis J. Budd*

Merry Tales
> *Introduction: Anne Bernays*
> *Afterword: Forrest G. Robinson*

The American Claimant
> *Introduction: Bobbie Ann Mason*
> *Afterword: Peter Messent*

The £1,000,000 Bank-Note and Other New Stories
> *Introduction: Malcolm Bradbury*
> *Afterword: James D. Wilson*

Tom Sawyer Abroad
> *Introduction: Nat Hentoff*
> *Afterword: M. Thomas Inge*

The Tragedy of Pudd'nhead Wilson and the Comedy
Those Extraordinary Twins
> *Introduction: Sherley Anne Williams*
> *Afterword: David Lionel Smith*

Speeches

Mark Twain

FOREWORD

SHELLEY FISHER FISHKIN

INTRODUCTION

HAL HOLBROOK

AFTERWORD

DAVID BARROW

New York   Oxford

OXFORD UNIVERSITY PRESS

1996

OXFORD UNIVERSITY PRESS

Oxford   New York

Athens, Auckland, Bangkok, Bogotá, Bombay

Buenos Aires, Calcutta, Cape Town, Dar es Salaam

Delhi, Florence, Hong Kong, Istanbul, Karachi

Kuala Lumpur, Madras, Madrid, Melbourne

Mexico City, Nairobi, Paris, Singapore

Taipei, Tokyo, Toronto

and associated companies in

Berlin, Ibadan

Copyright © 1996 by

Oxford University Press, Inc.

Introduction © 1996 by Hal Holbrook

Afterword © 1996 by David Barrow

Text design by Richard Hendel

Composition: David Thorne

Published by

Oxford University Press, Inc.

198 Madison Avenue, New York,

New York 10016

Oxford is a registered trademark of
Oxford University Press

All rights reserved.

No part of this publication may be
reproduced, stored in a retrieval system, or
transmitted, in any form or means, electronic,
mechanical, photocopying, recording, or
otherwise, without the prior permission of
Oxford University Press.

Library of Congress
Cataloging-in-Publication Data

Twain, Mark, 1835–1910.

[Speeches]

Mark Twain's speeches / by Mark Twain ; with
an introduction by Hal Holbrook; and an afterword
by David Barrow.

p. cm. — (The Oxford Mark Twain)

Originally published: New York:
Harper & Bros., 1910.

Includes bibliographical references.

1. Speeches, addresses, etc., American. I. Title.

II. Series: Twain, Mark, 1835-1910. Works. 1996.

PS1322.S5 1996

815'.4—dc20

96-15217

CIP

ISBN 0-19-510158-8 (trade ed.)

ISBN 0-19-511428-0 (lib. ed.)

ISBN 0-19-509088-8 (trade ed. set)

ISBN 0-19-511345-4 (lib. ed. set)

9 8 7 6 5 4 3 2 1

Printed in the United States of America
on acid-free paper

FRONTISPIECE

Samuel L. Clemens is photographed here in 1907,
three years before his death on April 21, 1910. *Mark
Twain's Speeches* appeared in print during the
summer of 1910. (The Mark Twain House, Hartford,
Connecticut)

CONTENTS

EDITOR'S NOTE

The Oxford Mark Twain consists of twenty-nine volumes of facsimiles of the first American editions of Mark Twain's works, with an editor's foreword, new introductions, afterwords, notes on the texts, and essays on the illustrations in volumes with artwork. The facsimiles have been reproduced from the originals unaltered, except that blank pages in the front and back of the books have been omitted, and any seriously damaged or missing pages have been replaced by pages from other first editions (as indicated in the notes on the texts).

In the foreword, introduction, afterword, and essays on the illustrations, the titles of Mark Twain's works have been capitalized according to modern conventions, as have the names of characters (except where otherwise indicated). In the case of discrepancies between the title of a short story, essay, or sketch as it appears in the original table of contents and as it appears on its own title page, the title page has been followed. The parenthetical numbers in the introduction, afterwords, and illustration essays are page references to the facsimiles.

FOREWORD

Shelley Fisher Fishkin

Samuel Clemens entered the world and left it with Halley's Comet, little dreaming that generations hence Halley's Comet would be less famous than Mark Twain. He has been called the American Cervantes, our Homer, our Tolstoy, our Shakespeare, our Rabelais. Ernest Hemingway maintained that "all modern American literature comes from one book by Mark Twain called *Huckleberry Finn*." President Franklin Delano Roosevelt got the phrase "New Deal" from *A Connecticut Yankee in King Arthur's Court. The Gilded Age* gave an entire era its name. "The future historian of America," wrote George Bernard Shaw to Samuel Clemens, "will find your works as indispensable to him as a French historian finds the political tracts of Voltaire."[1]

There is a Mark Twain Bank in St. Louis, a Mark Twain Diner in Jackson Heights, New York, a Mark Twain Smoke Shop in Lakeland, Florida. There are Mark Twain Elementary Schools in Albuquerque, Dayton, Seattle, and Sioux Falls. Mark Twain's image peers at us from advertisements for Bass Ale (his drink of choice was Scotch), for a gas company in Tennessee, a hotel in the nation's capital, a cemetery in California.

Ubiquitous though his name and image may be, Mark Twain is in no danger of becoming a petrified icon. On the contrary: Mark Twain lives. *Huckleberry Finn* is "the most taught novel, most taught long work, and most taught piece of American literature" in American schools from junior high to the graduate level.[2] Hundreds of Twain impersonators appear in theaters, trade shows, and shopping centers in every region of the country.[3] Scholars publish hundreds of articles as well as books about Twain every year, and he is the subject of daily exchanges on the Internet. A journalist somewhere in the world finds a reason to quote Twain just about every day. Television series such as *Bonanza, Star Trek: The Next Generation*, and *Cheers* broadcast episodes that feature Mark Twain as a character. Hollywood screenwriters regularly produce movies inspired by his works, and writers of mysteries and science fiction continue to weave him into their plots.[4]

A century after the American Revolution sent shock waves throughout Europe, it took Mark Twain to explain to Europeans and to his countrymen alike what that revolution had wrought. He probed the significance of this new land and its new citizens, and identified what it was in the Old World that America abolished and rejected. The founding fathers had thought through the political dimensions of making a new society; Mark Twain took on the challenge of interpreting the social and cultural life of the United States for those outside its borders as well as for those who were living the changes he discerned.

Americans may have constructed a new society in the eighteenth century, but they articulated what they had done in voices that were largely inter-changeable with those of Englishmen until well into the nineteenth century. Mark Twain became the voice of the new land, the leading translator of what and who the "American" was — and, to a large extent, is. Frances Trollope's *Domestic Manners of the Americans,* a best-seller in England, Hector St. John de Crèvecoeur's *Letters from an American Farmer,* and Tocqueville's *Democracy in America* all tried to explain America to Europeans. But Twain did more than that: he allowed European readers to *experience* this strange "new world." And he gave his countrymen the tools to do two things they had not quite had the confidence to do before. He helped them stand before the cultural icons of the Old World unembarrassed, unashamed of America's lack of palaces and shrines, proud of its brash practicality and bold inventiveness, unafraid to reject European models of "civilization" as tainted or corrupt. And he also helped them recognize their own insularity, boorishness, arrogance, or ignorance, and laugh at it — the first step toward transcending it and becoming more "civilized," in the best European sense of the word.

Twain often strikes us as more a creature of our time than of his. He appreciated the importance and the complexity of mass tourism and public relations, fields that would come into their own in the twentieth century but were only fledgling enterprises in the nineteenth. He explored the liberating potential of humor and the dynamics of friendship, parenting, and marriage. He narrowed the gap between "popular" and "high" culture, and he meditated on the enigmas of personal and national identity. Indeed, it would be difficult to find an issue on the horizon today that Twain did not touch on somewhere in his work. Heredity versus environment? Animal rights? The boundaries of gender? The place of black voices in the cultural heritage of the United States? Twain was there.

With startling prescience and characteristic grace and wit, he zeroed in on many of the key challenges — political, social, and technological — that would face his country and the world for the next hundred years: the challenge of race relations in a society founded on both chattel slavery and ideals of equality, and the intractable problem of racism in American life; the potential of new technologies to transform our lives in ways that can be both exhilarating and terrifying — as well as unpredictable; the problem of imperialism and the difficulties entailed in getting rid of it. But he never lost sight of the most basic challenge of all: each man or woman's struggle for integrity in the face of the seductions of power, status, and material things.

Mark Twain's unerring sense of the right word and not its second cousin taught people to pay attention when he spoke, in person or in print. He said things that were smart and things that were wise, and he said them incomparably well. He defined the rhythms of our prose and the contours of our moral map. He saw our best and our worst, our extravagant promise and our stunning failures, our comic foibles and our tragic flaws. Throughout the world he is viewed as the most distinctively American of American authors — and as one of the most universal. He is assigned in classrooms in Naples, Riyadh, Belfast, and Beijing, and has been a major influence on twentieth-century writers from Argentina to Nigeria to Japan. The Oxford Mark Twain celebrates the versatility and vitality of this remarkable writer.

The Oxford Mark Twain reproduces the first American editions of Mark Twain's books published during his lifetime.[5] By encountering Twain's works in their original format — typography, layout, order of contents, and illustrations — readers today can come a few steps closer to the literary artifacts that entranced and excited readers when the books first appeared. Twain approved of and to a greater or lesser degree supervised the publication of all of this material.[6] The Mark Twain House in Hartford, Connecticut, generously loaned us its originals.[7] When more than one copy of a first American edition was available, Robert H. Hirst, general editor of the Mark Twain Project, in cooperation with Marianne Curling, curator of the Mark Twain House (and Jeffrey Kaimowitz, head of Rare Books for the Watkinson Library of Trinity College, Hartford, where the Mark Twain House collection is kept), guided our decision about which one to use.[8] As a set, the volumes also contain more than eighty essays commissioned especially for The Oxford Mark Twain, in which distinguished contributors reassess Twain's achievement as a writer and his place in the cultural conversation that he did so much to shape.

Each volume of The Oxford Mark Twain is introduced by a leading American, Canadian, or British writer who responds to Twain — often in a very personal way — as a fellow writer. Novelists, journalists, humorists, columnists, fabulists, poets, playwrights — these writers tell us what Twain taught them and what in his work continues to speak to them. Reading Twain's books, both famous and obscure, they reflect on the genesis of his art and the characteristics of his style, the themes he illuminated, and the aesthetic strategies he pioneered. Individually and collectively their contributions testify to the place Mark Twain holds in the hearts of readers of all kinds and temperaments.

Scholars whose work has shaped our view of Twain in the academy today have written afterwords to each volume, with suggestions for further reading. Their essays give us a sense of what was going on in Twain's life when he wrote the book at hand, and of how that book fits into his career. They explore how each book reflects and refracts contemporary events, and they show Twain responding to literary and social currents of the day, variously accepting, amplifying, modifying, and challenging prevailing paradigms. Sometimes they argue that works previously dismissed as quirky or eccentric departures actually address themes at the heart of Twain's work from the start. And as they bring new perspectives to Twain's composition strategies in familiar texts, several scholars see experiments in form where others saw only formlessness, method where prior critics saw only madness. In addition to elucidating the work's historical and cultural context, the afterwords provide an overview of responses to each book from its first appearance to the present.

Most of Mark Twain's books involved more than Mark Twain's words: unique illustrations. The parodic visual send-ups of "high culture" that Twain himself drew for *A Tramp Abroad*, the sketch of financial manipulator Jay Gould as a greedy and sadistic "Slave Driver" in *A Connecticut Yankee in King Arthur's Court*, and the memorable drawings of Eve in *Eve's Diary* all helped Twain's books to be sold, read, discussed, and preserved. In their essays for each volume that contains artwork, Beverly R. David and Ray Sapirstein highlight the significance of the sketches, engravings, and photographs in the first American editions of Mark Twain's works, and tell us what is known about the public response to them.

The Oxford Mark Twain invites us to read some relatively neglected works by Twain in the company of some of the most engaging literary figures of our time. Roy Blount Jr., for example, riffs in a deliciously Twain-like manner on "An Item Which the Editor Himself Could Not Understand," which may well rank as one of the least-known pieces Twain ever published. Bobbie Ann Mason celebrates the "mad energy" of Twain's most obscure comic novel, *The American Claimant*, in which the humor "hurtles beyond tall tale into simon-pure absurdity."[9] Garry Wills finds that *Christian Science* "gets us very close to the heart of American culture." Lee Smith reads "Political Economy" as a sharp and funny essay on language. Walter Mosley sees "The Stolen White Elephant," a story "reduced to a series of ridiculous telegrams related by an untrustworthy narrator caught up in an adventure that is as impossible as it is ludicrous," as a stunningly compact and economical satire of a world we still recognize as our own. Anne Bernays returns to "The Private History of a Campaign That Failed" and finds "an antiwar manifesto that is also confession, dramatic monologue, a plea for understanding and absolution, and a romp that gradually turns into atrocity even as we watch." After revisiting Captain Stormfield's heaven, Frederik Pohl finds that there "is no imaginable place more pleasant to spend eternity." Indeed, Pohl writes, "one would almost be willing to die to enter it."

While less familiar works receive fresh attention in The Oxford Mark Twain, new light is cast on the best-known works as well. Judith Martin ("Miss Manners") points out that it is by reading a court etiquette book that Twain's pauper learns how to behave as a proper prince. As important as etiquette may be in the palace, Martin notes, it is even more important in the slums.

> That etiquette is a sorer point with the ruffians in the street than with the proud dignitaries of the prince's court may surprise some readers. As in our own streets, etiquette is always a more volatile subject among those who cannot count on being treated with respect than among those who have the power to command deference.

And taking a fresh look at *Adventures of Huckleberry Finn*, Toni Morrison writes,

> much of the novel's genius lies in its quiescence, the silences that pervade it and give it a porous quality that is by turns brooding and soothing. It lies in . . . the subdued images in which the repetition of a simple word, such as "lonesome," tolls like an evening bell; the moments when nothing is said, when scenes and incidents swell the heart unbearably precisely because unarticulated, and force an act of imagination almost against the will.

Engaging Mark Twain as one writer to another, several contributors to The Oxford Mark Twain offer new insights into the processes by which his books came to be. Russell Banks, for example, reads *A Tramp Abroad* as "an important revision of Twain's incomplete first draft of *Huckleberry Finn*, a second draft, if you will, which in turn made possible the third and final draft." Erica Jong suggests that *1601*, a freewheeling parody of Elizabethan manners and mores, written during the same summer Twain began *Huckleberry Finn*, served as "a warm-up for his creative process" and "primed the pump for other sorts of freedom of expression." And Justin Kaplan suggests that "one of the transcendent figures standing behind and shaping" *Joan of Arc* was Ulysses S. Grant, whose memoirs Twain had recently published, and who, like Joan, had risen unpredictably "from humble and obscure origins" to become a "military genius" endowed with "the gift of command, a natural eloquence, and an equally natural reserve."

As a number of contributors note, Twain was a man ahead of his times. *The Gilded Age* was the first "Washington novel," Ward Just tells us, because "Twain was the first to see the possibilities that had eluded so many others." Commenting on *The Tragedy of Pudd'nhead Wilson,* Sherley Anne Williams observes that "Twain's argument about the power of environment in shaping character runs directly counter to prevailing sentiment where the negro was concerned." Twain's fictional technology, wildly fanciful by the standards of his day, predicts developments we take for granted in ours. DNA cloning, fax machines, and photocopiers are all prefigured, Bobbie Ann Mason tells us, in *The American Claimant.* Cynthia Ozick points out that the "telelectrophonoscope" we meet in "From the 'London Times' of 1904" is suspiciously like what we know as "television." And Malcolm Bradbury suggests that in the "phrenophones" of "Mental Telegraphy" "the Internet was born."

Twain turns out to have been remarkably prescient about political affairs as well. Kurt Vonnegut sees in *A Connecticut Yankee* a chilling foreshadowing (or perhaps a projection from the Civil War) of "all the high-tech atrocities which followed, and which follow still." Cynthia Ozick suggests that "The Man That Corrupted Hadleyburg," along with some of the other pieces collected under that title — many of them written when Twain lived in a Vienna ruled by Karl Lueger, a demagogue Adolf Hitler would later idolize — shoot up moral flares that shed an eerie light on the insidious corruption, prejudice, and hatred that reached bitter fruition under the Third Reich. And Twain's portrait in this book of "the dissolving Austria-Hungary of the 1890s," in Ozick's view, presages not only the Sarajevo that would erupt in 1914 but also "the disintegrated components of the former Yugoslavia" and "the *fin-de-siècle* Sarajevo of our own moment."

Despite their admiration for Twain's ambitious reach and scope, contributors to The Oxford Mark Twain also recognize his limitations. Mordecai Richler, for example, thinks that "the early pages of *Innocents Abroad* suffer from being a tad broad, proffering more burlesque than inspired satire," perhaps because Twain was "trying too hard for knee-slappers." Charles Johnson notes that the Young Man in Twain's philosophical dialogue about free will and determinism (*What Is Man?*) "caves in far too soon," failing to challenge what through late-twentieth-century eyes looks like "pseudoscience" and suspect essentialism in the Old Man's arguments.

Some contributors revisit their first encounters with Twain's works, recalling what surprised or intrigued them. When David Bradley came across "Fenimore Cooper's Literary Offences" in his college library, he "did not at first realize that Twain was being his usual ironic self with all this business about the 'nineteen rules governing literary art in the domain of romantic fiction,' but by the time I figured out there was no such list outside Twain's own head, I had decided that the rules made *sense*. . . . It seemed to me they were a pretty good blueprint for writing — Negro writing included." Sherley Anne Williams remembers that part of what attracted her to *Pudd'nhead Wilson* when she first read it thirty years ago was "that Twain, writing at the end of the nineteenth century, could imagine negroes as characters, albeit white ones, who actually thought for and of themselves, whose actions were the product of their thinking rather than the spontaneous ephemera of physical instincts that stereotype assigned to blacks." Frederik Pohl recalls his first reading of *Huckleberry Finn* as "a watershed event" in his life, the first book he read as a child in which "bad people" ceased to exercise a monopoly on doing "bad things." In *Huckleberry Finn* "some seriously bad things — things like the possession and mistreatment of black slaves, like stealing and lying, even like killing other people in duels — were quite often done by people who not only thought of themselves as exemplarily moral but, by any other standards I knew how to apply, actually *were* admirable citizens." The world that

Tom and Huck lived in, Pohl writes, "was filled with complexities and contradictions," and resembled "the world I appeared to be living in myself."

Other contributors explore their more recent encounters with Twain, explaining why they have revised their initial responses to his work. For Toni Morrison, parts of *Huckleberry Finn* that she "once took to be deliberate evasions, stumbles even, or a writer's impatience with his or her material," now strike her "as otherwise: as entrances, crevices, gaps, seductive invitations flashing the possibility of meaning. Unarticulated eddies that encourage diving into the novel's undertow — the real place where writer captures reader." One such "eddy" is the imprisonment of Jim on the Phelps farm. Instead of dismissing this portion of the book as authorial bungling, as she once did, Morrison now reads it as Twain's commentary on the 1880s, a period that "saw the collapse of civil rights for blacks," a time when "the nation, as well as Tom Sawyer, was deferring Jim's freedom in agonizing play." Morrison believes that Americans in the 1880s were attempting "to bury the combustible issues Twain raised in his novel," and that those who try to kick Huck Finn out of school in the 1990s are doing the same: "The cyclical attempts to remove the novel from classrooms extend Jim's captivity on into each generation of readers."

Although imitation-Hemingway and imitation-Faulkner writing contests draw hundreds of entries annually, no one has ever tried to mount a faux-Twain competition. Why? Perhaps because Mark Twain's voice is too much a part of who we are and how we speak even today. Roy Blount Jr. suggests that it is impossible, "at least for an American writer, to parody Mark Twain. It would be like doing an impression of your father or mother: he or she is already there in your voice."

Twain's style is examined and celebrated in The Oxford Mark Twain by fellow writers who themselves have struggled with the nuances of words, the structure of sentences, the subtleties of point of view, and the trickiness of opening lines. Bobbie Ann Mason observes, for example, that "Twain loved the sound of words and he knew how to string them by sound, like different shades of one color: 'The earl's barbaric eye,' 'the Usurping Earl,' 'a double-dyed humbug.'" Twain "relied on the punch of plain words" to show writers how to move beyond the "wordy romantic rubbish" so prevalent in nineteenth-century fiction, Mason says; he "was one of the first writers in America to deflower literary language." Lee Smith believes that "American writers have benefited as much from the way Mark Twain opened up the possibilities of first-person narration as we have from his use of vernacular language." (She feels that "the ghost of Mark Twain was hovering someplace in the background" when she decided to write her novel *Oral History* from the standpoint of multiple first-person narrators.) Frederick Busch maintains that "A Dog's Tale" "boasts one of the great opening sentences" of all time: "My father was a St. Bernard, my mother was a collie, but I am a Presbyterian." And Ursula Le Guin marvels at the ingenuity of the following sentence that she encounters in *Extracts from Adam's Diary*.

> . . . This made her sorry for the creatures which live in there, which she calls fish, for she continues to fasten names on to things that don't need them and don't come when they are called by them, which is a matter of no consequence to her, as she is such a numskull anyway; so she got a lot of them out and brought them in last night and put them in my bed to keep warm, but I have noticed them now and then all day, and I don't see that they are any happier there than they were before, only quieter.[10]

Le Guin responds,

> Now, that is a pure Mark-Twain-tour-de-force sentence, covering an immense amount of territory in an effortless, aimless ramble that seems to be heading nowhere in particular and ends up with breathtaking accuracy at the gold mine. Any sensible child would find that funny, perhaps not following all its divagations but delighted by the swing of it, by the word "numskull," by the idea of putting fish in the bed; and as that child grew older and reread it, its reward would only grow; and if that grown-up child had to write an essay on the piece and therefore earnestly studied and pored over this sentence, she would end up in unmitigated admiration of its vocabulary, syntax, pacing, sense, and rhythm, above all the beautiful

timing of the last two words; and she would, and she does, still find it funny.

The fish surface again in a passage that Gore Vidal calls to our attention, from *Following the Equator*: "'The Whites always mean well when they take human fish out of the ocean and try to make them dry and warm and happy and comfortable in a chicken coop,' which is how, through civilization, they did away with many of the original inhabitants. Lack of empathy is a principal theme in Twain's meditations on race and empire."

Indeed, empathy — and its lack — is a principal theme in virtually all of Twain's work, as contributors frequently note. Nat Hentoff quotes the following thoughts from Huck in *Tom Sawyer Abroad*:

> I see a bird setting on a dead limb of a high tree, singing with its head tilted back and its mouth open, and before I thought I fired, and his song stopped and he fell straight down from the limb, all limp like a rag, and I run and picked him up and he was dead, and his body was warm in my hand, and his head rolled about this way and that, like his neck was broke, and there was a little white skin over his eyes, and one little drop of blood on the side of his head; and laws! I could n't see nothing more for the tears; and I hain't never murdered no creature since that war n't doing me no harm, and I ain't going to.[11]

"The Humane Society," Hentoff writes, "has yet to say anything as powerful — and lasting."

Readers of The Oxford Mark Twain will have the pleasure of revisiting Twain's Mississippi landmarks alongside Willie Morris, whose own lower Mississippi Valley boyhood gives him a special sense of connection to Twain. Morris knows firsthand the mosquitoes described in *Life on the Mississippi* — so colossal that "two of them could whip a dog" and "four of them could hold a man down"; in Morris's own hometown they were so large during the flood season that "local wags said they wore wristwatches." Morris's Yazoo City and Twain's Hannibal shared a "rough-hewn democracy . . . complicated by all the visible textures of caste and class, . . . harmless boyhood fun and mischief right along with . . . rank hypocrisies, churchgoing sanctimonies, racial hatred, entrenched and unrepentant greed."

For the West of Mark Twain's *Roughing It*, readers will have George Plimpton as their guide. "What a group these newspapermen were!" Plimpton writes about Twain and his friends Dan De Quille and Joe Goodman in Virginia City, Nevada. "Their roisterous carryings-on bring to mind the kind of frat-house enthusiasm one associates with college humor magazines like the *Harvard Lampoon*." Malcolm Bradbury examines Twain as "a living example of what made the American so different from the European." And Hal Holbrook, who has interpreted Mark Twain on stage for some forty years, describes how Twain "played" during the civil rights movement, during the Vietnam War, during the Gulf War, and in Prague on the eve of the demise of Communism.

Why do we continue to read Mark Twain? What draws us to him? His wit? His compassion? His humor? His bravura? His humility? His understanding of who and what we are in those parts of our being that we rarely open to view? Our sense that he knows we can do better than we do? Our sense that he knows we can't? E. L. Doctorow tells us that children are attracted to *Tom Sawyer* because in this book "the young reader confirms his own hope that no matter how troubled his relations with his elders may be, beneath all their disapproval is their underlying love for him, constant and steadfast." Readers in general, Arthur Miller writes, value Twain's "insights into America's always uncertain moral life and its shifting but everlasting hypocrisies"; we appreciate the fact that he "is not using his alienation from the public illusions of his hour in order to reject the country implicitly as though he could live without it, but manifestly in order to correct it." Perhaps we keep reading Mark Twain because, in Miller's words, he "wrote much more like a father than a son. He doesn't seem to be sitting in class taunting the teacher but standing at the head of it challenging his students to acknowledge their own humanity, that is, their immemorial attraction to the untrue."

Mark Twain entered the public eye at a time when many of his countrymen considered "American culture" an oxymoron; he died four years before a world conflagration that would lead many to question whether the contradiction in terms was not "European civilization" instead. In between he worked in journalism, printing, steamboating, mining, lecturing, publishing, and editing, in virtually every region of the country. He tried his hand at humorous sketches, social satire, historical novels, children's books, poetry, drama, science fiction, mysteries, romance, philosophy, travelogue, memoir, polemic, and several genres no one had ever seen before or has ever seen since. He invented a self-pasting scrapbook, a history game, a vest strap, and a gizmo for keeping bed sheets tucked in; he invested in machines and processes designed to revolutionize typesetting and engraving, and in a food supplement called "Plasmon." Along the way he cheerfully impersonated himself and prior versions of himself for doting publics on five continents while playing out a charming rags-to-riches story followed by a devastating riches-to-rags story followed by yet another great American comeback. He had a long-running real-life engagement in a sumptuous comedy of manners, and then in a real-life tragedy not of his own design: during the last fourteen years of his life almost everyone he ever loved was taken from him by disease and death.

Mark Twain has indelibly shaped our views of who and what the United States is as a nation and of who and what we might become. He understood the nostalgia for a "simpler" past that increased as that past receded — and he saw through the nostalgia to a past that was just as complex as the present. He recognized better than we did ourselves our potential for greatness and our potential for disaster. His fictions brilliantly illuminated the world in which he lived, changing it — and us — in the process. He knew that our feet often danced to tunes that had somehow remained beyond our hearing; with perfect pitch he played them back to us.

My mother read *Tom Sawyer* to me as a bedtime story when I was eleven. I thought Huck and Tom could be a lot of fun, but I dismissed Becky Thatcher as a bore. When I was twelve I invested a nickel at a local garage sale in a book that contained short pieces by Mark Twain. That was where I met Twain's Eve. Now, *that's* more like it, I decided, pleased to meet a female character I could identify *with* instead of against. Eve had spunk. Even if she got a lot wrong, you had to give her credit for trying. "The Man That Corrupted

Hadleyburg" left me giddy with satisfaction: none of my adolescent reveries of getting even with my enemies were half as neat as the plot of the man who got back at that town. "How I Edited an Agricultural Paper" set me off in uncontrollable giggles.

People sometimes told me that I looked like Huck Finn. "It's the freckles," they'd explain — not explaining anything at all. I didn't read *Huckleberry Finn* until junior year in high school in my English class. It was the fall of 1965. I was living in a small town in Connecticut. I expected a sequel to *Tom Sawyer*. So when the teacher handed out the books and announced our assignment, my jaw dropped: "Write a paper on how Mark Twain used irony to attack racism in *Huckleberry Finn*."

The year before, the bodies of three young men who had gone to Mississippi to help blacks register to vote — James Chaney, Andrew Goodman, and Michael Schwerner — had been found in a shallow grave; a group of white segregationists (the county sheriff among them) had been arrested in connection with the murders. America's inner cities were simmering with pent-up rage that began to explode in the summer of 1965, when riots in Watts left thirty-four people dead. None of this made any sense to me. I was confused, angry, certain that there was something missing from the news stories I read each day: the why. Then I met Pap Finn. And the Phelpses.

Pap Finn, Huck tells us, "had been drunk over in town" and "was just all mud." He erupts into a drunken tirade about "a free nigger . . . from Ohio — a mulatter, most as white as a white man," with "the whitest shirt on you ever see, too, and the shiniest hat; and there ain't a man in town that's got as fine clothes as what he had."

> . . . they said he was a p'fessor in a college, and could talk all kinds of languages, and knowed everything. And that ain't the wust. They said he could *vote*, when he was at home. Well, that let me out. Thinks I, what is the country a-coming to? It was 'lection day, and I was just about to go and vote, myself, if I warn't too drunk to get there; but when they told me there was a State in this country where they'd let that nigger vote, I drawed out. I says I'll never vote agin. Them's the very words I said. . . . And to see the

cool way of that nigger — why, he wouldn't a give me the road if I hadn't shoved him out o' the way.[12]

Later on in the novel, when the runaway slave Jim gives up his freedom to nurse a wounded Tom Sawyer, a white doctor testifies to the stunning altruism of his actions. The Phelpses and their neighbors, all fine, upstanding, well-meaning, churchgoing folk,

> agreed that Jim had acted very well, and was deserving to have some notice took of it, and reward. So every one of them promised, right out and hearty, that they wouldn't curse him no more.
>
> Then they come out and locked him up. I hoped they was going to say he could have one or two of the chains took off, because they was rotten heavy, or could have meat and greens with his bread and water, but they didn't think of it.[13]

Why did the behavior of these people tell me more about why Watts burned than anything I had read in the daily paper? And why did a drunk Pap Finn railing against a black college professor from Ohio whose vote was as good as his own tell me more about white anxiety over black political power than anything I had seen on the evening news?

Mark Twain knew that there was nothing, absolutely *nothing*, a black man could do — including selflessly sacrificing his freedom, the only thing of value he had — that would make white society see beyond the color of his skin. And Mark Twain knew that depicting racists with chilling accuracy would expose the viciousness of their world view like nothing else could. It was an insight echoed some eighty years after Mark Twain penned Pap Finn's rantings about the black professor, when Malcolm X famously asked, "Do you know what white racists call black Ph.D.'s?" and answered, "'*Nigger!*'"[14]

Mark Twain taught me things I needed to know. He taught me to understand the raw racism that lay behind what I saw on the evening news. He taught me that the most well-meaning people can be hurtful and myopic. He taught me to recognize the supreme irony of a country founded in freedom that continued to deny freedom to so many of its citizens. Every time I hear of another effort to kick Huck Finn out of school somewhere, I recall everything that Mark Twain taught *this* high school junior, and I find myself jumping into the fray.[15] I remember the black high school student who called CNN during the phone-in portion of a 1985 debate between Dr. John Wallace, a black educator spearheading efforts to ban the book, and myself. She accused Dr. Wallace of insulting her and all black high school students by suggesting they weren't smart enough to understand Mark Twain's irony. And I recall the black cameraman on the *CBS Morning News* who came up to me after he finished shooting another debate between Dr. Wallace and myself. He said he had never read the book by Mark Twain that we had been arguing about — but now he really wanted to. One thing that puzzled him, though, was why a white woman was defending it and a black man was attacking it, because as far as he could see from what we'd been saying, the book made whites look pretty bad.

As I came to understand *Huckleberry Finn* and *Pudd'nhead Wilson* as commentaries on the era now known as the nadir of American race relations, those books pointed me toward the world recorded in nineteenth-century black newspapers and periodicals and in fiction by Mark Twain's black contemporaries. My investigation of the role black voices and traditions played in shaping Mark Twain's art helped make me aware of their role in shaping all of American culture.[16] My research underlined for me the importance of changing the stories we tell about who we are to reflect the realities of what we've been.[17]

Ever since our encounter in high school English, Mark Twain has shown me the potential of American literature and American history to illuminate each other. Rarely have I found a contradiction or complexity we grapple with as a nation that Mark Twain had not puzzled over as well. He insisted on taking America seriously. And he insisted on *not* taking America seriously: "I think that there is but a single specialty with us, only one thing that can be called by the wide name 'American,'" he once wrote. "That is the national devotion to ice-water."[18]

Mark Twain threw back at us our dreams and our denial of those dreams, our greed, our goodness, our ambition, and our laziness, all rattling around together in that vast echo chamber of our talk — that sharp, spunky American talk that Mark Twain figured out how to write down without robbing it of its energy and immediacy. Talk shaped by voices that the official arbiters of "culture" deemed of no importance — voices of children, voices of slaves, voices of servants, voices of ordinary people. Mark Twain listened. And he made us listen. To the stories he told us, and to the truths they conveyed. He still has a lot to say that we need to hear.

Mark Twain lives — in our libraries, classrooms, homes, theaters, movie houses, streets, and most of all in our speech. His optimism energizes us, his despair sobers us, and his willingness to keep wrestling with the hilarious and horrendous complexities of it all keeps us coming back for more. As the twenty-first century approaches, may he continue to goad us, chasten us, delight us, berate us, and cause us to erupt in unrestrained laughter in unexpected places.

NOTES

1. Ernest Hemingway, *Green Hills of Africa* (New York: Charles Scribner's Sons, 1935), 22. George Bernard Shaw to Samuel L. Clemens, July 3, 1907, quoted in Albert Bigelow Paine, *Mark Twain: A Biography* (New York: Harper and Brothers, 1912), 3:1398.

2. Allen Carey-Webb, "Racism and *Huckleberry Finn*: Censorship, Dialogue and Change," *English Journal* 82, no. 7 (November 1993):22.

3. See Louis J. Budd, "Impersonators," in J. R. LeMaster and James D. Wilson, eds., *The Mark Twain Encyclopedia* (New York: Garland Publishing Company, 1993), 389–91.

4. See Shelley Fisher Fishkin, "Ripples and Reverberations," part 3 of *Lighting Out for the Territory: Reflections on Mark Twain and American Culture* (New York: Oxford University Press, 1996).

5. There are two exceptions. Twain published chapters from his autobiography in the *North American Review* in 1906 and 1907, but this material was not published in book form in Twain's lifetime; our volume reproduces the material as it appeared in the *North American Review*. The other exception is our final volume, *Mark Twain's Speeches*, which appeared two months after Twain's death in 1910.

An unauthorized handful of copies of *1601* was privately printed by an Alexander Gunn of Cleveland at the instigation of Twain's friend John Hay in 1880. The first American edition authorized by Mark Twain, however, was printed at the United States Military Academy at West Point in 1882; that is the edition reproduced here.

It should further be noted that four volumes — *The Stolen White Elephant and Other Detective Stories, Following the Equator and Anti-imperialist Essays, The Diaries of Adam and Eve,* and *1601, and Is Shakespeare Dead?*— bind together material originally published separately. In each case the first American edition of the material is the version that has been reproduced, always in its entirety. Because Twain constantly recycled and repackaged previously published works in his collections of short pieces, a certain amount of duplication is unavoidable. We have selected volumes with an eye toward keeping this duplication to a minimum.

Even the twenty-nine-volume Oxford Mark Twain has had to leave much out. No edition of Twain can ever claim to be "complete," for the man was too prolix, and the file drawers of both ephemera and as yet unpublished texts are deep.

6. With the possible exception of *Mark Twain's Speeches*. Some scholars suspect Twain knew about this book and may have helped shape it, although no hard evidence to that effect has yet surfaced. Twain's involvement in the production process varied greatly from book to book. For a fuller sense of authorial intention, scholars will continue to rely on the superb definitive editions of Twain's works produced by the Mark Twain Project at the University of California at Berkeley as they become available. Dense with annotation documenting textual emendation and related issues, these editions add immeasurably to our understanding of Mark Twain and the genesis of his works.

7. Except for a few titles that were not in its collection. The American Antiquarian Society in Worcester, Massachusetts, provided the first edition of *King Leopold's Soliloquy*; the Elmer Holmes Bobst Library of New York University furnished the 1906–7 volumes of the *North American Review* in which *Chapters from My Autobiography* first appeared; the Harry Ransom Humanities Research Center at the University of Texas at Austin made their copy of the West Point edition of *1601* available; and the Mark Twain Project provided the first edition of *Extract from Captain Stormfield's Visit to Heaven*.

8. The specific copy photographed for Oxford's facsimile edition is indicated in a note on the text at the end of each volume.

9. All quotations from contemporary writers in this essay are taken from their introductions to the volumes of The Oxford Mark Twain, and the quotations from Mark Twain's works are taken from the texts reproduced in The Oxford Mark Twain.

10. *The Diaries of Adam and Eve*, The Oxford Mark Twain [hereafter OMT] (New York: Oxford University Press, 1996), p. 33.

11. *Tom Sawyer Abroad*, OMT, p. 74.

12. *Adventures of Huckleberry Finn*, OMT, p. 49–50.

13. Ibid., p. 358.

14. Malcolm X, *The Autobiography of Malcolm X*, with the assistance of Alex Haley (New York: Grove Press, 1965), p. 284.

15. I do not mean to minimize the challenge of teaching this difficult novel, a challenge for which all teachers may not feel themselves prepared. Elsewhere I have developed some concrete strategies for approaching the book in the classroom, including teaching it in the context of the history of American race relations and alongside books by black writers. See Shelley Fisher Fishkin, "Teaching *Huckleberry Finn*," in James S. Leonard, ed., *Making Mark Twain Work in the Classroom* (Durham: Duke University Press, forthcoming). See also Shelley Fisher Fishkin, *Was Huck Black? Mark Twain and African-American Voices* (New York: Oxford University Press, 1993), pp. 106–8, and a curriculum kit in preparation at the Mark Twain House in Hartford, containing teaching suggestions from myself, David Bradley, Jocelyn Chadwick-Joshua, James Miller, and David E. E. Sloane.

16. See Fishkin, *Was Huck Black?* See also Fishkin, "Interrogating 'Whiteness,' Complicating 'Blackness': Remapping American Culture," in Henry Wonham, ed., *Criticism and the Color Line: Desegregating American Literary Studies* (New Brunswick: Rutgers UP, 1996, pp. 251–90 and in shortened form in *American Quarterly* 47, no. 3 (September 1995):428–66.

17. I explore the roots of my interest in Mark Twain and race at greater length in an essay entitled "Changing the Story," in Jeffrey Rubin-Dorsky and Shelley Fisher Fishkin, eds., *People of the Book: Thirty Scholars Reflect on Their Jewish Identity* (Madison: U of Wisconsin Press, 1996), pp. 47–63.

18. "What Paul Bourget Thinks of Us," *How to Tell a Story and Other Essays*, OMT, p. 197.

I told Professor Pearson that I doubted this voice he'd heard on the television documentary was really Mark Twain. Some months went by and he called me again. He had discovered that the television recording was originally made on wire in 1933 or 1934 in the home of Professor Packard of Harvard University, by the actor William Gillette. Gillette was making his last tour in the play *Secret Service*. He had lived only a few blocks from Mark Twain in Hartford and Twain had loaned him money to go to New York and pursue an acting career. So they were friends. The clincher was a preamble on the original tape during which other men in the room were heard urging "Bill" to recite his impersonation of Mark Twain doing the jumping frog story. Gillette demurred but finally gave in and delivered it. This whole introductory passage had been eliminated by some questionable character and the tape circulated as authentic Mark Twain. Professor "Sherlock" Holmes Pearson's sleuthing dashed everyone's hopes of finding a recording of Mark Twain's voice, although there was a persistent rumor that such a recording was lurking somewhere.

Years later, when I was doing Mark Twain at the Longacre Theatre in New York in 1966, a gentleman from Brooklyn wrote that he was coming to a matinee and would like to talk to me. He explained that he knew of a recording of Twain's voice. After the performance a courtly 92-year-old man came backstage and told me that he and his employer from the Columbia Vitaphone Company had gone to Mark Twain's home on Fifth Avenue in 1904 to record his voice on a wax cylinder. "Do you know where it is?" I asked, holding my breath. "It was stored in an attic and melted down," he said. To his knowledge there existed no other recording of Mark Twain's voice. That ended it. It appears the pursuit of his sound is left to our imagination.

He had a tenor singing voice. There's a clue. And we have many newspaper accounts describing the sound of his voice as well as his mannerisms and general appearance on the lecture platform.

> He speaks in a sort of mechanical drawl and with a most bored expression
> of countenance. . . . He jerks out a sentence or two and follows it with a si-

INTRODUCTION

Hal Holbrook

What did he sound like? I had read newspaper reports of his lectures which described his voice as a "nasal twang" or "a little buzz saw inside a corpse" and the *Detroit Free Press* referred to his "Down East" accent. Others called it a Missouri drawl. I learned early on in my research for the solo performance of Mark Twain that I would have to deal with inconsistency as well as the creative flights of the people doing the reporting. Some of them were trying to be funnier than Twain. And there was always the possibility that the man on the *Detroit Free Press* did not know a Down East accent from a Paiute Indian's.

Along about 1956 Professor Norman Holmes Pearson of Yale University called me up one day and said that he had heard a recording of Twain's voice on a television documentary, that he was suspicious of its authenticity and had acquired a copy. Would I listen to it and give him my opinion? I had met this eminent scholar at the Mark Twain House in Hartford and his call was a compliment. This was before I had acquired any wide reputation as an interpreter of Mark Twain, and I valued Professor Pearson's tacit imprimatur.

The recording was a rendition of the jumping frog story. The first thing that struck me about it was the obvious New England accent; having been brought up in New England, I knew what that sounded like. Then I remembered that in a letter to his wife in 1885, while on tour, Twain had listed timings for a Chicago lecture. He said the timing for the jumping frog story was the "fastest on record."[1] I timed Pearson's recording against my own reading of Twain's lecture version. Mark Twain's was thirteen minutes and the Pearson recording was nine. So something was off.

lence that is more suggestive than words. (*Washington Post*, November 25, 1884)

His deep voice and his pronunciation of many words are of Missouri, where he was brought up, his nasal twang is of New England where he has spent a good many years, and his drawl is of Mark Twain. (*Toronto Globe*, December 9, 1884)

That last description could send you in three different directions.

When Mark Twain walked on the stage [with] his unruly hair like a halo around his head, and his discouraged expression of countenance, he was welcomed with a prolonged clapping of hands. Without apparently recovering his spirits, he sauntered to the reading desk, felt for it with his right hand, and began. (*New York Sun*, November 19, 1884)[2]

I remember thinking of Jack Benny. The man they were describing was coming out deadpan and after a few lugubrious moments he was dropping comic bombshells and working the audience into a fit of startled laughter. He was obviously a performer and he was going for the funny bone. He had acquired the art of the tall story, that prize of our Wild West culture. You built the story up higher and higher, seeing how long you could sustain the ridiculousness of it before it crashed to the ground. A good example is "His Grandfather's Old Ram."

I studied pictures of Twain. A cartoon in a New York magazine showed him in his lecture platform garb: formal black suit with tails, white starched shirt, white tie — apparently the customary regalia for such an event in those days. But as I read more newspaper reviews of his lectures in various parts of the country, I got a clear picture of a man who was breaking all the rules. Instead of standing at the lectern and delivering his remarks in the normal elocutionary manner, he leaned against the lectern or slouched around the stage, sometimes with his hands in his pockets, speaking as if he were back home circling his dining table. Many of the sponsoring organizations of the time, like the Chautauquas, had a religious base, and this kind of behavior was considered frivolous and in poor taste. Mark Twain was severely criticized in some holy quarters. He didn't act right. I realized that what I had to do was find some way to represent this idiosyncratic behavior to a modern audience accustomed to informality and even questionable taste.

I thought about the cigar. Smoking cigars may have been Twain's favorite pastime, that and billiards. His friend William Dean Howells said that he smoked incessantly while visiting in Boston and even went to bed with a cigar clamped in his teeth. Howells was afraid he'd burn the house down, so he used to creep in and remove the cigar after Twain went to sleep. I figured smoking a cigar during a lecture would be considered eccentric, even in our day, so I adopted it.

Then I thought of the white suit. He liked to wear white in his later years — said it made him feel pure. Sometimes he paraded down Fifth Avenue in white on a Sunday morning while people were coming out of church, the men looking like "a flock of crows." If the white suit did not seem eccentric to a modern audience, at least it would capture their attention.

I was going to characterize him at the age of seventy because by then he had written practically everything I wanted him to say. In 1954, when I began the solo Twain, I was twenty-nine years old — forty-one years shy of the mark (sorry). My first makeup took one hour and fifteen minutes and I looked like a boy with white hair. By the time it grew into a four-hour job I was quite convincing.

I needed to have him move around. He was a restless talker at home and would get up from the dinner table and march around it while discharging his observations about God's pitiful invention, Man, into the clouds of cigar smoke curling around him. His first biographer, Albert Bigelow Paine, described his "ceaseless slippered shuffling walk . . . the white figure with its rocking, rolling movement . . . his deliberate speech — always deliberate save at rare intervals."[3] So I put a lectern on one side of the stage and on the other side a smallish library table and an armchair. The space in the middle was for wandering around or acting out scenes from his books. I would need an ashtray for the cigar, so that went on the table, along with a few books from which I would pretend to read when I got around to it. And a water pitcher and glass. These props would give me objects to fool with and would seem to distract me. I would have to drop cigar ashes, which would require me to cross the stage to the ashtray every once in a while, motivating my movements while he walked and talked. These devices were also chosen to help break the rules of the "lecture platform" and make audiences feel at home with him.

In 1956 I did Mark Twain in a nightclub in Greenwich Village with only the cigar as a prop. The club was called Upstairs at the Duplex and seated fifty-nine people, legally. I worked in the curve of a baby grand piano, very close to the audience, and did two or three shows a night. By then the make-up took two and a half hours. I stayed there for eight months and developed my first two hours of Twain material. I experimented with the pause. Twain loved fooling around with the pause, toying with it like a cat, taking chances with it, and there in the nightclub I was able to get familiar with the pause, especially in the late show when no one was in a hurry to go anywhere, the smoke drifting up through the spotlights and people simmered down from a nice load of whiskey or gin. I could take my time telling the stories, let the stuff sink in, play around with the easy nature of American humor. In the theater you go for laughs, but in that little club the laughs were chuckles and the audience was a friend in your lap. I learned to trust Twain's material.

I worked on new material constantly while doing a television and radio soap opera in the daytime, then memorized it on the IRT subway to Sheridan Square. I read patiently through all his books, very patiently, marking anything that might be useful for the stage and ticking off stories and anecdotes that had some dramatic life to them. Since a club show was only fifteen or twenty minutes long, many of these routines were not unlike his speeches. One of my earliest routines was carved out of his "Seventieth Birthday" speech, which I slimmed down and refined in front of audiences, keeping what got the best laughs. Another early selection was the "Italian Guide" sequence from *Innocents Abroad*. In this one I played Mark Twain impersonating two characters, an Italian guide and an American doctor. Tricky, but the audience seemed to enjoy it. Twain did the same thing in his lectures. He acted out scenes from his books. He was an actor at heart, a born one, according to Sir Henry Irving, the preeminent British actor of his day.

When I began getting engagements in colleges and theaters around the country I had to put together a longer show. My aim was to avoid formality, not to construct a program of "readings." That seemed deadly to me. Twain followed a formal structure in his lectures, but his speeches sounded improvised, and I wanted to merge both styles because I was working for a modern audience with a faster heartbeat. I started with the self-introduction he sometimes used on the platform, followed it with a joke about the lawyer who introduced him with his hands in his pockets ("a rare creature — a lawyer who kept his hands in his own pockets"), and that got the audience laughing. Then I would pull out the cigar and go into a routine on smoking and the dangers of abstinence. Finally, I'd get down to business with my program notes and start in on the lecture the audience expected to hear, but pretty soon I'd lose track of that and get reminded of something else, and that would lead me into a routine on politics. Along about this time I'd remember a book I wrote called *Innocents Abroad*, and we were into the "Italian Guide." Or something else.

It was a meandering structure, purposefully improvisational, to keep the audience off guard and wondering what was coming next. It seemed to me that the most effective way to program an evening of Mark Twain was to give the impression that I was making it up on my feet, that I was taking chances. That would be more dangerous and create suspense. That was the effect I think he tried to achieve himself, particularly in his speeches. He rehearsed them with intense zeal (so did I) until he drilled them into his head. Then he strove to make the performance look spontaneous. This speaking style seemed to suit his style of writing. He was, after all, the first American author to write the way Americans speak. Bernard DeVoto caught the spirit of Twain's genius when he said,

It is a literature of oral anecdote, whose purpose is the embodiment of character and the revelation of a *point*, whose aim is the entertainment of listeners, and whose origin is the life immediately at hand.[4]

It was in 1957, in Little Rock, Arkansas, that I first became aware of the potential for social commentary in Mark Twain's work. Until then I had been trying to put together a funny show, born in a nightclub, one that I hoped would survive on a variety of stages. I had played some pretty strange ones, from the curve of that piano to the basketball floors of rural schools with kids sitting on windowsills, so I knew that keeping the audience entertained meant the difference between life and death. But when President Eisenhower called out the troops to put down the racial explosion at Central High School in Little Rock, Mark Twain's social conscience began to cast its shadow over me. By some strange twist of fate (later to be repeated in the 1960s) I was scheduled to perform Mark Twain near Little Rock not long after the riots there. I did not yet have material in my repertoire that specifically commented on racial injustice. All I had was the Sherburn-Boggs selection from *Huckleberry Finn*, which ends with Colonel Sherburn's blistering speech to the mob that has come to lynch him. Although a white man is speaking to a white mob, Mark Twain is making a thinly veiled statement about the Ku Klux Klan. The portrait of sudden violence in the shooting of Boggs, of ignorance and the mob mentality that sweeps people along, was eerily appropriate to this modern-day crisis in Little Rock, and Twain's setting did happen to be a town in Arkansas. So that was the selection I chose to deliver.

I don't know how much the audience got out of it. I do know that my mind was honed like a silver blade on the point I wanted to get across. I hope it came through. I think it did to some of them. When I got back to New York City I started reading with a different appetite. I began exploring the social commentary of Mark Twain and in time there opened before me a mine of gold that I had overlooked. I found nuggets lying all around in those great books and essays and speeches and suddenly the show took on a feeling of importance it had never had before. I didn't know it then, but the civil rights movement had begun.

I read "To the Person Sitting in Darkness" and "To My Missionary Critics," "The United States of Lyncherdom," the wonderful material about the damned human race in the last volume of Paine's biography of Twain, much of it later included in *Letters to the Earth*; I read *Pudd'nhead Wilson*. I began to put together in my mind another Huckleberry number which would express the message of the entire book. In 1958 Philip S. Foner's riveting *Mark Twain: Social Critic* was published. It was a nest of mercurial opinions by Twain which led me in the direction of the material I developed later, when the 1960s matured and the passions of the civil rights movement and the Vietnam War struck fire together. I was creating a show which almost seemed to be commenting on the news of the day.

The *Mark Twain Tonight!* which opened at the Longacre Theatre in 1966 was judged very topical. It talked about the Silent Lie, how you could lie by remaining quiet in the shadow of a great injustice, as people did during the movement to abolish slavery.[5] Then came the new Huckleberry number, in which Huck characterizes his father giving that sublimely racist speech about the "free nigger from Ohio" and then grapples with the awful decision to turn Jim in: yes or no. When the dust settled down on that scene, I had Twain deliver his personal observation on how racism can be trained into you.

The Vietnam War was heating up while I was at the Longacre Theatre, so in the second act I moved from racism to patriotism, the right to speak your mind in times of national stress. In *Letters from the Earth*, I found this about our Philippine war: "*Our Country, right or wrong!* . . . every man who failed to shout it . . . was proclaimed a traitor — none but those others were patriots." He could have been talking about the war we were being drawn into in Vietnam. "Who is 'the Country'? Is it the Government? . . . The Government is merely a servant, . . . a temporary one . . . . If you alone of all the nation shall decide one way, and that way be the right way according to your convictions of the right, you have done your duty by yourself and by your country — hold up your head!"[6] Edited together from bits and pieces of Twain, this had an electric effect upon the audience in 1966. It reminded us that dissent is a tradition of our democracy, something we forget about six and a half days of every week.

I've been working this material for over forty years now and I see no shrinkage in its timeliness. Twain was talking about the human race, which seems always to run after itself in circles. On May 31, 1985, I gave a performance at the Jiri Wolker Theatre in Prague, before the Communist walls came down. At the beginning of the second act I started with the Silent Lie routine. The audience became profoundly attentive. After the line "when whole nations of people conspire to propagate gigantic mute lies like that one, in the interest of tyrannies and shams," someone in the audience started to applaud. Then someone else joined in. Just two people clapping. I felt a sudden concern for their safety and quickly continued. But the air was charged. In all the shows I've done, there were only two other performances where an audience clapped at that particular moment. The first was in Hamburg, Germany, in 1961. The second was in Oxford, Mississippi, on October 9, 1962, during the riots over the admission of the first black student, James Meredith, to the University of Mississippi.

Sometimes one piece of material from the repertoire will burn with relevance for a few years and then cool down as other social issues flare up. But then a routine which has occupied a modest niche, useful but not triumphant, will catch fire and smile out its timely perception of our foolish world.

Such is the case with a forty-year-old routine lifted from the "Seventieth Birthday" speech. (Here, as in many other routines in my show, the text has been altered slightly to simplify it for the stage.) "I have never taken any exercise except sleeping and resting . . . . I could never see any benefit in being tired." Then I splice in a remark attributed to Twain: "When the urge to exercise comes over me I lie down until it passes away." This has always been fun to do, but ever since the symbol of America became a pair of sneakers and the passion for health superseded any lingering passion for intelligence, Twain's commentary has become more than just a joke. It has a slim barb in it which the audience enjoys.

Sometimes events inspire me to construct a new routine. A few years ago we were in another war, this one in the desert, against Iraq. Everyone could see it coming, and as it built to a declaration I worried that the country would once again fly into the conflicting passions which had polarized us during the Vietnam War. Everyone would start shouting back and forth and the losers would be our soldiers: the men and women who had to go over there and lay their lives on the line and then come home to a nation that never thanked them for the job they'd been told to do. Whether the Gulf War was politically right or wrong, it was too sad to think of these soldiers coming back to experience the same cruel emptiness the Vietnam veterans have lived with for years — never to be thanked except for that eloquent black wall in Washington. I could sense that most people felt the same way I did. So I put together a number called "Opinions," whose point is that we should stop shouting at each other and start listening to what the other person is trying to say.

"Opinions" is made up of material from seven different sources, edited and arranged for the stage. The idea for it popped out of a paragraph from *Christian Science*. "When I, a thoughtful and unbiased Presbyterian, examine the Koran, I know that beyond any question every Mohammedan is insane . . . . I cannot prove to him that he is insane, because you can never prove anything to a lunatic." There follows a line I added for transition ("But it is perfectly clear to me"), and then back to the same passage in *Christian Science* (edited from first-person plural to first-person singular): "I know exactly where to put my finger upon his insanity. It is where his opinion differs from mine."[7] The "Opinions" selection ends with a paragraph from chapter 53 of *Following the Equator* (my words are in brackets):

> Reverence for one's own sacred things . . . religion, flag, laws, and respect for one's own beliefs — these are feelings which we cannot even help. . . . They are involuntary, like breathing. There is no personal merit in breathing. But the reverence which is difficult, and which has personal merit in it, is the respect which you [we] pay, without compulsion, to the political or religious attitudes of a man whose beliefs are not yours [ours]. You [We] can't revere his gods or his politics, and no one expects you [us] to do that, but you [we] could respect his belief in them if you [we] tried hard enough. . . . But it is very, very difficult; it is next to impossible, and so we hardly ever try. If the man doesn't believe as we do, we say he is a crank, and that settles it. I mean it does nowadays, because now we can't burn him.[8]

What makes Mark Twain so palatable even when he's beating up on us? I think it's that he includes himself in the beating.

> The human race is a race of cowards. And I am not only marching in that procession, I am carrying the banner.[9]

He too is culpable; that, together with his honesty and his passion, helps us swallow his harshest criticism of us. It also allows him to put a lemon twist of humor into it.

In the beginning I tried to put together a funny show. One that would survive in a nightclub and on the humble stages of America. Then our reasonably ordered world began to break apart. The civil rights movement exploded and has become a lasting warfare. In the 1960s debate over the war in Vietnam joined the passions generated by racial inequality. Restraint and respect for civility were thrown aside. The traditional rebellion of youth became violent to the point of anarchy; Dylan put it to music and Elvis made it sensual. Now, thirty years later, staring at the troubled wake behind us, at the old harbors we've abandoned, we find ourselves at sea without a star to bring us home, sails flapping lugubriously in every squall, and we cannot find our way because the crew is undisciplined and there is no captain to guide us.

What would he say about all this? Our world is losing its humaneness. Anger is loose among us, riding in the streets, spilling over again and again after all these years of trying to contain it. Everybody wants what they ain't got, and sweating hard for it seems to take too much time. Our young wear the smile of cynicism to mask their pain. And immorality is on the prowl.

> That California get-rich-quick disease of my youth spread like wildfire. It produced a civilization which has destroyed the simplicity and repose of life, its poetry, its soft romantic dreams and visions, and replaced them with the money fever, sordid ideals, vulgar ambitions and the sleep which does not refresh. It has created a thousand useless luxuries and turned them into necessities and satisfied nothing. It has dethroned God and set up a shekel in his place.[10]

The great thing about Mark Twain is that he makes you smile, because he speaks the truth so well even when it has a bitter taste. And it goes to your heart. Sometimes it makes you cry. Perhaps this is why he survives and why people still want to listen to him.

NOTES

1. *The Love Letters of Mark Twain*, ed. Dixon Wecter (New York: Harper and Brothers, 1949), p. 230.

2. These newspaper accounts are reprinted in Guy A. Cardwell, *Twins of Genius* (Ann Arbor: Michigan State College Press, 1953), pp. 23, 28, 20.

3. Albert Bigelow Paine, *Mark Twain: A Biography* (New York: Harper and Brothers, 1912), 4:1323.

4. Bernard DeVoto, *Mark Twain's America* (Boston: Little, Brown, 1932), p. 92.

5. "My First Lie, and How I Got Out of It," *The Man That Corrupted Hadleyburg and Other Stories and Essays* (New York: Harper and Brothers, 1900), pp. 147–49.

6. See *Letters from the Earth*, ed. Bernard DeVoto (New York: Harper and Brothers, 1962), pp. 108–9.

7. See *Christian Science, with Notes Containing Corrections to Date* (New York: Harper and Brothers, 1907), bk. 1, ch. 5, pp. 40–41.

8. See *Following the Equator: A Journey Around the World* (Hartford: American Publishing Company, 1897), ch. 53, p. 514.

9. See prefatory note, *Mark Twain in Eruption*, ed. Bernard DeVoto (New York: Harper and Brothers, 1940).

10. See *Letters from the Earth*, p. 98.

MARK TWAIN'S SPEECHES

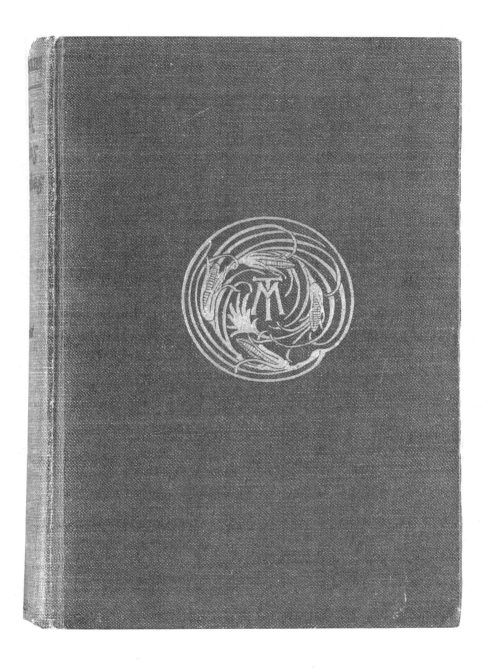

Mark Twain

MARK TWAIN'S SPEECHES

WITH AN INTRODUCTION BY
WILLIAM DEAN HOWELLS

NEW YORK AND LONDON
HARPER & BROTHERS PUBLISHERS
1910

Copyright, 1910, by HARPER & BROTHERS

All rights reserved

Published June, 1910
Printed in the United States of America

CONTENTS

CONTENTS

CONTENTS

CONTENTS

INTRODUCTION

THESE speeches will address themselves to the minds and hearts of those who read them, but not with the effect they had with those who heard them; Clemens himself would have said, not with half the effect. I have noted elsewhere how he always held that the actor doubled the value of the author's words; and he was a great actor as well as a great author. He was a most consummate actor, with this difference from other actors, that he was the first to know the thoughts and invent the fancies to which his voice and action gave the color of life. Representation is the art of other actors; his art was creative as well as representative; it was nothing at second hand.

I never heard Clemens speak when I thought he quite failed; some burst or spurt redeemed him when he seemed flagging short of the goal, and, whoever else was in the running, he came in ahead. His near-failures were the error of a rare trust to the spontaneity in which other speakers confide, or are believed to confide, when they are on their feet. He knew that from the beginning of oratory

the orator's spontaneity was for the silence and
solitude of the closet where he mused his words
to an imagined audience; that this was the use of
orators from Demosthenes and Cicero up and
down. He studied every word and syllable, and
memorized them by a system of mnemonics peculiar to himself, consisting of an arbitrary arrangement of things on a table—knives, forks,
salt-cellars; inkstands, pens, boxes, or whatever
was at hand—which stood for points and clauses
and climaxes, and were at once indelible diction
and constant suggestion. He studied every tone
and every gesture, and he forecast the result with
the real audience from its result with that imagined audience. Therefore, it was beautiful to see
him and to hear him; he rejoiced in the pleasure
he gave and the blows of surprise which he dealt;
and because he had his end in mind, he knew when
to stop.

I have been talking of his method and manner;
the matter the reader has here before him; and
it is good matter, glad, honest, kind, just.

W. D. HOWELLS.

PREFACE

FROM THE PREFACE TO THE ENGLISH EDITION OF
"MARK TWAIN'S SKETCHES"

IF I were to sell the reader a barrel of molasses, and he, instead of sweetening his substantial dinner with the same at judicious intervals, should eat the entire barrel at one sitting, and then abuse me for making him sick, I would say that he deserved to be made sick for not knowing any better how to utilize the blessings this world affords. And if I sell to the reader this volume of nonsense, and he, instead of seasoning his graver reading with a chapter of it now and then, when his mind demands such relaxation, unwisely overdoses himself with several chapters of it at a single sitting, he will deserve to be nauseated, and he will have nobody to blame but himself if he is. There is no more sin in publishing an entire volume of nonsense than there is in keeping a candy-store with no hardware in it. It lies wholly with the customer whether he will injure himself by means of either, or will derive from them the benefits which they will afford him if he uses their possibilities judiciously.

Respectfully submitted,

THE AUTHOR.

MARK TWAIN'S SPEECHES

MARK TWAIN'S SPEECHES

THE STORY OF A SPEECH

An address delivered in 1877, and a review of it twenty-nine years later. The original speech was delivered at a dinner given by the publishers of The Atlantic Monthly *in honor of the seventieth anniversary of the birth of John Greenleaf Whittier, at the Hotel Brunswick, Boston, December 17, 1877.*

THIS is an occasion peculiarly meet for the digging up of pleasant reminiscences concerning literary folk; therefore I will drop lightly into history myself. Standing here on the shore of the Atlantic and contemplating certain of its largest literary billows, I am reminded of a thing which happened to me thirteen years ago, when I had just succeeded in stirring up a little Nevadian literary puddle myself, whose spume-flakes were beginning to blow thinly Californiaward. I started an inspection tramp through the southern mines of California. I was callow and conceited, and I resolved to try the virtue of my *nom de guerre*.

I very soon had an opportunity. I knocked at a miner's lonely log cabin in the foot-hills of the Sierras just at nightfall. It was snowing at the time. A jaded, melancholy man of fifty, barefooted, opened the door to me. When he heard my *nom de guerre* he looked more dejected than before. He let me in—pretty reluctantly, I thought—and after the customary bacon and beans, black coffee and hot whiskey, I took a pipe. This sorrowful man had not said three words up to this time. Now he spoke up and said, in the voice of one who is secretly suffering, "You're the fourth—I'm going to move." "The fourth what?" said I. "The fourth littery man that has been here in twenty-four hours—I'm going to move." "You don't tell me!" said I; "who were the others?" "Mr. Longfellow, Mr. Emerson, and Mr. Oliver Wendell Holmes—consound the lot!"

You can easily believe I was interested. I supplicated—three hot whiskeys did the rest—and finally the melancholy miner began. Said he:

"They came here just at dark yesterday evening, and I let them in of course. Said they were going to the Yosemite. They were a rough lot, but that's nothing; everybody looks rough that travels afoot. Mr. Emerson was a seedy little bit of a chap, red-headed. Mr. Holmes was as fat as a balloon; he weighed as much as three hundred, and had double chins all the way down to his stomach. Mr. Longfellow was built like a prize-fighter. His head was cropped and bristly, like as if he had a wig made of hair-brushes. His nose lay straight down his face, like a finger with the end joint tilted up. They had been drinking, I could see that. And what queer talk they used! Mr. Holmes inspected this cabin, then he took me by the buttonhole, and says he:

> "'Through the deep caves of thought
> I hear a voice that sings,
> Build thee more stately mansions,
> O my soul!'

"Says I, 'I can't afford it, Mr. Holmes, and moreover I don't want to.' Blamed if I liked it pretty well, either, coming from a stranger, that way. However, I started to get out my bacon and beans, when Mr. Emerson came and looked on awhile, and then *he* takes me aside by the buttonhole and says:

> "'Give me agates for my meat;
> Give me cantharids to eat;
> From air and ocean bring me foods,
> From all zones and altitudes.'

"Says I, 'Mr. Emerson, if you'll excuse me, this ain't no hotel.' You see it sort of riled me—I warn't used to the ways of littery swells. But I went on a-sweating over my work, and next comes

3

Mr. Longfellow and buttonholes me, and interrupts me. Says he:

> "'Honor be to Mudjekeewis!
> You shall hear how Pau-Puk-Keewis—'

"But I broke in, and says I, 'Beg your pardon, Mr. Longfellow, if you'll be so kind as to hold your yawp for about five minutes and let me get this grub ready, you'll do me proud.' Well, sir, after they'd filled up I set out the jug. Mr. Holmes looks at it, and then he fires up all of a sudden and yells:

> "'Flash out a stream of blood-red wine!
> For I would drink to other days.'

"By George, I was getting kind of worked up. I don't deny it, I was getting kind of worked up. I turns to Mr. Holmes, and says I, 'Looky here, my fat friend, I'm a-running this shanty, and if the court knows herself, you'll take whiskey straight or you'll go dry.' Them's the very words I said to him. Now I don't want to sass such famous littery people, but you see they kind of forced me. There ain't nothing onreasonable 'bout me; I don't mind a passel of guests a-treadin' on my tail three or four times, but when it comes to *standing* on it it's different, 'and if the court knows herself,' I says, 'you'll take whiskey straight or you'll go dry.' Well, between drinks they'd swell around the cabin and strike attitudes and

4

spout; and pretty soon they got out a greasy old deck and went to playing euchre at ten cents a corner—on trust. I began to notice some pretty suspicious things. Mr. Emerson dealt, looked at his hand, shook his head, says:

    "'I am the doubter and the doubt—'

and ca'mly bunched the hands and went to shuffling for a new layout. Says he:

> "'They reckon ill who leave me out;
>   They know not well the subtle ways I keep.
>   I pass and deal *again!*'

Hang'd if he didn't go ahead and do it, too! Oh, he was a cool one! Well, in about a minute things were running pretty tight, but all of a sudden I see by Mr. Emerson's eye he judged he had 'em. He had already corralled two tricks, and each of the others one. So now he kind of lifts a little in his chair and says:

> "'I tire of globes and aces!—
>   Too long the game is played!'

—and down he fetched a right bower. Mr. Longfellow smiles as sweet as pie and says:

> "'Thanks, thanks to thee, my worthy friend,
>   For the lesson thou hast taught,'

—and blamed if he didn't down with *another* right bower! Emerson claps his hand on his bowie,

2

Longfellow claps his on his revolver, and I went under a bunk. There was going to be trouble; but that monstrous Holmes rose up, wobbling his double chins, and says he, 'Order, gentlemen; the first man that draws, I'll lay down on him and smother him!' All quiet on the Potomac, you bet!

"They were pretty how-come-you-so by now, and they begun to blow. Emerson says, 'The nobbiest thing I ever wrote was " Barbara Friet-chie."' Says Longfellow, 'It don't begin with my " Biglow Papers."' Says Holmes, 'My " Thana-topsis " lays over 'em both.' They mighty near ended in a fight. Then they wished they had some more company—and Mr. Emerson pointed to me and says:

> " 'Is yonder squalid peasant all
> That this proud nursery could breed ?'

He was a-whetting his bowie on his boot—so I let it pass. Well, sir, next they took it into their heads that they would like some music; so they made me stand up and sing " When Johnny Comes Marching Home " till I dropped—at thirteen minutes past four this morning. That's what I've been through, my friend. When I woke at seven, they were leaving, thank goodness, and Mr. Longfellow had my only boots on, and his'n under his arm. Says I, 'Hold on, there, Evangeline, what are you going to do with *them?*' He says, 'Going to make tracks with 'em; because:

6

THE STORY OF A SPEECH

> "'Lives of great men all remind us
> We can make our lives sublime;
> And, departing, leave behind us
> Footprints on the sands of time.'

As I said, Mr. Twain, you are the fourth in twenty-four hours—and I'm going to move; I ain't suited to a littery atmosphere."

I said to the miner, "Why, my dear sir, *these* were not the gracious singers to whom we and the world pay loving reverence and homage; these were impostors."

The miner investigated me with a calm eye for a while; then said he, "Ah! impostors, were they? Are *you?*"

I did not pursue the subject, and since then I have not travelled on my *nom de guerre* enough to hurt. Such was the reminiscence I was moved to contribute, Mr. Chairman. In my enthusiasm I may have exaggerated the details a little, but you will easily forgive me that fault, since I believe it is the first time I have ever deflected from perpendicular fact on an occasion like this.

From Mark Twain's Autobiography.

January 11, 1906.

Answer to a letter received this morning:

DEAR MRS. H.,—I am forever your debtor for reminding me of that curious passage in my life. During the first year or two after it happened, I could not bear to think of it. My pain and shame were so intense, and my sense of having been an imbecile so settled, established and confirmed, that I drove the episode entirely from my mind—and so all these twenty-eight or twenty-nine years I have lived in the conviction that my performance of that time was coarse, vulgar, and destitute of humor. But your suggestion that you and your family found humor in it twenty-eight years ago moved me to look into the matter. So I commissioned a Boston typewriter to delve among the Boston papers of that bygone time and send me a copy of it.

It came this morning, and if there is any vulgarity about it I am not able to discover it. If it isn't innocently and ridiculously funny, I am no judge. I will see to it that you get a copy.

What I have said to Mrs. H. is true. I did suffer during a year or two from the deep humiliations of that episode. But at last, in 1888, in Venice, my wife and I came across Mr. and Mrs. A. P. C., of Concord, Massachusetts, and a friendship began then of the sort which nothing but death terminates. The C.'s were very bright people and in every way charming and companionable. We were together a month or two in Venice and several months in Rome, afterward, and one day that lamented break of mine was mentioned. And when I was on the point of lathering those people for bringing it to my mind when I had gotten the memory of it almost squelched, I perceived with joy that the C.'s were

8

indignant about the way that my performance had been received in Boston. They poured out their opinions most freely and frankly about the frosty attitude of the people who were present at that performance, and about the Boston newspapers for the position they had taken in regard to the matter. That position was that I had been irreverent beyond belief, beyond imagination. Very well; I had accepted that as a fact for a year or two, and had been thoroughly miserable about it whenever I thought of it—which was not frequently, if I could help it. Whenever I thought of it I wondered how I ever could have been inspired to do so unholy a thing. Well, the C.'s comforted me, but they did not persuade me to continue to think about the unhappy episode. I resisted that. I tried to get it out of my mind, and let it die, and I succeeded. Until Mrs. H.'s letter came, it had been a good twenty-five years since I had thought of that matter; and when she said that the thing was funny I wondered if possibly she might be right. At any rate, my curiosity was aroused, and I wrote to Boston and got the whole thing copied, as above set forth.

I vaguely remember some of the details of that gathering—dimly I can see a hundred people— no, perhaps fifty—shadowy figures sitting at tables feeding, ghosts now to me, and nameless forevermore. I don't know who they were, but I can very distinctly see, seated at the grand table

and facing the rest of us, Mr. Emerson, super-
naturally grave, unsmiling; Mr. Whittier, grave,
lovely, his beautiful spirit shining out of his face;
Mr. Longfellow, with his silken white hair and his
benignant face; Dr. Oliver Wendell Holmes, flashing smiles and affection and all good-fellowship
everywhere like a rose-diamond whose facets are
being turned toward the light first one way and
then another—a charming man, and always fas-
cinating, whether he was talking or whether he
was sitting still (what *he* would call still, but
what would be more or less motion to other people). I can see those figures with entire distinct-
ness across this abyss of time.

One other feature is clear—Willie Winter (for
these past thousand years dramatic editor of the
New York Tribune, and still occupying that high
post in his old age) was there. He was much
younger then than he is now, and he showed it.
It was always a pleasure to me to see Willie Winter
at a banquet. During a matter of twenty years
I was seldom at a banquet where Willie Winter
was not also present, and where he did not read
a charming poem written for the occasion. He
did it this time, and it was up to standard: dainty,
happy, choicely phrased, and as good to listen to
as music, and sounding exactly as if it was pour-
ing unprepared out of heart and brain.

Now at that point ends all that was pleasurable
about that notable celebration of Mr. Whittier's

seventieth birthday—because *I* got up at that
point and followed Winter, with what I have no
doubt I supposed would be the gem of the evening—the gay oration above quoted from the Boston paper.   I had written it all out the day before
and had perfectly memorized it, and I stood up
there at my genial and happy and self-satisfied
ease, and began to deliver it.   Those majestic
guests, that row of venerable and still active vol-
canoes, listened, as did everybody else in the
house, with attentive interest.   Well, I delivered
myself of—we'll say the first two hundred words
of my speech.   I was expecting no returns from
that part of the speech, but this was not the case
as regarded the rest of it.   I arrived now at the
dialogue: "The old miner said, 'You are the
fourth, I'm going to move.'   'The fourth what?'
said I.   He answered, 'The fourth littery man
that has been here in twenty-four hours.   I am
going to move.'   'Why, you don't tell me,' said
I.   'Who were the others?'   'Mr. Longfellow, Mr.
Emerson, Mr. Oliver Wendell Holmes, consound
the lot—' "

Now, then, the house's *attention* continued, but
the expression of interest in the faces turned to a
sort of black frost.   I wondered what the trouble
was.   I didn't know.   I went on, but with difficulty—I struggled along, and entered upon that
miner's fearful description of the bogus Emerson,
the bogus Holmes, the bogus Longfellow, always

hoping—but with a gradually perishing hope—
that somebody would laugh, or that somebody
would at least smile, but nobody did. I didn't
know enough to give it up and sit down, I was
too new to public speaking, and so I went on
with this awful performance, and carried it clear
through to the end, in front of a body of people
who seemed turned to stone with horror. It was
the sort of expression their faces would have worn
if I had been making these remarks about the
Deity and the rest of the Trinity; there is no
milder way in which to describe the petrified
condition and the ghastly expression of those
people.

When I sat down it was with a heart which
had long ceased to beat. I shall never be as
dead again as I was then. I shall never be as
miserable again as I was then. I speak now as
one who doesn't know what the condition of
things may be in the next world, but in this one I
shall never be as wretched again as I was then.
Howells, who was near me, tried to say a comforting word, but couldn't get beyond a gasp.
There was no use—he understood the whole size
of the disaster. He had good intentions, but the
words froze before they could get out. It was
an atmosphere that would freeze anything. If
Benvenuto Cellini's salamander had been in that
place he would not have survived to be put into
Cellini's autobiography. There was a frightful

pause. There was an awful silence, a desolating silence. Then the next man on the list had to get up—there was no help for it. That was Bishop—Bishop had just burst handsomely upon the world with a most acceptable novel, which had appeared in The *Atlantic Monthly*, a place which would make any novel respectable and any author noteworthy. In this case the novel itself was recognized as being, without extraneous help, respectable. Bishop was away up in the public favor, and he was an object of high interest, consequently there was a sort of national expectancy in the air; we may say our American millions were standing, from Maine to Texas and from Alaska to Florida, holding their breath, their lips parted, their hands ready to applaud, when Bishop should get up on that occasion, and for the first time in his life speak in public. It was under these damaging conditions that he got up to "make good," as the vulgar say. I had spoken several times before, and that is the reason why I was able to go on without dying in my tracks, as I ought to have done—but Bishop had had no experience. He was up facing those awful deities —facing those other people, those strangers— facing human beings for the first time in his life, with a speech to utter. No doubt it was well packed away in his memory, no doubt it was fresh and usable, until I had been heard from. I suppose that after that, and under the smothering pall of that dreary silence, it began to waste away and disappear out of his head like the rags breaking from the edge of a fog, and presently there wasn't any fog left. He didn't go on—he didn't last long. It was not many sentences after his first before he began to hesitate, and break, and lose his grip, and totter, and wobble, and at last he slumped down in a limp and mushy pile.

Well, the programme for the occasion was probably not more than one - third finished, but it ended there. Nobody rose. The next man hadn't strength enough to get up, and everybody looked so dazed, so stupefied, paralyzed, it was impossible for anybody to do anything, or even try. Nothing could go on in that strange atmosphere. Howells mournfully, and without words, hitched himself to Bishop and me and supported us out of the room. It was very kind—he was most generous. He towed us tottering away into some room in that building, and we sat down there. I don't know what my remark was now, but I know the nature of it. It was the kind of remark you make when you know that nothing in the world can help your case. But Howells was honest—he had to say the heart-breaking things he did say: that there was no help for this calamity, this shipwreck, this cataclysm; that this was the most disastrous thing that had ever happened in anybody's history—and then he added, "That is, for *you*—and consider what you have done for Bishop. It is bad enough in your case, you deserve to suffer. You have committed this crime, and you deserve to have all you are going to get. But here is an innocent man. Bishop had never done you any harm, and see what you have done to him. He can never hold his head up again. The world can never look upon Bishop as being a live person. He is a corpse."

That is the history of that episode of twenty-eight years ago, which pretty nearly killed me with shame during that first year or two whenever it forced its way into my mind.

Now then, I take that speech up and examine it. As I said, it arrived this morning, from Boston. I have read it twice, and unless I am an idiot, it hasn't a single defect in it from the first word to the last. It is just as good as good can be. It is smart; it is saturated with humor. There isn't a suggestion of coarseness or vulgarity in it anywhere. What could have been the matter with that house? It is amazing, it is incredible, that they didn't shout with laughter, and those deities the loudest of them all. Could the fault have been with me? Did I lose courage when I saw those great men up there whom I was going to describe in such a strange fashion? If that happened, if I showed doubt, that can account for it, for you can't be successfully funny if you show that you are afraid of it. Well, I can't account for it, but if I had those beloved and revered old literary immortals back here now on the platform at Carnegie Hall I would take that same old speech, deliver it, word for word, and melt them till they'd run all over that stage. Oh, the fault must have been with *me*, it is not in the speech at all.

PLYMOUTH ROCK AND THE PILGRIMS

Address at the First Annual Dinner, N. E Society, Philadelphia, December 22, 1881

On calling upon Mr. Clemens to make response, President Rollins said:

"This sentiment has been assigned to one who was never *exactly* born in New England, nor, perhaps, were any of his ancestors. He is not *technically*, therefore, of New England descent. Under the painful circumstances in which he has found himself, however, he has done the best he could—he has had all his children born there, and has made of *himself* a New England *ancestor*. He is a self-made man. More than this, and better even, in cheerful, hopeful, helpful literature he is of New England *ascent*. To *ascend* there in anything that's reasonable is difficult, for—confidentially, with the door shut—we all know that they are the brightest, ablest sons of that goodly land who never leave it, and it is among and above *them* that Mr. Twain has made his brilliant and permanent ascent—become a man of mark."

I RISE to protest. I have kept still for years, but really I think there is no sufficient justification for this sort of thing. What do you want to celebrate those people for?—those ancestors of

yours of 1620—the *Mayflower* tribe, I mean.
What do you want to celebrate *them* for? Your
pardon: the gentleman at my left assures me that
you are not celebrating the Pilgrims themselves,
but the landing of the Pilgrims at Plymouth
Rock on the 22d of December. So you are celebrating their landing. Why, the other pretext
was thin enough, but this is thinner than ever;
the other was tissue, tinfoil, fish-bladder, but this
is gold-leaf. Celebrating their landing! What
was there remarkable about it, I would like to
know? What can you be thinking of? Why,
those Pilgrims had been at sea three or four
months. It was the very middle of winter: it
was as cold as death off Cape Cod there. Why
shouldn't they come ashore? If they *hadn't*
landed there would be some reason for celebrating
the fact. It would have been a case of monumental leatherheadedness which the world would
not willingly let die. If it had been *you*, gentlemen, you probably wouldn't have landed, but
you have no shadow of right to be celebrating,
in your ancestors, gifts which they did not exercise, but only transmitted. Why, to be celebrating the mere landing of the Pilgrims—to be
trying to make out that this most natural and
simple and customary procedure was an extraordinary circumstance — a circumstance to be
amazed at, and admired, aggrandized and glorified, at orgies like this for two hundred and sixty

18

years—hang it, a horse would have known enough
to land; a horse— Pardon again; the gentleman
on my right assures me that it was not merely
the landing of the Pilgrims that we are celebrating, but the Pilgrims themselves. So we have
struck an inconsistency here—one says it was the
landing, the other says it was the Pilgrims. It
is an inconsistency characteristic of your intractable and disputatious tribe, for you never agree
about anything but Boston. Well, then, what do
you want to celebrate those Pilgrims for? They
were a mighty hard lot—you know it. I grant
you, without the slightest unwillingness, that they
were a deal more gentle and merciful and just than
were the people of Europe of that day; I grant you
that they are better than their predecessors. But
what of that?—that is nothing. People always
progress. You are better than your fathers and
grandfathers were (this is the first time I have
ever aimed a measureless slander at the departed,
for I consider such things improper). Yes, those
among you who have not been in the penitentiary,
if such there be, are better than your fathers and
grandfathers were; but is that any sufficient reason
for getting up annual dinners and celebrating you?
No, by no means—by no means. Well, I repeat,
those Pilgrims were a hard lot. They took good
care of themselves, but they abolished everybody
else's ancestors. I am a border-ruffian from the
State of Missouri. I am a Connecticut Yankee

by adoption. In me, you have Missouri morals, Connecticut culture; this, gentlemen, is the combination which makes the perfect man. But where are my ancestors? Whom shall I celebrate? Where shall I find the raw material?

My first American ancestor, gentlemen, was an Indian — an early Indian. Your ancestors skinned him alive, and I am an orphan. Not one drop of my blood flows in that Indian's veins to-day. I stand here, lone and forlorn, without an ancestor. They skinned him! I do not object to that, if they needed his fur; but alive, gentlemen—alive! They skinned him alive—and before company! That is what rankles. Think how he must have felt; for he was a sensitive person and easily embarrassed. If he had been a bird, it would have been all right, and no violence done to his feelings, because he would have been considered "dressed." But he was not a bird, gentlemen, he was a man, and probably one of the most undressed men that ever was. I ask you to put yourselves in his place. I ask it as a favor; I ask it as a tardy act of justice; I ask it in the interest of fidelity to the traditions of your ancestors; I ask it that the world may contemplate, with vision unobstructed by disguising swallow-tails and white cravats, the spectacle which the true New England Society ought to present. Cease to come to these annual orgies in this hollow modern mockery—the surplusage of raiment. Come in character; come in the summer grace, come in the unadorned simplicity, come in the free and joyous costume which your sainted ancestors provided for mine.

Later ancestors of mine were the Quakers William Robinson, Marmaduke Stevenson, *et al*. Your tribe chased them out of the country for their religion's sake; promised them death if they came back; for your ancestors had forsaken the homes they loved, and braved the perils of the sea, the implacable climate, and the savage wilderness, to acquire that highest and most precious of boons, freedom for every man on this broad continent to worship according to the dictates of his own conscience—and they were not going to allow a lot of pestiferous Quakers to interfere with it. Your ancestors broke forever the chains of political slavery, and gave the vote to every man in this wide land, excluding none!—none except those who did not belong to the orthodox church. Your ancestors—yes, they were a hard lot; but, nevertheless, they gave us religious liberty to worship as they required us to worship, and political liberty to vote as the church required; and so I the bereft one, I the forlorn one, am here to do my best to help you celebrate them right.

The Quaker woman Elizabeth Hooton was an ancestress of mine. Your people were pretty severe with her—you will confess that. But, poor thing! I believe they changed her opinions before she died, and took her into their fold; and so we have every reason to presume that when she died she went to the same place which your ancestors went to. It is a great pity, for she was a good woman. Roger Williams was an ancestor of mine. I don't really remember what your people did with him. But they banished him to Rhode Island, anyway. And then, I believe, recognizing that this was really carrying harshness to an unjustifiable extreme, they took pity on him and burned him. They were a hard lot! All those Salem witches were ancestors of mine! Your people made it tropical for them. Yes, they did; by pressure and the gallows they made such a clean deal with them that there hasn't been a witch and hardly a halter in our family from that day to this, and that is one hundred and eighty-nine years. The first slave brought into New England out of Africa by your progenitors was an ancestor of mine—for I am of a mixed breed, an infinitely shaded and exquisite Mongrel. I'm not one of your sham meerschaums that you can color in a week. No, my complexion is the patient art of eight generations. Well, in my own time, I had acquired a lot of my kin—by purchase, and swapping around, and one way and another—and was getting along very well. Then, with the inborn perversity of your lineage, you got up a war, and took them all away from me. And so, again am I bereft, again am I forlorn; no drop of my blood flows in the veins of any living being who is marketable.

O my friends, hear me and reform! I seek your good, not mine. You have heard the speeches. Disband these New England societies—nurseries of a system of steadily augmenting laudation and hosannaing, which, if persisted in uncurbed, may some day in the remote future beguile you into prevaricating and bragging. Oh, stop, stop, while you are still temperate in your appreciation of your ancestors! Hear me, I beseech you; get up an auction and sell Plymouth Rock! The Pilgrims were a simple and ignorant race. They never had seen any good rocks before, or at least any that were not watched, and so they were excusable for hopping ashore in frantic delight and clapping an iron fence around this one. But you, gentlemen, are educated; you are enlightened; you know that in the rich land of your nativity, opulent New England, overflowing with rocks, this one isn't worth, at the outside, more than thirty-five cents. Therefore, sell it, before it is injured by exposure, or at least throw it open to the patent-medicine advertisements, and let it earn its taxes.

Yes, hear your true friend—your only true friend—list to his voice. Disband these societies, hotbeds of vice, of moral decay—perpetuators of ancestral superstition. Here on this board I see

water, I see milk, I see the wild and deadly lemon-
ade. These are but steps upon the downward
path. Next we shall see tea, then chocolate, then
coffee—hotel coffee. A few more years—all too
few, I fear—mark my words, we shall have cider!
Gentlemen, pause ere it be too late. You are on
the broad road which leads to dissipation, physical ruin, moral decay, gory crime and the gallows! I beseech you, I implore you, in the name
of your anxious friends, in the name of your suffering families, in the name of your impending
widows and orphans, stop ere it be too late. Disband these New England societies, renounce these
soul-blistering saturnalia, cease from varnishing
the rusty reputations of your long-vanished ancestors—the super-high-moral old iron-clads of
Cape Cod, the pious buccaneers of Plymouth
Rock—go home, and try to learn to behave!

However, chaff and nonsense aside, I think I
honor and appreciate your Pilgrim stock as much
as you do yourselves, perhaps; and I endorse and
adopt a sentiment uttered by a grandfather of
mine once—a man of sturdy opinions, of sincere
make of mind, and not given to flattery. He
said: "People may talk as they like about that
Pilgrim stock, but, after all's said and done, it
would be pretty hard to improve on those people;
and, as for me, I don't mind coming out flatfooted
and saying there ain't any way to improve on
them—except having them born in Missouri!"

COMPLIMENTS AND DEGREES

Delivered at the Lotos Club, January 11, 1908

In introducing Mr. Clemens, Frank R. Lawrence, the President of the Lotos Club, recalled the fact that the first club dinner in the present club-house, some fourteen years ago, was in honor of Mark Twain.

I WISH to begin this time at the beginning, lest I forget it altogether; that is to say, I wish to thank you for this welcome that you are giving, and the welcome which you gave me seven years ago, and which I forgot to thank you for at that time. I also wish to thank you for the welcome you gave me fourteen years ago, which I also forgot to thank you for at the time.

I hope you will continue this custom to give me a dinner every seven years before I join the hosts in the other world—I do not know which world.

Mr. Lawrence and Mr. Porter have paid me many compliments. It is very difficult to take compliments. I do not care whether you deserve the compliments or not, it is just as difficult to take them. The other night I was at the Engineers' Club, and enjoyed the sufferings of Mr.

25

Carnegie. They were complimenting him there; there it was all compliments, and none of them deserved. They say that you cannot live by bread alone, but I can live on compliments.

I do not make any pretence that I dislike compliments. The stronger the better, and I can manage to digest them. I think I have lost so much by not making a collection of compliments, to put them away and take them out again once in a while. When in England I said that I would start to collect compliments, and I began there and I have brought some of them along.

The first one of these lies—I wrote them down and preserved them—I think they are mighty good and extremely just. It is one of Hamilton Mabie's compliments. He said that La Salle was the first one to make a voyage of the Mississippi, but Mark Twain was the first to chart, light, and navigate it for the whole world.

If that had been published at the time that I issued that book [*Life on the Mississippi*], it would have been money in my pocket. I tell you, it is a talent by itself to pay compliments gracefully and have them ring true. It's an art by itself.

Here is another compliment by Albert Bigelow Paine, my biographer. He is writing four octavo volumes about me, and he has been at my elbow two and one-half years.

I just suppose that he does not know me, but says he knows me. He says "Mark Twain is not

26

merely a great writer, a great philosopher, a great man; he is the supreme expression of the human being, with his strength and his weakness." What a talent for compression! It takes a genius in compression to compact as many facts as that.

W. D. Howells spoke of me as first of Hartford, and ultimately of the solar system, not to say of the universe.

You know how modest Howells is. If it can be proved that my fame reaches to Neptune and Saturn, that will satisfy even me. You know how modest and retiring Howells seems to be, but deep down he is as vain as I am.

Mr. Howells had been granted a degree at Oxford, whose gown was red. He had been invited to an exercise at Columbia, and upon inquiry had been told that it was usual to wear the black gown. Later he had found that three other men wore bright gowns, and he had lamented that he had been one of the black mass, and not a red torch.

Edison wrote: "The average American loves his family. If he has any love left over for some other person, he generally selects Mark Twain."

Now here's the compliment of a little Montana girl which came to me indirectly. She was in a room in which there was a large photograph of me. After gazing at it steadily for a time, she said:

"We've got a John the Baptist like that." She also said: "Only ours has more trimmings."

I suppose she meant the halo. Now here is a gold-miner's compliment. It is forty-two years old. It was my introduction to an audience to which I lectured in a log school-house. There were no ladies there. I wasn't famous then. They didn't know me. Only the miners were there, with their breeches tucked into their boot-tops and with clay all over them. They wanted some one to introduce me, and they selected a miner, who protested, saying:

"I don't know anything about this man. Any-how, I only know two things about him. One is, he has never been in jail, and the other is, I don't know why."

There's one thing I want to say about that English trip. I knew his Majesty the King of England long years ago, and I didn't meet him for the first time then. One thing that I regret was that some newspapers said I talked with the Queen of England with my hat on. I don't do that with any woman. I did not put it on until she asked me to. Then she told me to put it on, and it's a command there. I thought I had car-ried my American democracy far enough. So I put it on. I have no use for a hat, and never did have.

Who was it who said that the police of London knew me? Why, the police know me everywhere. There never was a day over there when a police-man did not salute me, and then put up his hand

and stop the traffic of the world. They treated me as though I were a duchess.

The happiest experience I had in England was at a dinner given in the building of the *Punch* publication, a humorous paper which is appreciated by all Englishmen. It was the greatest privilege ever allowed a foreigner. I entered the dining-room of the building, where those men get together who have been running the paper for over fifty years. We were about to begin dinner when the toastmaster said: "Just a minute; there ought to be a little ceremony." Then there was that meditating silence for a while, and out of a closet there came a beautiful little girl dressed in pink, holding in her hand a copy of the previous week's paper, which had in it my cartoon. It broke me all up. I could not even say "Thank you." That was the prettiest incident of the dinner, the delight of all that wonderful table. When she was about to go, I said, "My child, you are not going to leave me; I have hardly got acquainted with you." She replied, "You know I've got to go; they never let me come in here before, and they never will again." That is one of the beautiful incidents that I cherish.

[At the conclusion of his speech, and while the diners were still cheering him, Colonel Porter brought forward the red-and-gray gown of the Oxford "doctor," and Mr. Clemens was made to

don it. The diners rose to their feet in their enthusiasm. With the mortar - board on his head,
and looking down admiringly at himself, Mr.
Twain said:]

I like that gown. I always did like red. The
redder it is the better I like it. I was born for a
savage. Now, whoever saw any red like this?
There is no red outside the arteries of an archangel that could compare with this. I know you
all envy me. I am going to have luncheon shortly
with ladies—just ladies. I will be the only lady of
my sex present, and I shall put on this gown and
make those ladies look dim.

BOOKS, AUTHORS, AND HATS

ADDRESS AT THE PILGRIMS' CLUB LUNCHEON, GIVEN
IN HONOR OF MR. CLEMENS AT THE SAVOY
HOTEL, LONDON, JUNE 25, 1907.

Mr. Birrell, M.P., Chief-Secretary for Ireland, in
introducing Mr. Clemens said: "We all love Mark
Twain, and we are here to tell him so. One more point
—all the world knows it, and that is why it is dangerous to omit it—our guest is a distinguished citizen of
the Great Republic beyond the seas. In America his
Huckleberry Finn and his *Tom Sawyer* are what
Robinson Crusoe and *Tom Brown's School Days* have
been to us. They are racy of the soil. They are
books to which it is impossible to place any period of
termination. I will not speak of the classics—
reminiscences of much evil in our early lives. We
do not meet here to-day as critics with our apprecia-
tions and depreciations, our twopenny little prefaces
or our forewords. I am not going to say what the
world a thousand years hence will think of Mark
Twain. Posterity will take care of itself, will read
what it wants to read, will forget what it chooses to
forget, and will pay no attention whatsoever to our
critical mumblings and jumblings. Let us therefore
be content to say to our friend and guest that we are
here speaking for ourselves and for our children, to
say what he has been to us. I remember in Liver-

pool, in 1867, first buying the copy, which I still preserve, of the celebrated *Jumping Frog*. It had a few
words of preface which reminded me then that our
guest in those days was called 'the wild humorist of
the Pacific slope,' and a few lines later down, 'the
moralist of the Main.' That was some forty years
ago. Here he is, still the humorist, still the moralist.
His humor enlivens and enlightens his morality, and
his morality is all the better for his humor. That is
one of the reasons why we love him. I am not here
to mention any book of his—that is a subject of dis-
pute in my family circle, which is the best and which
is the next best—but I must put in a word, lest I
should not be true to myself—a terrible thing—for
his *Joan of Arc*, a book of chivalry, of nobility, and
of manly sincerity for which I take this opportunity
of thanking him. But you can all drink this toast,
each one of you with his own intention. You can
get into it what meaning you like. Mark Twain is a
man whom English and Americans do well to honor.
He is the true consolidator of nations. His delightful humor is of the kind which dissipates and destroys
national prejudices. His truth and his honor, his
love of truth, and his love of honor, overflow all
boundaries. He has made the world better by his
presence. We rejoice to see him here. Long may
he live to reap the plentiful harvest of hearty, honest
human affection!''

PILGRIMS, I desire first to thank those undergraduates of Oxford. When a man has
grown so old as I am, when he has reached the
verge of seventy-two years, there is nothing that
carries him back to the dreamland of his life, to

32

his boyhood, like recognition of those young hearts up yonder. And so I thank them out of my heart. I desire to thank the Pilgrims of New York also for their kind notice and message which they have cabled over here. Mr. Birrell says he does not know how he got here. But he will be able to get away all right—he has not drunk anything since he came here. I am glad to know about those friends of his, Otway and Chatterton—fresh, new names to me. I am glad of the disposition he has shown to rescue them from the evils of poverty, and if they are still in London, I hope to have a talk with them. For a while I thought he was going to tell us the effect which my book had upon his growing manhood. I thought he was going to tell us how much that effect amounted to, and whether it really made him what he now is, but with the discretion born of Parliamentary experience he dodged that, and we do not know now whether he read the book or not. He did that very neatly. I could not do it any better myself.

My books have had effects, and very good ones, too, here and there, and some others not so good. There is no doubt about that. But I remember one monumental instance of it years and years ago. Professor Norton, of Harvard, was over here, and when he came back to Boston I went out with Howells to call on him. Norton was allied in some way by marriage with Darwin.

33

Mr. Norton was very gentle in what he had to say, and almost delicate, and he said: "Mr. Clemens, I have been spending some time with Mr. Darwin in England, and I should like to tell you something connected with that visit. You were the object of it, and I myself would have been very proud of it, but you may not be proud of it. At any rate, I am going to tell you what it was, and to leave to you to regard it as you please. Mr. Darwin took me up to his bedroom and pointed out certain things there—pitcher-plants, and so on, that he was measuring and watching from day to day—and he said: 'The chambermaid is permitted to do what she pleases in this room, but she must never touch those plants and never touch those books on that table by that candle. With those books I read myself to sleep every night.' Those were your own books." I said: "There is no question to my mind as to whether I should regard that as a compliment or not. I do regard it as a very great compliment and a very high honor that that great mind, laboring for the whole human race, should rest itself on my books. I am proud that he should read himself to sleep with them."

Now, I could not keep that to myself—I was so proud of it. As soon as I got home to Hartford I called up my oldest friend—and dearest enemy on occasion—the Rev. Joseph Twichell, my pastor, and I told him about that, and, of course, he was full of interest and venom. Those people who get no compliments like that feel like that. He went off. He did not issue any applause of any kind, and I did not hear of that subject for some time. But when Mr. Darwin passed away from this life, and some time after Darwin's *Life and Letters* came out, the Rev. Mr. Twichell procured an early copy of that work and found something in it which he considered applied to me. He came over to my house—it was snowing, raining, sleeting, but that did not make any difference to Twichell. He produced the book, and turned over and over, until he came to a certain place, when he said: "Here, look at this letter from Mr. Darwin to Sir Joseph Hooker." What Mr. Darwin said—I give you the idea and not the very words—was this: I do not know whether I ought to have devoted my whole life to these drudgeries in natural history and the other sciences or not, for while I may have gained in one way I have lost in another. Once I had a fine perception and appreciation of high literature, but in me that quality is atrophied. "That was the reason," said Mr. Twichell, "he was reading your books."

Mr. Birrell has touched lightly—very lightly, but in not an uncomplimentary way—on my position in this world as a moralist. I am glad to have that recognition, too, because I have suffered since I have been in this town; in the first place, right away, when I came here, from a newsman going

35

around with a great red, highly displayed placard in the place of an apron. He was selling newspapers, and there were two sentences on that placard which would have been all right if they had been punctuated; but they ran those two sentences together without a comma or anything, and that would naturally create a wrong impression, because it said, "Mark Twain arrives Ascot Cup stolen." No doubt many a person was misled by those sentences joined together in that unkind way. I have no doubt my character has suffered from it. I suppose I ought to defend my character, but how can I defend it? I can say here and now—and anybody can see by my face that I am sincere, that I speak the truth—that I have never seen that Cup. I have not got the Cup—I did not have a chance to get it. I have always had a good character in that way. I have hardly ever stolen anything, and if I did steal anything I had discretion enough to know about the value of it first. I do not steal things that are likely to get myself into trouble. I do not think any of us do that. I know we all take things—that is to be expected—but really, I have never taken anything, certainly in England, that amounts to any great thing. I do confess that when I was here seven years ago I stole a hat, but that did not amount to anything. It was not a good hat, and was only a clergyman's hat, anyway.

I was at a luncheon party, and Archdeacon Wilberforce was there also. I dare say he is Archdeacon now—he was a canon then—and he was serving in the Westminster battery, if that is the proper term—I do not know, as you mix military and ecclesiastical things together so much. He left the luncheon table before I did. He began this. I did steal his hat, but he began by taking mine. I make that interjection because I would not accuse Archdeacon Wilberforce of stealing my hat—I should not think of it. I confine that phrase to myself. He merely took my hat. And with good judgment, too—it was a better hat than his. He came out before the luncheon was over, and sorted the hats in the hall, and selected one which suited. It happened to be mine. He went off with it. When I came out by-and-by there was no hat there which would go on my head except his, which was left behind. My head was not the customary size just at that time. I had been receiving a good many very nice and complimentary attentions, and my head was a couple of sizes larger than usual, and his hat just suited me. The bumps and corners were all right intellectually. There were results pleasing to me —possibly so to him. He found out whose hat it was, and wrote me saying it was pleasant that all the way home, whenever he met anybody his gravities, his solemnities, his deep thoughts, his eloquent remarks were all snatched up by the people he met, and mistaken for brilliant humorisms.

I had another experience. It was not unpleasing. I was received with a deference which was entirely foreign to my experience by everybody whom I met, so that before I got home I had a much higher opinion of myself than I have ever had before or since. And there is in that very connection an incident which I remember at that old date which is rather melancholy to me, because it shows how a person can deteriorate in a mere seven years. It is seven years ago. I have not that hat now. I was going down Pall-Mall, or some other of your big streets, and I recognized that that hat needed ironing. I went into a big shop and passed in my hat, and asked that it might be ironed. They were courteous, very courteous, even courtly. They brought that hat back to me presently very sleek and nice, and I asked how much there was to pay. They replied that they did not charge the clergy anything. I have cherished the delight of that moment from that day to this. It was the first thing I did the other day to go and hunt up that shop and hand in my hat to have it ironed. I said when it came back, "How much to pay?" They said, "Ninepence." In seven years I have acquired all that worldliness, and I am sorry to be back where I was seven years ago.

But now I am chaffing and chaffing and chaffing

here, and I hope you will forgive me for that; but when a man stands on the verge of seventy-two you know perfectly well that he never reached that place without knowing what this life is— heartbreaking bereavement. And so our reverence is for our dead. We do not forget them; but our duty is toward the living; and if we can be cheerful, cheerful in spirit, cheerful in speech and in hope, that is a benefit to those who are around us.

My own history includes an incident which will always connect me with England in a pathetic way, for when I arrived here seven years ago with my wife and my daughter—we had gone around the globe lecturing to raise money to clear off a debt—my wife and one of my daughters started across the ocean to bring to England our eldest daughter. She was twenty-four years of age and in the bloom of young womanhood, and we were unsuspecting. When my wife and daughter—and my wife has passed from this life since—when they had reached mid-Atlantic, a cablegram—one of those heartbreaking cablegrams which we all in our days have to experience—was put into my hand. It stated that that daughter of ours had gone to her long sleep. And so, as I say, I cannot always be cheerful, and I cannot always be chaffing; I must sometimes lay the cap and bells aside, and recognize that I am of the human race like the rest, and must have

39

my cares and griefs. And therefore I noticed what Mr. Birrell said—I was so glad to hear him say it—something that was in the nature of these verses here at the top of this:

> " He lit our life with shafts of sun
>   And vanquished pain.
> Thus two great nations stand as one
>   In honoring Twain."

I am very glad to have those verses. I am very glad and very grateful for what Mr. Birrell said in that connection. I have received since I have been here, in this one week, hundreds of letters from all conditions of people in England—men, women, and children—and there is in them compliment, praise, and, above all and better than all, there is in them a note of affection. Praise is well, compliment is well, but affection—that is the last and final and most precious reward that any man can win, whether by character or achievement, and I am very grateful to have that reward. All these letters make me feel that here in England—as in America—when I stand under the English flag, I am not a stranger. I am not an alien, but at home.

DEDICATION SPEECH

AT THE DEDICATION OF THE COLLEGE OF THE CITY OF
NEW YORK, MAY 14, 1908

*Mr. Clemens wore his gown as Doctor of Laws, Oxford
University.   Ambassador Bryce and Mr. Choate had
made the formal addresses.*

HOW difficult, indeed, is the higher education.
Mr. Choate needs a little of it.   He is not
only short as a statistician of New York, but he
is off, far off, in his mathematics.   The four
thousand citizens of Greater New York, indeed!

But I don't think it was wise or judicious on
the part of Mr. Choate to show this higher education he has obtained.   He sat in the lap of that
great education (I was there at the time), and
see the result—the lamentable result.   Maybe if
he had had a sandwich here to sustain him the
result would not have been so serious.

For seventy-two years I have been striving to
acquire that higher education which stands for
modesty and diffidence, and it doesn't work.

And then look at Ambassador Bryce, who referred
to his alma mater, Oxford.   He might just as well
have included me.   Well, I am a later production.

If I am the latest graduate, I really and sincerely hope I am not the final flower of its seven
centuries; I hope it may go on for seven ages longer.

DIE SCHRECKEN DER DEUTSCHEN SPRACHE

ADDRESS TO THE VIENNA PRESS CLUB, NOVEMBER 21, 1897, AS DELIVERED IN GERMAN

ES hat mich tief gerührt, meine Herren, hier so gastfreundlich empfangen zu werden, von Kollegen aus meinem eigenen Berufe, in diesem von meiner eigenen Heimath so weit entferntem Lande. Mein Herz ist voller Dankbarkeit, aber meine Armuth an deutschen Worten zwingt mich zu groszer Sparzamkeit des Ausdruckes. Entschuldigen Sie, meine Herren, dasz ich verlese, was ich Ihnen sagen will. (Er las aber nicht, Anm. d. Ref.) Die deutsche Sprache spreche ich nicht gut, doch haben mehrere Sächverständige mich versichert, dasz ich sie schreibe wie ein Engel. Mag sein—ich weisz nicht. Habe bis jetzt keine Bekanntschaften mit Engeln gehabt. Das kommt später—wenn's dem lieben Gott gefällt—es hat keine Eile.

Seit lange, meine Herren, habe ich die leidenschaftliche Sehnsucht gehegt, eine Rede auf Deutsch zu halten, aber man hat mir's nie erlauben wollen. Leute, die kein Gefühl für die Kunst

THE HORRORS OF THE GERMAN LANGUAGE

ADDRESS TO THE VIENNA PRESS CLUB, NOVEMBER
21, 1897

[A LITERAL TRANSLATION]

IT has me deeply touched, my gentlemen, here
so hospitably received to be. From colleagues
out of my own profession, in this from my
own home so far distant land. My heart is full
of gratitude, but my poverty of German words
forces me to greater economy of expression. Excuse you, my gentlemen, that I read off, what I
you say will. [But he didn't read].

The German language speak I not good, but
have numerous connoisseurs me assured that I
her write like an angel. Maybe—maybe—I know
not. Have till now no acquaintance with the
angels had. That comes later—when it the dear
God please—it has no hurry.

Since long, my gentlemen, have I the passionate
longing nursed a speech on German to hold, but

hatten, legten mir immer Hindernisse in den Weg und vereitelten meinen Wunsch—zuweilen durch Vorwände, häufig durch Gewalt. Immer sagten diese Leute zu mir: "Schweigen Sie, Ew. Hochwohlgeboren! Ruhe, um Gotteswillen! Suche eine andere Art und Weise, Dich lästig zu machen."

Im jetzigen Fall, wie gewöhnlich, ist es mir schwierig geworden, mir die Erlaubnisz zu verschaffen. Das Comite bedauerte sehr, aber es konnte mir die Erlaubnisz nicht bewilligen wegen eines Gesetzes, das von der Concordia verlangt, sie soll die deutsche Sprache schützen. Du liebe Zeit! Wieso hätte man mir das sagen können— mögen—dürfen—sollen? Ich bin ja der treueste Freund der deutschen Sprache—und nicht nur jetzt, sondern von lange her—ja vor zwanzig Jahren schon. Und nie habe ich das Verlangen gehabt, der edlen Sprache zu schaden, im Gegentheil, nur gewünscht, sie zu verbessern; ich wollte sie blos reformiren. Es ist der Traum meines Lebens gewesen. Ich habe schon Besuche bei den verschiedenen deutschen Regierungen abgestattet und um Kontrakte gebeten. Ich bin jetzt nach Oesterreich in demselben Auftrag gekommen. Ich wurde nur einige Aenderungen anstreben. Ich wurde blos die Sprachmethode— die uppige, weitschweifige Konstruktion—zusammenrucken; die ewige Parenthese unterdrücken, abschaffen, vernichten; die Einführung von mehr

44

one has me not permitted. Men, who no feeling for the art had, laid me ever hindrance in the way and made naught my desire—sometimes by excuses, often by force. Always said these men to me: "Keep you still, your Highness! Silence! For God's sake seek another way and means yourself obnoxious to make."

In the present case, as usual it is me difficult become, for me the permission to obtain. The committee sorrowed deeply, but could me the permission not grant on account of a law which from the Concordia demands she shall the German language protect. Du liebe Zeit! How so had one to me this say could—might—dared—should? I am indeed the truest friend of the German language—and not only now, but from long since —yes, before twenty years already. And never have I the desire had the noble language to hurt; to the contrary, only wished she to improve—I would her only reform. It is the dream of my life been. I have already visits by the various German governments paid and for contracts prayed. I am now to Austria in the same task come. I would only some changes effect. I would only the language method—the luxurious, elaborate construction compress, the eternal parenthesis suppress, do away with, annihilate; the introduction of more than thirteen subjects in one sentence forbid; the verb so far to the

als dreizehn Subjekten in einen Satz verbieten;
das Zeitwort so weit nach vorne rücken, bis man
es ohne Fernrohr entdecken kann. Mit einem
Wort, meine Herren, ich möchte Ihre geliebte
Sprache vereinfachen, auf dasz, meine Herren,
wenn Sie sie zum Gebet brauchen, man sie dort
oben versteht.

Ich flehe Sie an, von mir sich berathen zu lassen,
führen Sie diese erwähnten Reformen aus. Dann
werden Sie eine prachtvolle Sprache besitzen und
nachher, wenn Sie Etwas sagen wollen, werden Sie
wenigstens selber verstehen, was Sie gesagt haben.
Aber öfters heutzutage, wenn Sie einen meilen-
langen Satz von sich gegeben und Sie sich etwas
angelehnt haben, um auszuruhen, dann müssen
Sie eine rührende Neugierde empfinden, selbst
herauszubringen, was Sie eigentlich gesprochen
haben. Vor mehreren Tagen hat der Korrespond-
ent einer hiesigen Zeitung einen Satz zustande
gebracht welcher hundertundzwölf Worte enthielt
und darin waren sieben Parenthese eingeschachtelt
und es wurde Das Subjekt siebenmal gewechselt.
Denken Sie nur, meine Herren, im Laufe der
Reise eines einzigen Satzes musz das arme, ver-
folgte, ermüdete Subjekt siebenmal umsteigen.

Nun, wenn wir die erwähnten Reformen aus-
führen, wird's nicht mehre so arg sein. Doch
noch eins. Ich möchte gern das trennbare
Zeitwort auch ein Bischen reformiren. Ich
mochte Niemand thun lassen, was Schiller gethan:

46

front pull that one it without a telescope discover can. With one word, my gentlemen, I
would your beloved language simplify so that,
my gentlemen, when you her for prayer need, One
her yonder-up understands.

I beseech you, from me yourself counsel to let,
execute these mentioned reforms. Then will
you an elegant language possess, and afterward,
when you some thing say will, will you at least
yourself understand what you said had. But often
nowadays, when you a mile-long sentence from
you given and you yourself somewhat have rested,
then must you have a touching inquisitiveness
have yourself to determine what you actually
spoken have. Before several days has the correspondent of a local paper a sentence constructed
which hundred and twelve words contain, and
therein were seven parentheses smuggled in, and
the subject seven times changed. Think you
only, my gentlemen, in the course of the voyage of a single sentence must the poor, persecuted, fatigued subject seven times change position!

Now, when we the mentioned reforms execute,
will it no longer so bad be. Doch noch eins. I
might gladly the separable verb also a little bit
reform. I might none do let what Schiller did:
he has the whole history of the **Thirty Years'**

47

Der hat die ganze Geschichte des dreizigjährigen Krieges zwischen die zwei Glieder eines trennbaren Zeitwortes eingezwängt. Das hat sogar Deutschland selbst empört; und man hat Schiller die Erlaubnisz verweigert, die Geschichte des hundert jährigen Krieges zu verfassen—Gott sei's gedankt. Nachdem alle diese Reformen festgestellt sein werden, wird die deutsche Sprache die edelste und die schönste auf der Welt sein.

Da Ihnen jetzt, meine Herren, der Charackter meiner Mission bekannt ist, bitte ich Sie, so freundlich zu sein und mir Ihre werthvolle Hilfe zu schenken. Herr Pötzl hat das Publikum glauben machen wollen, dasz ich nach Wien gekommen bin, um die Brücken zu verstopfen und den Verkehr zu hindern, während ich Beobachtungen sammle und aufzeichne. Lassen Sie sich aber nicht von ihm anführen. Meine häufige Anwesenheit auf den Brücken hat einen ganz unschuldigen Grund. Dort giebt's den nöthigen Raum. Dort kann man einen edlen, langen, deutschen Satz ausdehnen, die Brückengeländer entlang, und seinen ganzen Inhalt mit einem Blick übersehen. Auf das eine Ende des Geländers klebe ich das erste Glied eines trennbaren Zeitwortes und das Schluszglied klebe ich an's andere Ende — dann breite ich den Leib des Satzes dazwischen aus. Gewöhnlich sind für meinen Zweck die Brücken der Stadt lang genug: wenn ich aber Pötzl's Schriften studiren will, fahre ich

48

THE GERMAN LANGUAGE

War between the two members of a separable verb in-pushed. That has even Germany itself aroused, and one has Schiller the permission refused the History of the Hundred Years' War to compose—God be it thanked! After all these reforms established be will, will the German language the noblest and the prettiest on the world be.

Since to you now, my gentlemen, the character of my mission known is, beseech I you so friendly to be and to me your valuable help grant. Mr. Pötzl has the public believed make would that I to Vienna come am in order the bridges to clog up and the traffic to hinder, while I observations gather and note. Allow you yourselves but not from him deceived. My frequent presence on the bridges has an entirely innocent ground. Yonder gives it the necessary space, yonder can one a noble long German sentence elaborate, the bridge-railing along, and his whole contents with one glance overlook. On the one end of the railing pasted I the first member of a separable verb and the final member cleave I to the other end—then spread the body of the sentence between it out! Usually are for my purposes the bridges of the city long enough; when I but Pötzl's writings study will I ride out and use the glorious endless imperial bridge. But this is a calumny; Pötzl writes the prettiest German. Perhaps not so

hinaus und benutze die herrliche unendliche Reichsbrücke. Aber das ist eine Verleumdung. Pötzl schreibt das schönste Deutsch. Vielleicht nicht so biegsam wie das meinige, aber in manchen Kleinigkeiten viel besser. Entschuldigen Sie diese Schmeicheleien. Die sind wohl verdient. Nun bringe ich meine Rede um—nein—ich wollte sagen, ich bringe sie zum Schlusz. Ich bin ein Fremder—aber hier, unter Ihnen, habe ich es ganz vergessen. Und so, wieder, und noch wieder —biete ich Ihnen meinen herzlichsten Dank!

pliable as the mine, but in many details much
better. Excuse you these flatteries. These are
well deserved.

Now I my speech execute—no, I would say I
bring her to the close. I am a foreigner—but
here, under you, have I it entirely forgotten. And
so again and yet again proffer I you my heartiest
thanks."

GERMAN FOR THE HUNGARIANS

Address at the Jubilee Celebration of the
Emancipation of the Hungarian Press,
March 26, 1899

*The Ministry and members of Parliament were pres-
ent.   The subject was the "Ausgleich"—i. e., the arrangement for the apportionment of the taxes between
Hungary and Austria.   Paragraph 14 of the ausgleich
fixes the proportion each country must pay to the
support of the army.   It is the paragraph which
caused the trouble and prevented its renewal.*

NOW that we are all here together, I think it
will be a good idea to arrange the ausgleich.
If you will act for Hungary I shall be quite willing
to act for Austria, and this is the very time for it.
There couldn't be a better, for we are all feeling
friendly, fair-minded, and hospitable now, and full
of admiration for each other, full of confidence in
each other, full of the spirit of welcome, full of
the grace of forgiveness, and the disposition to
let bygones be bygones.

Let us not waste this golden, this beneficent,
this providential opportunity.   I am willing to
make any concession you want, just so we get it

settled. I am not only willing to let grain come in free, I am willing to pay the freight on it, and you may send delegates to the Reichsrath if you like. All I require is that they shall be quiet, peaceable people like your own deputies, and not disturb our proceedings.

If you want the Gegenseitigengeldbeitragendenverhältnismässigkeiten rearranged and readjusted I am ready for that. I will let you off at twenty-eight per cent. — twenty-seven — even twenty-five if you insist, for there is nothing illiberal about me when I am out on a diplomatic debauch.

Now, in return for these concessions, I am willing to take anything in reason, and I think we may consider the business settled and the ausgleich ausgegloschen at last for ten solid years, and we will sign the papers in blank, and do it here and now.

Well, I am unspeakably glad to have that ausgleich off my hands. It has kept me awake nights for anderthalbjahr.

But I never could settle it before, because always when I called at the Foreign Office in Vienna to talk about it, there wasn't anybody at home, and that is not a place where you can go in and see for yourself whether it is a mistake or not, because the person who takes care of the front door there is of a size that discourages liberty of action and the free spirit of investigation. To think the

5 53

ausgleich is abgemacht at last! It is a grand and beautiful consummation, and I am glad I came.

The way I feel now I do honestly believe I would rather be just my own humble self at this moment than paragraph 14.

A NEW GERMAN WORD

To aid a local charity Mr. Clemens appeared before a fashionable audience in Vienna, March 10, 1899, reading his sketch " The Lucerne Girl," and describing how he had been interviewed and ridiculed. He said in part:

I HAVE not sufficiently mastered German to allow my using it with impunity. My collection of fourteen - syllable German words is still incomplete. But I have just added to that collection a jewel—a veritable jewel. I found it in a telegram from Linz, and it contains ninety-five letters:

Personaleinkommensteuerschätzungskommissionsmitgliedsreisekostenrechnungsergänzungsrevisionsfund

If I could get a similar word engraved upon my tombstone I should sleep beneath it in peace.

UNCONSCIOUS PLAGIARISM

DELIVERED AT THE DINNER GIVEN BY THE PUB-
LISHERS OF "THE ATLANTIC MONTHLY" TO
OLIVER WENDELL HOLMES, IN HONOR
OF HIS SEVENTIETH BIRTHDAY,
AUGUST 29, 1879

I WOULD have travelled a much greater distance than I have come to witness the paying of honors to Doctor Holmes; for my feeling toward him has always been one of peculiar warmth. When one receives a letter from a great man for the first time in his life, it is a large event to him, as all of you know by your own experience. You never can receive letters enough from famous men afterward to obliterate that one, or dim the memory of the pleasant surprise it was, and the gratification it gave you. Lapse of time cannot make it commonplace or cheap.

Well, the first great man who ever wrote me a letter was our guest—Oliver Wendell Holmes. He was also the first great literary man I ever stole anything from—and that is how I came to write to him and he to me. When my first book was new, a friend of mine said to me, "The dedication is very neat." Yes, I said, I thought it was. My friend said, "I always admired it, even before I saw it in *The Innocents Abroad*." I naturally said: "What do you mean? Where did you ever see it before?" "Well, I saw it first some years ago as Doctor Holmes's dedication to his *Songs in Many Keys*." Of course, my first impulse was to prepare this man's remains for burial, but upon reflection I said I would reprieve him for a moment or two and give him a chance to prove his assertion if he could. We stepped into a book-store, and he did prove it. I had really stolen that dedication, almost word for word. I could not imagine how this curious thing had happened; for I knew one thing—that a certain amount of pride always goes along with a teaspoonful of brains, and that this pride protects a man from deliberately stealing other people's ideas. That is what a teaspoonful of brains will do for a man—and admirers had often told me I had nearly a basketful—though they were rather reserved as to the size of the basket.

However, I thought the thing out, and solved the mystery. Two years before, I had been laid up a couple of weeks in the Sandwich Islands, and had read and re-read Doctor Holmes's poems till my mental reservoir was filled up with them to the brim. The dedication lay on the top, and handy, so, by-and-by, I unconsciously stole it. Perhaps I unconsciously stole the rest of the volume, too, for many people have told me that my book was pretty poetical, in one way or another. Well, of course, I wrote Doctor Holmes and told him I hadn't meant to steal, and he wrote back and said in the kindest way that it was all right and no harm done; and added that he believed we all unconsciously worked over ideas gathered in reading and hearing, imagining they were original with ourselves. He stated a truth, and did it in such a pleasant way, and salved over my sore spot so gently and so healingly, that I was rather glad I had committed the crime, for the sake of the letter. I afterward called on him and told him to make perfectly free with any ideas of mine that struck him as being good protoplasm for poetry. He could see by that that there wasn't anything mean about me; so we got along right from the start. I have not met Doctor Holmes many times since; and lately he said— However, I am wandering wildly away from the one thing which I got on my feet to do; that is, to make my compliments to you, my fellow-teachers of the great public, and likewise to say that I am right glad to see that Doctor Holmes is still in his prime and full of generous life; and as age is not determined by years, but by trouble and infirmities of mind and body, I hope it may be a very long time yet before any one can truthfully say, "He is growing old."

THE WEATHER

ADDRESS AT THE NEW ENGLAND SOCIETY'S SEVENTY-FIRST ANNUAL DINNER, NEW YORK CITY

The next toast was: "The Oldest Inhabitant—The Weather of New England."
> Who can lose it and forget it?
> Who can have it and regret it?

> "Be interposer 'twixt us Twain."
> —*Merchant of Venice.*

I REVERENTLY believe that the Maker who made us all makes everything in New England but the weather. I don't know who makes that, but I think it must be raw apprentices in the weather-clerk's factory who experiment and learn how, in New England, for board and clothes, and then are promoted to make weather for countries that require a good article, and will take their custom elsewhere if they don't get it. There is a sumptuous variety about the New England weather that compels the stranger's admiration—and regret. The weather is always doing something there; always attending strictly to business; always getting up new designs and trying them on the people to see how they will go. But it gets

59

through more business in spring than in any other season. In the spring I have counted one hundred and thirty-six different kinds of weather inside of four-and-twenty hours. It was I that made the fame and fortune of that man that had that marvellous collection of weather on exhibition at the Centennial, that so astounded the foreigners. He was going to travel all over the world and get specimens from all the climes. I said, "Don't you do it; you come to New England on a favorable spring day." I told him what we could do in the way of style, variety, and quantity. Well, he came and he made his collection in four days. As to variety, why, he confessed that he got hundreds of kinds of weather that he had never heard of before. And as to quantity— well, after he had picked out and discarded all that was blemished in any way, he not only had weather enough, but weather to spare; weather to hire out; weather to sell; to deposit; weather to invest; weather to give to the poor. The people of New England are by nature patient and forbearing, but there are some things which they will not stand. Every year they kill a lot of poets for writing about "Beautiful Spring." These are generally casual visitors, who bring their notions of spring from somewhere else, and cannot, of course, know how the natives feel about spring. And so the first thing they know the opportunity to inquire how they feel has permanently gone by. Old Probabilities has a mighty reputation for accurate prophecy, and thoroughly well deserves it. You take up the paper and observe how crisply and confidently he checks off what to-day's weather is going to be on the Pacific, down South, in the Middle States, in the Wisconsin region. See him sail along in the joy and pride of his power till he gets to New England, and then see his tail drop. *He* doesn't know what the weather is going to be in New England. Well, he mulls over it, and by-and-by he gets out something about like this: Probably northeast to southwest winds, varying to the southward and westward and eastward, and points between, high and low barometer swapping around from place to place; probable areas of rain, snow, hail, and drought, succeeded or preceded by earthquakes, with thunder and lightning. Then he jots down his postscript from his wandering mind, to cover accidents. "But it is possible that the programme may be wholly changed in the mean time." Yes, one of the brightest gems in the New England weather is the dazzling uncertainty of it. There is only one thing certain about it: you are certain there is going to be plenty of it—a perfect grand review; but you never can tell which end of the procession is going to move first. You fix up for the drought; you leave your umbrella in the house and sally out, and two to one you get drowned. You make up your mind that the earthquake is due; you stand from under, and take hold of something to steady yourself, and the first thing you know you get struck by lightning. These are great disappointments; but they can't be helped. The lightning there is peculiar; it is so convincing, that when it strikes a thing it doesn't leave enough of that thing behind for you to tell whether— Well, you'd think it was something valuable, and a Congressman had been there. And the thunder. When the thunder begins to merely tune up and scrape and saw, and key up the instruments for the performance, strangers say, "Why, what awful thunder you have here!" But when the baton is raised and the real concert begins, you'll find that stranger down in the cellar with his head in the ash-barrel. Now as to the *size* of the weather in New England—lengthways, I mean. It is utterly disproportioned to the size of that little country. Half the time, when it is packed as full as it can stick, you will see that New England weather sticking out beyond the edges and projecting around hundreds and hundreds of miles over the neighboring States. She can't hold a tenth part of her weather. You can see cracks all about where she has strained herself trying to do it. I could speak volumes about the inhuman perversity of the New England weather, but I will give but a single specimen. I like to hear rain on a tin roof. So I covered part of my **roof** with tin, with an eye to that luxury. Well, sir, do you think it ever rains on that tin? No, sir; skips it every time. Mind, in this speech I have been trying merely to do honor to the New England weather—no language could do it justice. But, after all, there is at least one or two things about that weather (or, if you please, effects produced by it) which we residents would not like to part with. If we hadn't our bewitching autumn foliage, we should still have to credit the weather with one feature which compensates for all its bullying vagaries—the ice-storm: when a leafless tree is clothed with ice from the bottom to the top —ice that is as bright and clear as crystal; when every bough and twig is strung with ice-beads, frozen dew-drops, and the whole tree sparkles cold and white, like the Shah of Persia's diamond plume. Then the wind waves the branches and the sun comes out and turns all those myriads of beads and drops to prisms that glow and burn and flash with all manner of colored fires, which change and change again with inconceivable rapidity from blue to red, from red to green, and green to gold—the tree becomes a spraying fountain, a very explosion of dazzling jewels; and it stands there the acme, the climax, the supremest possibility in art or nature, of bewildering, intoxicating, intolerable magnificence. One cannot make the words too strong.

THE BABIES

DELIVERED AT THE BANQUET, IN CHICAGO, GIVEN
BY THE ARMY OF THE TENNESSEE TO THEIR
FIRST COMMANDER, GENERAL U. S.
GRANT, NOVEMBER, 1879

*The fifteenth regular toast was " The Babies.—As
they comfort us in our sorrows, let us not forget them
in our festivities."*

I LIKE that. We have not all had the good
fortune to be ladies. We have not all been
generals, or poets, or statesmen; but when the
toast works down to the babies, we stand on
common ground. It is a shame that for a thousand years the world's banquets have utterly
ignored the baby, as if he didn't amount to anything. If you will stop and think a minute—if
you will go back fifty or one hundred years to
your early married life and recontemplate your
first baby—you will remember that he amounted
to a good deal, and even something over. You
soldiers all know that when that little fellow
arrived at family headquarters you had to hand
in your resignation. He took entire command.
You became his lackey, his mere body-servant,

and you had to stand around too. He was not a commander who made allowances for time, distance, weather, or anything else. You had to execute his order whether it was possible or not. And there was only one form of marching in his manual of tactics, and that was the double-quick. He treated you with every sort of insolence and disrespect, and the bravest of you didn't dare to say a word. You could face the death-storm at Donelson and Vicksburg, and give back blow for blow; but when he clawed your whiskers, and pulled your hair, and twisted your nose, you had to take it. When the thunders of war were sounding in your ears you set your faces toward the batteries, and advanced with steady tread; but when he turned on the terrors of his war-whoop you advanced in the other direction, and mighty glad of the chance, too. When he called for soothing-syrup, did you venture to throw out any side-remarks about certain services being unbecoming an officer and a gentleman? No. You got up and *got* it. When he ordered his pap bottle and it was not warm, did you talk back? Not you. You went to work and *warmed* it. You even descended so far in your menial office as to take a suck at that warm, insipid stuff yourself, to see if it was right—three parts water to one of milk, a touch of sugar to modify the colic, and a drop of peppermint to kill those immortal hiccoughs. I can taste that stuff yet. And how many things you learned as you went along! Sentimental young folks still take stock in that beautiful old saying that when the baby smiles in his sleep, it is because the angels are whispering to him. Very pretty, but too thin—simply wind on the stomach, my friends. If the baby proposed to take a walk at his usual hour, two o'clock in the morning, didn't you rise up promptly and remark, with a mental addition which would not improve a Sunday-school book *much*, that that was the very thing you were about to propose yourself? Oh! you were under good discipline, and as you went fluttering up and down the room in your undress uniform, you not only prattled undignified baby-talk, but even tuned up your martial voices and tried to *sing!—Rock-a-by Baby in the Tree-top*, for instance. What a spectacle for an Army of the Tennessee! And what an affliction for the neighbors, too; for it is not everybody within a mile around that likes military music at three in the morning. And when you had been keeping this sort of thing up two or three hours, and your little velvet-head intimated that nothing suited him like exercise and noise, what did you do? You simply *went* on until you dropped in the last ditch. The idea that a *baby* doesn't *amount* to anything! Why, *one* baby is just a house and a front yard full by itself. *One* baby can furnish more business than you and your whole Interior

66

Department can attend to. He is enterprising, irrepressible, brimful of lawless activities. Do what you please, you can't make him stay on the reservation. Sufficient unto the day is one baby. As long as you are in your right mind don't you ever pray for twins. Twins amount to a permanent riot. And there ain't any real difference between triplets and an insurrection.

Yes, it was high time for a toast-master to recognize the importance of the babies. Think what is in store for the present crop! Fifty years from now we shall all be dead, I trust, and then this flag, if it still survive (and let us hope it may), will be floating over a Republic numbering 200,-000,000 souls, according to the settled laws of our increase. Our present schooner of State will have grown into a political leviathan—a *Great Eastern*. The cradled babies of to-day will be on deck. Let them be well trained, for we are going to leave a big contract on their hands. Among the three or four million cradles now rocking in the land are some which this nation would preserve for ages as sacred things, if we could know which ones they are. In one of these cradles the unconscious Farragut of the future is at this moment teething — think of it! — and putting in a world of dead earnest, unarticulated, but perfectly justifiable profanity over it, too. In another the future renowned astronomer is blinking at the shining Milky Way with but a languid in-

terest—poor little chap!—and wondering what
has become of that other one they call the wet-
nurse. In another the future great historian
is lying—and doubtless will continue to lie until
his earthly mission is ended. In another the future
President is busying himself with no profounder
problem of state than what the mischief has
become of his hair so early; and in a mighty array
of other cradles there are now some 60,000 future
office-seekers, getting ready to furnish him occasion to grapple with that same old problem a
second time. And in still one more cradle, somewhere under the flag, the future illustrious com-
mander-in-chief of the American armies is so little
burdened with his approaching grandeurs and re-
sponsibilities as to be giving his whole strategic
mind at this moment to trying to find out some
way to get his big toe into his mouth—an achievement which, meaning no disrespect, the illustrious
guest of this evening turned *his* entire attention to
some fifty-six years ago; and if the child is but a
prophecy of the man, there are mighty few who
will doubt that he *succeeded*.

OUR CHILDREN AND GREAT DISCOVERIES

DELIVERED AT THE AUTHORS' CLUB, NEW YORK

OUR children — yours — and — mine. They seem like little things to talk about — our children, but little things often make up the sum of human life—that's a good sentence. I repeat it, little things often produce great things. Now, to illustrate, take Sir Isaac Newton—I presume some of you have heard of Mr. Newton. Well, once when Sir Isaac Newton—a mere lad—got over into the man's apple orchard—I don't know what he was doing there—I didn't come all the way from Hartford to q-u-e-s-t-i-o-n Mr. Newton's honesty—but when he was there — in the main orchard—he saw an apple fall and he was a-t-t-racted toward it, and that led to the discovery — not of Mr. Newton — but of the great law of *attraction* and gravitation.

And there was once another great discoverer— I've forgotten his name, and I don't remember what he discovered, but I know it was something very important, and I hope you will all tell your children about it when you get home. Well, when the great discoverer was once loafin' around down in Virginia, and a-puttin' in his time flirting with Pocahontas—oh! Captain John Smith, that was the man's name—and while he and Poca were sitting in Mr. Powhatan's garden, he accidentally put his arm around her and picked something— a simple weed, which proved to be tobacco—and now we find it in every Christian family, shedding its civilizing influence broadcast throughout the whole religious community.

Now there was another great man, I can't think of his name either, who used to loaf around and watch the great chandelier in the cathedral at Pisa, which set him to thinking about the great law of gunpowder, and eventually led to the discovery of the cotton-gin.

Now, I don't say this as an inducement for our young men to loaf around like Mr. Newton and Mr. Galileo and Captain Smith, but they were once little babies two days old, and they show what little things have sometimes accomplished.

EDUCATING THEATRE-GOERS

The children of the Educational Alliance gave a performance of "The Prince and the Pauper" on the afternoon of April 14, 1907, in the theatre of the Alliance Building in East Broadway. The audience was composed of nearly one thousand children of the neighborhood. Mr. Clemens, Mr. Howells, and Mr. Daniel Frohman were among the invited guests.

I HAVE not enjoyed a play so much, so heartily, and so thoroughly since I played Miles Hendon twenty-two years ago. I used to play in this piece ("The Prince and the Pauper") with my children, who, twenty-two years ago, were little youngsters. One of my daughters was the Prince, and a neighbor's daughter was the Pauper, and the children of other neighbors played other parts. But we never gave such a performance as we have seen here to-day. It would have been beyond us.

My late wife was the dramatist and stage-manager. Our coachman was the stage-manager, second in command. We used to play it in this simple way, and the one who used to bring in the crown on a cushion—he was a little fellow then—is now a clergyman way up high—six or seven

71

feet high—and growing higher all the time. We played it well, but not as well as you see it here, for you see it done by practically trained professionals.

I was especially interested in the scene which we have just had, for Miles Hendon was my part. I did it as well as a person could who never remembered his part. The children all knew their parts. They did not mind if I did not know mine. I could thread a needle nearly as well as the player did whom you saw to-day. The words of my part I could supply on the spot. The words of the song that Miles Hendon sang here I did not catch. But I was great in that song.

[Then Mr. Clemens hummed a bit of doggerel that the reporter made out as this:

> " There was a woman in her town,
> She loved her husband well,
> But another man just twice as well."

"How is that?" demanded Mr. Clemens. Then resuming:]

It was so fresh and enjoyable to make up a new set of words each time that I played the part.

If I had a thousand citizens in front of me, I would like to give them information, but you children already know all that I have found out about the Educational Alliance. It's like a man living within thirty miles of Vesuvius and never knowing about a volcano. It's like living for a lifetime in Buffalo, eighteen miles from Niagara, and never going to see the Falls. So I had lived in New York and knew nothing about the Educational Alliance.

This theatre is a part of the work, and furnishes pure and clean plays. This theatre is an influence. Everything in the world is accomplished by influences which train and educate. When you get to be seventy-one and a half, as I am, you may think that your education is over, but it isn't.

If we had forty theatres of this kind in this city of four millions, how they would educate and elevate! We should have a body of educated theatre-goers.

It would make better citizens, honest citizens. One of the best gifts a millionaire could make would be a theatre here and a theatre there. It would make of you a real Republic, and bring about an educational level.

THE EDUCATIONAL THEATRE

On November 19, 1907, Mr. Clemens entertained a party of six or seven hundred of his friends, inviting them to witness the representation of "The Prince and the Pauper," played by boys and girls of the East Side at the Children's Educational Theatre, New York.

JUST a word or two to let you know how deeply I appreciate the honor which the children who are the actors and frequenters of this cozy playhouse have conferred upon me. They have asked me to be their ambassador to invite the hearts and brains of New York to come down here and see the work they are doing. I consider it a grand distinction to be chosen as their intermediary. Between the children and myself there is an indissoluble bond of friendship.

I am proud of this theatre and this performance —proud, because I am naturally vain—vain of myself and proud of the children.

I wish we could reach more children at one time. I am glad to see that the children of the East Side have turned their backs on the Bowery theatres to come to see the pure entertainments presented here.

THE EDUCATIONAL THEATRE

This Children's Theatre is a great educational institution. I hope the time will come when it will be part of every public school in the land. I may be pardoned in being vain. I was born vain, I guess. [At this point the stage-manager's whistle interrupted Mr. Clemens.] That settles it; there's my cue to stop. I was to talk until the whistle blew, but it blew before I got started. It takes me longer to get started than most people. I guess I was born at slow speed. My time is up, and if you'll keep quiet for two minutes I'll tell you something about Miss Herts, the woman who conceived this splendid idea. She is the originator and the creator of this theatre. Educationally, this institution coins the gold of young hearts into external good.

[On April 23, 1908, he spoke again at the same place]

I will be strictly honest with you; I am only fit to be honorary president. It is not to be expected that I should be useful as a real president. But when it comes to things ornamental I, of course, have no objection. There is, of course, no competition. I take it as a very real compliment because there are thousands of children who have had a part in this request. It is promotion in truth.

It is a thing worth doing that is done here. You have seen the children play. You saw how little

Sally reformed her burglar. She could reform any burglar. She could reform me. This is the only school in which can be taught the highest and most difficult lessons—morals. In other schools the way of teaching morals is revolting. Here the children who come in thousands live through each part.

They are terribly anxious for the villain to get his bullet, and that I take to be a humane and proper sentiment. They spend freely the ten cents that is not saved without a struggle. It comes out of the candy money, and the money that goes for chewing-gum and other necessaries of life. They make the sacrifice freely. This is the only school which they are sorry to leave.

POETS AS POLICEMEN

Mr. Clemens was one of the speakers at the Lotos Club dinner to Governor Odell, March 24, 1900. The police problem was referred to at length.

LET us abolish policemen who carry clubs and revolvers, and put in a squad of poets armed to the teeth with poems on Spring and Love. I would be very glad to serve as commissioner, not because I think I am especially qualified, but because I am too tired to work and would like to take a rest.

Howells would go well as my deputy. He is tired too, and needs a rest badly.

I would start in at once to elevate, purify, and depopulate the red-light district. I would assign the most soulful poets to that district, all heavily armed with their poems. Take Chauncey Depew as a sample. I would station them on the corners after they had rounded up all the depraved people of the district so they could not escape, and then have them read from their poems to the poor unfortunates. The plan would be very effective in causing an emigration of the depraved element.

PUDD'NHEAD WILSON DRAMATIZED

When Mr. Clemens arrived from Europe in 1895 one of the first things he did was to see the dramatization of Pudd'nhead Wilson. *The audience becoming aware of the fact that Mr. Clemens was in the house called upon him for a speech.*

NEVER in my life have I been able to make a speech without preparation, and I assure you that this position in which I find myself is one totally unexpected.

I have been hemmed in all day by William Dean Howells and other frivolous persons, and I have been talking about everything in the world except that of which speeches are constructed. Then, too, seven days on the water is not conducive to speech-making. I will only say that I congratulate Mr. Mayhew; he has certainly made a delightful play out of my rubbish. His is a charming gift. Confidentially I have always had an idea that I was well equipped to write plays, but I have never encountered a manager who has agreed with me.

DALY THEATRE

Address at a Dinner After the One Hundredth Performance of "The Taming of the Shrew."

Mr. Clemens made the following speech, which he incorporated afterward in Following the Equator.

I AM glad to be here. This is the hardest theatre in New York to get into, even at the front door. I never got in without hard work. I am glad we have got so far in at last. Two or three years ago I had an appointment to meet Mr. Daly on the stage of this theatre at eight o'clock in the evening. Well, I got on a train at Hartford to come to New York and keep the appointment. All I had to do was to come to the back door of the theatre on Sixth Avenue. I did not believe that; I did not believe it could be on Sixth Avenue, but that is what Daly's note said—come to that door, walk right in, and keep the appointment. It look-ed very easy. It looked easy enough, but I had not much confidence in the Sixth Avenue door.

Well, I was kind of bored on the train, and I bought some newspapers — New Haven newspapers—and there was not much news in them, so I read the advertisements. There was one advertisement of a bench-show. I had heard of bench - shows, and I often wondered what there was about them to interest people. I had seen bench-shows—lectured to bench-shows, in fact—but I didn't want to advertise them or to brag about them. Well, I read on a little, and learned that a bench-show was not a bench-show — but dogs, not benches at all—only dogs. I began to be interested, and as there was nothing else to do I read every bit of the advertisement, and learned that the biggest thing in this show was a St. Bernard dog that weighed one hundred and forty-five pounds. Before I got to New York I was so interested in the bench-shows that I made up my mind to go to one the first chance I got. Down on Sixth Avenue, near where that back door might be, I began to take things leisurely. I did not like to be in too much of a hurry. There was not anything in sight that looked like a back door. The nearest approach to it was a cigar store. So I went in and bought a cigar, not too expensive, but it cost enough to pay for any information I might get and leave the dealer a fair profit. Well, I did not like to be too abrupt, to make the man think me crazy, by asking him if that was the way to Daly's Theatre, so I started gradually to lead up to the subject, asking him first if that was the way to Castle Garden. When I got to the real

question, and he said he would show me the way,
I was astonished. He sent me through a long
hallway, and I found myself in a back yard.
Then I went through a long passageway and into
a little room, and there before my eyes was a big
St. Bernard dog lying on a bench. There was
another door beyond and I went there, and was
met by a big, fierce man with a fur cap on and
coat off, who remarked, "Phwat do yez want?"
I told him I wanted to see Mr. Daly. "Yez can't
see Mr. Daly this time of night," he responded.
I urged that I had an appointment with Mr. Daly,
and gave him my card, which did not seem to
impress him much. "Yez can't get in and yez
can't shmoke here. Throw away that cigar. If
yez want to see Mr. Daly, yez 'll have to be after
going to the front door and buy a ticket, and
then if yez have luck and he's around that way
yez may see him." I was getting discouraged,
but I had one resource left that had been of good
service in similar emergencies. Firmly but kindly
I told him my name was Mark Twain, and I
awaited results. There was none. He was not
fazed a bit. "Phwere's your order to see Mr.
Daly?" he asked. I handed him the note, and he
examined it intently. "My friend," I remarked,
"you can read that better if you hold it the other
side up." But he took no notice of the suggestion,
and finally asked: "Where's Mr. Daly's name?"
"There it is," I told him, "on the top of the page."

"That's all right," he said, "that's where he always puts it; but I don't see the 'W' in his name," and he eyed me distrustfully. Finally he asked, "Phwat do yez want to see Mr. Daly for?" "Business." "Business?" "Yes." It was my only hope. "Phwat kind—theatres?" That was too much. "No." "What kind of shows, then?" "Bench-shows." It was risky, but I was desperate. "Bench - shows, is it — where?" The big man's face changed, and he began to look interested. "New Haven." "New Haven, it is? Ah, that's going to be a fine show. I'm glad to see you. Did you see a big dog in the other room?" "Yes." "How much do you think that dog weighs?" "One hundred and forty-five pounds." "Look at that, now! He's a good judge of dogs, and no mistake. He weighs all of one hundred and thirty-eight. Sit down and shmoke—go on and shmoke your cigar, I'll tell Mr. Daly you are here." In a few minutes I was on the stage shaking hands with Mr. Daly, and the big man standing around glowing with satisfaction. "Come around in front," said Mr. Daly, "and see the performance. I will put you into my own box." And as I moved away I heard my honest friend mutter, "Well, he desarves it."

THE DRESS OF CIVILIZED WOMAN

A LARGE part of the daughter of civilization is her dress—as it should be. Some civilized women would lose half their charm without dress, and some would lose all of it. The daughter of modern civilization dressed at her utmost best is a marvel of exquisite and beautiful art and expense. All the lands, all the climes, and all the arts are laid under tribute to furnish her forth. Her linen is from Belfast, her robe is from Paris, her lace is from Venice, or Spain, or France, her feathers are from the remote regions of Southern Africa, her furs from the remoter region of the iceberg and the aurora, her fan from Japan, her diamonds from Brazil, her bracelets from California, her pearls from Ceylon, her cameos from Rome. She has gems and trinkets from buried Pompeii, and others that graced comely Egyptian forms that have been dust and ashes now for forty centuries. Her watch is from Geneva, her card-case is from China, her hair is from—from—I don't know where her hair is from; I never could find out; that is, her other hair—her public hair, her Sunday hair; I don't mean the hair she goes to bed with. . . .

And that reminds me of a trifle. Any time you want to you can glance around the carpet of a Pullman car, and go and pick up a hair-pin; but not to save your life can you get any woman in that car to acknowledge that hair-pin. Now, isn't that strange? But it's true. The woman who has never swerved from cast-iron veracity and fidelity in her whole life will, when confronted with this crucial test, deny her hair-pin. She will deny that hair-pin before a hundred witnesses. I have stupidly got into more trouble and more hot water trying to hunt up the owner of a hair-pin in a Pullman than by any other indiscretion of my life.

DRESS REFORM AND COPYRIGHT

When the present copyright law was under discussion, Mr. Clemens appeared before the committee. He had sent Speaker Cannon the following letter:

"DEAR UNCLE JOSEPH,—Please get me the thanks of Congress, not next week but right away. It is very necessary. Do accomplish this for your affectionate old friend right away—by persuasion if you can, by violence if you must, for it is imperatively necessary that I get on the floor of the House for two or three hours and talk to the members, man by man, in behalf of support, encouragement, and protection of one of the nation's most valuable assets and industries —its literature. I have arguments with me—also a barrel with liquid in it.

"Give me a chance. Get me the thanks of Congress. Don't wait for others—there isn't time; furnish them to me yourself and let Congress ratify later. I have stayed away and let Congress alone for seventy-one years and am entitled to the thanks. Congress knows this perfectly well, and I have long felt hurt that this quite proper and earned expression of gratitude has been merely felt by the House and never publicly uttered.

"Send me an order on the sergeant-at-arms quick. When shall I come?

"With love and a benediction,

"MARK TWAIN."

While waiting to appear before the committee, Mr. Clemens talked to the reporters:

WHY don't you ask why I am wearing such apparently unseasonable clothes? I'll tell you. I have found that when a man reaches the advanced age of seventy-one years, as I have, the continual sight of dark clothing is likely to have a depressing effect upon him. Light-colored clothing is more pleasing to the eye and enlivens the spirit. Now, of course, I cannot compel every one to wear such clothing just for my especial benefit, so I do the next best thing and wear it myself.

Of course, before a man reaches my years the fear of criticism might prevent him from indulging his fancy. I am not afraid of that. I am decidedly for pleasing color combinations in dress. I like to see the women's clothes, say, at the opera. What can be more depressing than the sombre black which custom requires men to wear upon state occasions? A group of men in evening clothes looks like a flock of crows, and is just about as inspiring.

After all, what is the purpose of clothing? Are not clothes intended primarily to preserve dignity and also to afford comfort to their wearer? Now I know of nothing more uncomfortable than the present-day clothes of men. The finest clothing made is a person's own skin, but, of course, society demands something more than this.

DRESS REFORM AND COPYRIGHT

The best-dressed man I have ever seen, however, was a native of the Sandwich Islands who attracted my attention thirty years ago. Now, when that man wanted to don especial dress to honor a public occasion or a holiday, why, he occasionally put on a pair of spectacles. Otherwise the clothing with which God had provided him sufficed.

Of course, I have ideas of dress reform. For one thing, why not adopt some of the women's styles? Goodness knows, they adopt enough of ours. Take the peek-a-boo waist, for instance. It has the obvious advantages of being cool and comfortable, and in addition it is almost always made up in pleasing colors which cheer and do not depress.

It is true that I dressed the Connecticut Yankee at King Arthur's Court in a plug-hat, but, let's see, that was twenty-five years ago. Then no man was considered fully dressed until he donned a plug - hat. Nowadays I think that no man is dressed until he leaves it home. Why, when I left home yesterday they trotted out a plug-hat for me to wear.

"You must wear it," they told me; "why, just think of going to Washington without a plug-hat!" But I said no; I would wear a derby or nothing. Why, I believe I could walk along the streets of New York—I never do—but still I think I could —and I should never see a well-dressed man wearing a plug-hat. If I did I should suspect him of something. I don't know just what, but I would suspect him.

Why, when I got up on the second story of that Pennsylvania ferry-boat coming down here yesterday I saw Howells coming along. He was the only man on the boat with a plug-hat, and I tell you he felt ashamed of himself. He said he had been persuaded to wear it against his better sense. But just think of a man nearly seventy years old who has not a mind of his own on such matters!

"Are you doing any work now?" the youngest and most serious reporter asked.

Work? I retired from work on my seventieth birthday. Since then I have been putting in merely twenty-six hours a day dictating my autobiography, which, as John Phœnix said in regard to his autograph, may be relied upon as authentic, as it is written exclusively by me. But it is not to be published in full until I am thoroughly dead. I have made it as caustic, fiendish, and devilish as possible. It will fill many volumes, and I shall continue writing it until the time comes for me to join the angels. It is going to be a terrible autobiography. It will make the hair of some folks curl. But it cannot be published until I am dead, and the persons mentioned in it and their children and grandchildren are dead. It is something awful!

"Can you tell us the names of some of the notables that are here to see you off?"

I don't know. I am so shy. My shyness takes a peculiar phase. I never look a person in the face. The reason is that I am afraid they may know me and that I may not know them, which makes it very embarrassing for both of us. I always wait for the other person to speak. I know lots of people, but I don't know who they are. It is all a matter of ability to observe things. I never observe anything now. I gave up the habit years ago. You should keep a habit up if you want to become proficient in it. For instance, I was a pilot once, but I gave it up, and I do not believe the captain of the *Minneapolis* would let me navigate his ship to London. Still, if I think that he is not on the job I may go up on the bridge and offer him a few suggestions.

COLLEGE GIRLS

Five hundred undergraduates, under the auspices of the Woman's University Club, New York, welcomed Mr. Clemens as their guest, April 3, 1906, and gave him the freedom of the club, which the chairman explained was freedom to talk individually to any girl present.

I'VE worked for the public good thirty years, so for the rest of my life I shall work for my personal contentment. I am glad Miss Neron has fed me, for there is no telling what iniquity I might wander into on an empty stomach—I mean, an empty mind.

I am going to tell you a practical story about how once upon a time I was blind—a story I should have been using all these months, but I never thought about telling it until the other night, and now it is too late, for on the nineteenth of this month I hope to take formal leave of the platform forever at Carnegie Hall—that is, take leave so far as talking for money and for people who have paid money to hear me talk. I shall continue to infest the platform on these conditions —that there is nobody in the house who has paid to hear me, that I am not paid to be heard, and that there will be none but young women students in the audience. [Here Mr. Clemens told the story of how he took a girl to the theatre while he was wearing tight boots, which appears elsewhere in this volume, and ended by saying: "And now let this be a lesson to you—I don't know what kind of a lesson; I'll let you think it out."]

GIRLS

IN my capacity of publisher I recently received a manuscript from a teacher which embodied a number of answers given by her pupils to questions propounded. These answers show that the children had nothing but the sound to go by—the sense was perfectly empty. Here are some of their answers to words they were asked to define: Auriferous—pertaining to an orifice; ammonia—the food of the gods; equestrian—one who asks questions; parasite—a kind of umbrella; ipecac—a man who likes a good dinner. And here is the definition of an ancient word honored by a great party: Republican—a sinner mentioned in the Bible. And here is an innocent deliverance of a zoological kind: "There are a good many donkeys in the theological gardens." Here also is a definition which really isn't very bad in its way: Demagogue—a vessel containing beer and other liquids. Here, too, is a sample of a boy's composition on girls, which, I must say, I rather like:

"Girls are very stuckup and dignified in their manner and behaveyour. They think more of dress than anything and like to play with dowls and rags. They cry if they see a cow in a far distance and are afraid of guns. They stay at home all the time and go to church every Sunday. They are al-ways sick. They are al-ways funy and making fun of boys hands and they say how dirty. They cant play marbles. I pity them poor things. They make fun of boys and then turn round and love them. I don't belave they ever kiled a cat or anything. They look out every nite and say, 'Oh, a'nt the moon lovely!' Thir is one thing I have not told and that is they al-ways now their lessons bettern boys."

THE LADIES

Delivered at the Anniversary Festival, 1872, of the Scottish Corporation of London

Mr. Clemens replied to the toast " The Ladies."

I AM proud, indeed, of the distinction of being chosen to respond to this especial toast, to "The Ladies," or to women if you please, for that is the preferable term, perhaps; it is certainly the older, and therefore the more entitled to reverence. I have noticed that the Bible, with that plain, blunt honesty which is such a conspicuous characteristic of the Scriptures, is always particular to never refer to even the illustrious mother of all mankind as a "lady," but speaks of her as a woman. It is odd, but you will find it is so. I am peculiarly proud of this honor, because I think that the toast to women is one which, by right and by every rule of gallantry, should take precedence of all others—of the army, of the navy, of even royalty itself—perhaps, though the latter is not necessary in this day and in this land, for the reason that, tacitly, you do drink a broad general health to all good women when you drink the health of the Queen of England and the Princess of Wales. I have in mind a poem just now which is familiar to you all, familiar to everybody. And what an inspiration that was, and how instantly the present toast recalls the verses to all our minds when the most noble, the most gracious, the purest, and sweetest of all poets says:

> " Woman! O woman!——er——
> Wom——"

However, you remember the lines; and you remember how feelingly, how daintily, how almost imperceptibly the verses raise up before you, feature by feature, the ideal of a true and perfect woman; and how, as you contemplate the finished marvel, your homage grows into worship of the intellect that could create so fair a thing out of mere breath, mere words. And you call to mind now, as I speak, how the poet, with stern fidelity to the history of all humanity, delivers this beautiful child of his heart and his brain over to the trials and sorrows that must come to all, sooner or later, that abide in the earth, and how the pathetic story culminates in that apostrophe— so wild, so regretful, so full of mournful retrospection. The lines run thus:

> " Alas!—alas!—a—alas!
> —— Alas! — —— — alas!"

—and so on. I do not remember the rest; but,

95

taken together, it seems to me that poem is the noblest tribute to woman that human genius has ever brought forth—and I feel that if I were to talk hours I could not do my great theme completer or more graceful justice than I have now done in simply quoting that poet's matchless words. The phases of the womanly nature are infinite in their variety. Take any type of woman, and you shall find in it something to respect, something to admire, something to love. And you shall find the whole joining you heart and hand. Who was more patriotic than Joan of Arc? Who was braver? Who has given us a grander instance of self-sacrificing devotion? Ah! you remember, you remember well, what a throb of pain, what a great tidal wave of grief swept over us all when Joan of Arc fell at Waterloo. Who does not sorrow for the loss of Sappho, the sweet singer of Israel? Who among us does not miss the gentle ministrations, the softening influences, the humble piety of Lucretia Borgia? Who can join in the heartless libel that says woman is extravagant in dress when he can look back and call to mind our simple and lowly mother Eve arrayed in her modification of the Highland costume? Sir, women have been soldiers, women have been painters, women have been poets. As long as language lives the name of Cleopatra will live. And not because she conquered George III.—but because she wrote those divine lines:

THE LADIES

"Let dogs delight to bark and bite,
For God hath made them so."

The story of the world is adorned with the
names of illustrious ones of our own sex—some
of them sons of St. Andrew, too—Scott, Bruce,
Burns, the warrior Wallace, Ben Nevis—the gifted
Ben Lomond, and the great new Scotchman, Ben
Disraeli.* Out of the great plains of history
tower whole mountain ranges of sublime women—
the Queen of Sheba, Josephine, Semiramis, Sairey
Gamp; the list is endless—but I will not call the
mighty roll, the names rise up in your own memories at the mere suggestion, luminous with the
glory of deeds that cannot die, hallowed by the
loving worship of the good and the true of all
epochs and all climes. Suffice it for our pride
and our honor that we in our day have added to it
such names as those of Grace Darling and Florence
Nightingale. Woman is all that she should be—
gentle, patient, longsuffering, trustful, unselfish,
full of generous impulses. It is her blessed mission to comfort the sorrowing, plead for the erring,
encourage the faint of purpose, succor the distressed, uplift the fallen, befriend the friendless—
in a word, afford the healing of her sympathies
and a home in her heart for all the bruised and

---

*Mr. Benjamin Disraeli, at that time Prime Minister of Eng-
land, had just been elected Lord Rector of Glasgow University,
and had made a speech which gave rise to a world of
discussion.

97

persecuted children of misfortune that knock at its hospitable door. And when I say, God bless her, there is none among us who has known the ennobling affection of a wife, or the steadfast devotion of a mother but in his heart will say, Amen!

WOMAN'S PRESS CLUB

On October 27, 1900, the New York Woman's Press Club gave a tea in Carnegie Hall. Mr. Clemens was the guest of honor.

IF I were asked an opinion I would call this an ungrammatical nation. There is no such thing as perfect grammar, and I don't always speak good grammar myself. But I have been fore-gathering for the past few days with professors of American universities, and I've heard them all say things like this: "He don't like to do it." [There was a stir.] Oh, you'll hear that to-night if you listen, or, "He would have liked to have done it." You'll catch some educated Americans saying that. When these men take pen in hand they write with as good grammar as any. But the moment they throw the pen aside they throw grammatical morals aside with it.

To illustrate the desirability and possibility of concentration, I must tell you a story of my little six-year-old daughter. The governess had been teaching her about the reindeer, and, as the custom was, she related it to the family. She reduced the history of that reindeer to two or

99

three sentences when the governess could not have put it into a page. She said: "The reindeer is a very swift animal. A reindeer once drew a sled four hundred miles in two hours." She appended the comment: "This was regarded as extraordinary." And concluded: "When that reindeer was done drawing that sled four hundred miles in two hours it died."

As a final instance of the force of limitations in the development of concentration, I must mention that beautiful creature, Helen Keller, whom I have known for these many years. I am filled with the wonder of her knowledge, acquired because shut out from all distraction. If I could have been deaf, dumb, and blind I also might have arrived at something.

VOTES FOR WOMEN

AT THE ANNUAL MEETING OF THE HEBREW TECH-
NICAL SCHOOL FOR GIRLS, HELD IN THE
TEMPLE EMMANUEL, JANUARY
20, 1901

*Mr. Clemens was introduced by President Meyer,
who said: "In one of Mr. Clemens's works he expressed
his opinion of men, saying he had no choice between
Hebrew and Gentile, black men or white; to him all
men were alike. But I never could find that he expressed
his opinion of women; perhaps that opinion was so
exalted that he could not express it. We shall now
be called to hear what he thinks of women."*

LADIES AND GENTLEMEN,—It is a small
help that I can afford, but it is just such help
that one can give as coming from the heart
through the mouth. The report of Mr. Meyer
was admirable, and I was as interested in it as
you have been. Why, I'm twice as old as he,
and I've had so much experience that I would say
to him, when he makes his appeal for help: "Don't
make it for to-day or to-morrow, but collect the
money on the spot."

We are all creatures of sudden impulse. We

must be worked up by steam, as it were. Get them to write their wills now, or it may be too late by-and-by. Fifteen or twenty years ago I had an experience I shall never forget. I got into a church which was crowded by a sweltering and panting multitude. The city missionary of our town—Hartford—made a telling appeal for help. He told of personal experiences among the poor in cellars and top lofts requiring instances of devotion and help. The poor are always good to the poor. When a person with his millions gives a hundred thousand dollars it makes a great noise in the world, but he does not miss it; it's the widow's mite that makes no noise but does the best work.

I remember on that occasion in the Hartford church the collection was being taken up. The appeal had so stirred me that I could hardly wait for the hat or plate to come my way. I had four hundred dollars in my pocket, and I was anxious to drop it in the plate and wanted to borrow more. But the plate was so long in coming my way that the fever-heat of beneficence was going down lower and lower—going down at the rate of a hundred dollars a minute. The plate was passed too late. When it finally came to me, my enthusiasm had gone down so much that I kept my four hundred dollars—and stole a dime from the plate. So, you see, time sometimes leads to crime.

Oh, many a time have I thought of that and

regretted it, and I adjure you all to give while the fever is on you.

Referring to woman's sphere in life, I'll say that woman is always right. For twenty-five years I've been a woman's rights man. I have always believed, long before my mother died, that, with her gray hairs and admirable intellect, perhaps she knew as much as I did. Perhaps she knew as much about voting as I.

I should like to see the time come when women shall help to make the laws. I should like to see that whip-lash, the ballot, in the hands of women. As for this city's government, I don't want to say much, except that it is a shame—a shame; but if I should live twenty-five years longer—and there is no reason why I shouldn't—I think I'll see women handle the ballot. If women had the ballot to-day, the state of things in this town would not exist.

If all the women in this town had a vote to-day they would elect a mayor at the next election, and they would rise in their might and change the awful state of things now existing here.

WOMAN—AN OPINION

ADDRESS AT AN EARLY BANQUET OF THE WASHING-
TON CORRESPONDENTS' CLUB

*The twelfth toast was as follows: "Woman—The
pride of any profession, and the jewel of ours."*

M R. PRESIDENT,—I do not know why I
should be singled out to receive the greatest
distinction of the evening—for so the office of
replying to the toast of woman has been regarded
in every age. I do not know why I have received
this distinction, unless it be that I am a trifle less
homely than the other members of the club.
But be this as it may, Mr. President, I am proud
of the position, and you could not have chosen
any one who would have accepted it more gladly,
or labored with a heartier good-will to do the
subject justice than I—because, sir, I love the
sex. I love all the women, irrespective of age
or color.

Human intellect cannot estimate what we owe
to woman, sir. She sews on our buttons; she
mends our clothes; she ropes us in at the church

fairs; she confides in us; she tells us whatever she can find out about the little private affairs of the neighbors; she gives us good advice, and plenty of it; she soothes our aching brows; she bears our children—ours as a general thing. In all relations of life, sir, it is but a just and graceful tribute to woman to say of her that she is a brick.

Wheresoever you place woman, sir—in whatever position or estate—she is an ornament to the place she occupies, and a treasure to the world. [Here Mr. Clemens paused, looked inquiringly at his hearers, and remarked that the applause should come in at this point. It came in. He resumed his eulogy.] Look at Cleopatra!—look at Desdemona!—look at Florence Nightingale!—look at Joan of Arc!—look at Lucretia Borgia! [Disapprobation expressed.] Well [said Mr. Clemens, scratching his head, doubtfully], suppose we let Lucretia slide. Look at Joyce Heth!—look at Mother Eve! You need not look at her unless you want to, but [said Mr. Clemens, reflectively, after a pause] Eve was ornamental, sir—particularly before the fashions changed. I repeat, sir, look at the illustrious names of history. Look at the Widow Machree!—look at Lucy Stone!—look at Elizabeth Cady Stanton!—look at George Francis Train! And, sir, I say it with bowed head and deepest veneration—look at the mother of Washington! She raised a boy that could not tell a lie—could not tell a lie! But he never had any chance. It might have been different if he had belonged to the Washington Newspaper Correspondents' Club.

I repeat, sir, that in whatever position you place a woman she is an ornament to society and a treasure to the world. As a sweetheart, she has few equals and no superiors; as a cousin, she is convenient; as a wealthy grandmother with an incurable distemper, she is precious; as a wet-nurse, she has no equal among men.

What, sir, would the people of the earth be without woman? They would be scarce, sir, almighty scarce. Then let us cherish her; let us protect her; let us give her our support, our encouragement, our sympathy, ourselves—if we get a chance.

But, jesting aside, Mr. President, woman is lovable, gracious, kind of heart, beautiful—worthy of all respect, of all esteem, of all deference. Not any here will refuse to drink her health right cordially in this bumper of wine, for each and every one has personally known, and loved, and honored the very best one of them all—his own mother.

ADVICE TO GIRLS

In 1907 a young girl whom Mr. Clemens met on the steamer Minnehaha *called him "grandpa," and he called her his granddaughter. She was attending St. Timothy's School, at Catonsville, Maryland, and Mr. Clemens promised her to see her graduate. He accordingly made the journey from New York on June 10, 1909, and delivered a short address.*

I DON'T know what to tell you girls to do. Mr. Martin has told you everything you ought to do, and now I must give you some don'ts.

There are three things which come to my mind which I consider excellent advice:

First, girls, don't smoke—that is, don't smoke to excess. I am seventy-three and a half years old, and have been smoking seventy-three of them. But I never smoke to excess—that is, I smoke in moderation, only one cigar at a time.

Second, don't drink — that is, don't drink to excess.

Third, don't marry—I mean, to excess.

Honesty is the best policy. That is an old proverb; but you don't want ever to forget it in your journey through life.

TAXES AND MORALS

ADDRESS DELIVERED IN NEW YORK, JANUARY 22,
1906

*At the twenty-fifth anniversary of the founding of
Tuskeegee Institute by Booker Washington, Mr. Choate
presided, and in introducing Mr. Clemens made fun of
him because he made play his work, and that when he
worked hardest he did so lying in bed.*

I CAME here in the responsible capacity of
policeman to watch Mr. Choate. This is an
occasion of grave and serious importance, and it
seems necessary for me to be present, so that if he
tried to work off any statement that required correction, reduction, refutation, or exposure, there
would be a tried friend of the public to protect
the house. He has not made one statement
whose veracity fails to tally exactly with my own
standard. I have never seen a person improve so.
This makes me thankful and proud of a country
that can produce such men—two such men.
And all in the same country. We can't be with
you always; we are passing away, and then—well,
everything will have to stop, I reckon. It is a

sad thought. But in spirit I shall still be with you. Choate, too—if he can.

Every born American among the eighty millions, let his creed or destitution of creed be what it may, is indisputably a Christian to this degree— that his moral constitution is Christian.

There are two kinds of Christian morals, one private and the other public. These two are so distinct, so unrelated, that they are no more akin to each other than are archangels and politicians. During three hundred and sixty-three days in the year the American citizen is true to his Christian private morals, and keeps undefiled the nation's character at its best and highest; then in the other two days of the year he leaves his Christian private morals at home and carries his Christian public morals to the tax office and the polls, and does the best he can to damage and undo his whole year's faithful and righteous work. Without a blush he will vote for an unclean boss if that boss is his party's Moses, without compunction he will vote against the best man in the whole land if he is on the other ticket. Every year in a number of cities and States he helps put corrupt men in office, whereas if he would but throw away his Christian public morals, and carry his Christian private morals to the polls, he could promptly purify the public service and make the possession of office a high and honorable distinction.

Once a year he lays aside his Christian private morals and hires a ferry-boat and piles up his bonds in a warehouse in New Jersey for three days, and gets out his Christian public morals and goes to the tax office and holds up his hands and swears he wishes he may never-never if he's got a cent in the world, so help him. The next day the list appears in the papers—a column and a quarter of names, in fine print, and every man in the list a billionaire and member of a couple of churches. I know all those people. I have friendly, social, and criminal relations with the whole lot of them. They never miss a sermon when they are so's to be around, and they never miss swearing-off day, whether they are so's to be around or not.

I used to be an honest man. I am crumbling. No—I have crumbled. When they assessed me at $75,000 a fortnight ago I went out and tried to borrow the money, and couldn't; then when I found they were letting a whole crop of millionaires live in New York at a third of the price they were charging me I was hurt, I was indignant, and said: "This is the last feather. I am not going to run this town all by myself." In that moment—in that memorable moment—I began to crumble. In fifteen minutes the disintegration was complete. In fifteen minutes I had become just a mere moral sand-pile; and I lifted up my hand along with those seasoned and experienced deacons and swore off every rag of personal property I've got in the world, clear down to cork leg, glass eye, and what is left of my wig.

Those tax officers were moved; they were profoundly moved. They had long been accustomed to seeing hardened old grafters act like that, and they could endure the spectacle; but they were expecting better things of me, a chartered, professional moralist, and they were saddened.

I fell visibly in their respect and esteem, and I should have fallen in my own, except that I had already struck bottom, and there wasn't any place to fall to.

At Tuskeegee they will jump to misleading conclusions from insufficient evidence, along with Doctor Parkhurst, and they will deceive the student with the superstition that no gentleman ever swears.

Look at those good millionaires; aren't they gentlemen? Well, they swear. Only once in a year, maybe, but there's enough bulk to it to make up for the lost time. And do they lose anything by it? No, they don't; they save enough in three minutes to support the family seven years. When they swear, do we shudder? No—unless they say "damn!" Then we do. It shrivels us all up. Yet we ought not to feel so about it, because we all swear—everybody. Including the ladies. Including Doctor Parkhurst, that strong and brave and excellent citizen, but superficially educated.

For it is not the word that is the sin, it is the spirit back of the word. When an irritated lady says " oh!" the spirit back of it is "damn!" and that is the way it is going to be recorded against her. It always makes me so sorry when I hear a lady swear like that. But if she says "damn," and says it in an amiable, nice way, it isn't going to be recorded at all.

The idea that no gentleman ever swears is all wrong; he can swear and still be a gentleman if he does it in a nice and benevolent and affectionate way. The historian, John Fiske, whom I knew well and loved, was a spotless and most noble and upright Christian gentleman, and yet he swore once. Not exactly that, maybe; still, he—but I will tell you about it.

One day, when he was deeply immersed in his work, his wife came in, much moved and profoundly distressed, and said: "I am sorry to disturb you, John, but I must, for this is a serious matter, and needs to be attended to at once."

Then, lamenting, she brought a grave accusation against their little son. She said: "He has been saying his Aunt Mary is a fool and his Aunt Martha is a damned fool." Mr. Fiske reflected upon the matter a minute, then said: "Oh, well, it's about the distinction I should make between them myself."

TAXES AND MORALS

Mr. Washington, I beg you to convey these teachings to your great and prosperous and most beneficent educational institution, and add them to the prodigal mental and moral riches wherewith you equip your fortunate protégés for the struggle of life.

TAMMANY AND CROKER

Mr. Clemens made his debut as a campaign orator on October 7, 1901, advocating the election of Seth Low for Mayor, not as a Republican, but as a member of the "Acorns," which he described as a "third party having no political affiliation, but was concerned only in the selection of the best candidates and the best member."

GREAT BRITAIN had a Tammany and a Croker a good while ago. This Tammany was in India, and it began its career with the spread of the English dominion after the Battle of Plassey. Its first boss was Clive, a sufficiently crooked person sometimes, but straight as a yardstick when compared with the corkscrew crookedness of the second boss, Warren Hastings.

That old-time Tammany was the East India Company's government, and had its headquarters at Calcutta. Ostensibly it consisted of a Great Council of four persons, of whom one was the Governor-General, Warren Hastings; really it consisted of one person—Warren Hastings; for by usurpation he concentrated all authority in himself and governed the country like an autocrat.

Ostensibly the Court of Directors, sitting in London and representing the vast interests of the stockholders, was supreme in authority over the Calcutta Great Council, whose membership it appointed and removed at pleasure, whose policies it dictated, and to whom it conveyed its will in the form of sovereign commands; but whenever it suited Hastings, he ignored even that august body's authority and conducted the mighty affairs of the British Empire in India to suit his own notions.

At his mercy was the daily bread of every official, every trader, every clerk, every civil servant, big and little, in the whole huge India Company's machine, and the man who hazarded his bread by any failure of subserviency to the boss lost it.

Now then, let the supreme masters of British India, the giant corporation of the India Company of London, stand for the voters of the city of New York; let the Great Council of Calcutta stand for Tammany; let the corrupt and money-grubbing great hive of serfs which served under the Indian Tammany's rod stand for New York Tammany's serfs; let Warren Hastings stand for Richard Croker, and it seems to me that the parallel is exact and complete. And so let us be properly grateful and thank God and our good luck that we didn't invent Tammany.

Edmund Burke, regarded by many as the greatest orator of all times, conducted the case against Warren Hastings in that renowned trial which lasted years, and which promises to keep its renown for centuries to come. I wish to quote some of the things he said. I wish to imagine him arrainging Mr. Croker and Tammany before the voters of New York City and pleading with them for the overthrow of that combined iniquity of the 5th of November, and will substitute for "My Lords," read "Fellow-Citizens"; for "Kingdom," read "City"; for "Parliamentary Process," read "Political Campaign"; for "Two Houses," read "Two Parties," and so it reads:

"Fellow - citizens, I must look upon it as an auspicious circumstance to this cause, in which the honor of the city is involved, that from the first commencement of our political compaign to this the hour of solemn trial not the smallest difference of opinion has arisen between the two parties.

"You will see, in the progress of this cause, that there is not only a long, connected, systematic series of misdemeanors, but an equally connected system of maxims and principles invented to justify them. Upon both of these you must judge.

"It is not only the interest of the city of New York, now the most considerable part of the city of the Americans, which is concerned, but the credit and honor of the nation itself will be decided by this decision."

TAMMANY AND CROKER

At a later meeting of the Acorn Club, Mr. Clemens said:

Tammany is dead, and there's no use in blackguarding a corpse.

The election makes me think of a story of a man who was dying. He had only two minutes to live, so he sent for a clergyman and asked him, "Where is the best place to go to?" He was undecided about it. So the minister told him that each place had its advantages—heaven for climate, and hell for society.

MUNICIPAL CORRUPTION

ADDRESS AT THE CITY CLUB DINNER, JANUARY 4, 1901

Bishop Potter told how an alleged representative of Tammany Hall asked him in effect if he would cease his warfare upon the Police Department if a certain captain and inspector were dismissed. He replied that he would never be satisfied until the "man at the top" and the "system" which permitted evils in the Police Department were crushed.

THE Bishop has just spoken of a condition of things which none of us can deny, and which ought not to exist; that is, the lust of gain—a lust which does not stop short of the penitentiary or the jail to accomplish its ends. But we may be sure of one thing, and that is that this sort of thing is not universal. If it were, this country would not be. You may put this down as a fact: that out of every fifty men, forty-nine are clean. Then why is it, you may ask, that the forty-nine don't have things the way they want them? I'll tell you why it is. A good deal has been said here to-night about what is to be accomplished by organization. That's just the thing. It's be-

118

cause the fiftieth fellow and his pals are organized and the other forty-nine are not that the dirty one rubs it into the clean fellows every time.

You may say organize, organize, organize; but there may be so much organization that it will interfere with the work to be done. The Bishop here had an experience of that sort, and told all about it down-town the other night. He was painting a barn—it was his own barn—and yet he was informed that his work must stop; he was a non-union painter, and couldn't continue at that sort of job.

Now, all these conditions of which you complain should be remedied, and I am here to tell you just how to do it. I've been a statesman without salary for many years, and I have accomplished great and widespread good. I don't know that it has benefited anybody very much, even if it was good; but I do know that it hasn't harmed me very much, and is hasn't made me any richer.

We hold the balance of power. Put up your best men for office, and we shall support the better one. With the election of the best man for Mayor would follow the selection of the best man for Police Commissioner and Chief of Police.

My first lesson in the craft of statesmanship was taken at an early age. Fifty-one years ago I was fourteen years old, and we had a society in the town I lived in, patterned after the Freemasons, or the Ancient Order of United Farmers, or some such thing—just what it was patterned after doesn't matter. It had an inside guard and an outside guard, and a past-grand warden, and a lot of such things, so as to give dignity to the organization and offices to the members.

Generally speaking it was a pretty good sort of organization, and some of the very best boys in the village, including—but I mustn't get personal on an occasion like this—and the society would have got along pretty well had it not been for the fact that there were a certain number of the members who could be bought. They got to be an infernal nuisance. Every time we had an election the candidates had to go around and see the purchasable members. The price per vote was paid in doughnuts, and it depended somewhat on the appetites of the individuals as to the price of the votes.

This thing ran along until some of us, the really very best boys in the organization, decided that these corrupt practices must stop, and for the purpose of stopping them we organized a third party. We had a name, but we were never known by that name. Those who didn't like us called us the Anti-Doughnut party, but we didn't mind that.

We said: "Call us what you please; the name doesn't matter. We are organized for a principle." By-and-by the election came around, and we made a big mistake. We were triumphantly beaten. That taught us a lesson. Then and there we decided never again to nominate anybody for anything. We decided simply to force the other two parties in the society to nominate their very best men. Although we were organized for a principle, we didn't care much about that. Principles aren't of much account anyway, except at election-time. After that you hang them up to let them season.

The next time we had an election we told both the other parties that we'd beat any candidates put up by any one of them of whom we didn't approve. In that election we did business. We got the man we wanted. I suppose they called us the Anti-Doughnut party because they couldn't buy us with their doughnuts. They didn't have enough of them. Most reformers arrive at their price sooner or later, and I suppose we would have had our price; but our opponents weren't offering anything but doughnuts, and those we spurned.

Now it seems to me that an Anti-Doughnut party is just what is wanted in the present emergency. I would have the Anti-Doughnuts felt in every city and hamlet and school district in this State and in the United States. I was an Anti-Doughnut in my boyhood, and I'm an Anti-Doughnut still. The modern designation is Mugwump. There used to be quite a number of us

Mugwumps, but I think I'm the only one left. I had a vote this fall, and I began to make some inquiries as to what I had better do with it.

I don't know anything about finance, and I never did, but I know some pretty shrewd financiers, and they told me that Mr. Bryan wasn't safe on any financial question. I said to myself, then, that it wouldn't do for me to vote for Bryan, and I rather thought—I know now—that McKinley wasn't just right on this Philippine question, and so I just didn't vote for anybody. I've got that vote yet, and I've kept it clean, ready to deposit at some other election. It wasn't cast for any wildcat financial theories, and it wasn't cast to support the man who sends our boys as volunteers out into the Philippines to get shot down under a polluted flag.

MUNICIPAL GOVERNMENT

ADDRESS AT THE ANNUAL DINNER OF THE ST. NICHO-
LAS SOCIETY, NEW YORK, DECEMBER 6, 1900

*Doctor Mackay, in his response to the toast "St. Nicho-
las," referred to Mr. Clemens, saying: "Mark Twain is as
true a preacher of true righteousness as any bishop, priest,
or minister of any church to-day, because he moves men
to forget their faults by cheerful well-doing instead of
making them sour and morbid by everlastingly bending
their attention to the seamy and sober side of life."*

MR. CHAIRMAN AND GENTLEMEN OF
THE ST. NICHOLAS SOCIETY,—These
are, indeed, prosperous days for me. Night before last, in a speech, the Bishop of the Diocese
of New York complimented me for my contribu-
tion to theology, and to-night the Reverend Doctor Mackay has elected me to the ministry. I
thanked Bishop Potter then for his compliment,
and I thank Doctor Mackay now for that promotion. I think that both have discerned in me
what I long ago discerned, but what I was afraid
the world would never learn to recognize.

In this absence of nine years I find a great improvement in the city of New York. I am glad
to speak on that as a toast—"The City of New

York." Some say it has improved because I have been away. Others, and I agree with them, say it has improved because I have come back. We must judge of a city, as of a man, by its external appearances and by its inward character. In externals the foreigner coming to these shores is more impressed at first by our sky-scrapers. They are new to him. He has not done anything of the sort since he built the tower of Babel. The foreigner is shocked by them.

In the daylight they are ugly. They are—well, too chimneyfied and too snaggy—like a mouth that needs attention from a dentist; like a cemetery that is all monuments and no gravestones. But at night, seen from the river where they are columns towering against the sky, all sparkling with light, they are fairylike; they are beauty more satisfactory to the soul and more enchanting than anything that man has dreamed of since the Arabian nights. We can't always have the beautiful aspect of things. Let us make the most of our sights that are beautiful and let the others go. When your foreigner makes disagreeable comments on New York by daylight, float him down the river at night.

What has made these sky-scrapers possible is the elevator. The cigar-box which the European calls a "lift" needs but to be compared with our elevators to be appreciated. The lift stops to reflect between floors. That is all right in a hearse,

but not in elevators. The American elevator acts
like the man's patent purge—it worked. As the
inventor said, "This purge doesn't waste any
time fooling around; it attends strictly to business."

That New-Yorkers have the cleanest, quickest,
and most admirable system of street railways in
the world has been forced upon you by the
abnormal appreciation you have of your hackman. We ought always to be grateful to him
for that service. Nobody else would have brought
such a system into existence for us. We ought
to build him a monument. We owe him one as
much as we owe one to anybody. Let it be a
tall one. Nothing permanent, of course; build it
of plaster, say. Then gaze at it and realize how
grateful we are—for the time being—and then
pull it down and throw it on the ash-heap. That's
the way to honor your public heroes.

As to our streets, I find them cleaner than they
used to be. I miss those dear old landmarks, the
symmetrical mountain ranges of dust and dirt
that used to be piled up along the streets for the
wind and rain to tear down at their pleasure.
Yes, New York is cleaner than Bombay. I realize
that I have been in Bombay, that I now am in
New York; that it is not my duty to flatter
Bombay, but rather to flatter New York.

Compared with the wretched attempts of London to light that city, New York may fairly be

said to be a well-lighted city. Why, London's attempt at good lighting is almost as bad as London's attempt at rapid transit. There is just one good system of rapid transit in London—the "Tube," and that, of course, had been put in by Americans. Perhaps, after a while, those Americans will come back and give New York also a good underground system. Perhaps they have already begun. I have been so busy since I came back that I haven't had time as yet to go down cellar.

But it is by the laws of the city, it is by the manners of the city, it is by the ideals of the city, it is by the customs of the city and by the municipal government which all these elements correct, support, and foster, by which the foreigner judges the city. It is by these that he realizes that New York may, indeed, hold her head high among the cities of the world. It is by these standards that he knows whether to class the city higher or lower than the other municipalities of the world.

Gentlemen, you have the best municipal government in the world—the purest and the most fragrant. The very angels envy you, and wish they could establish a government like it in heaven. You got it by a noble fidelity to civic duty. You got it by stern and ever-watchful exertion of the great powers with which you are charged by the rights which were handed down to you by your forefathers, by your manly refusal to let base men invade the high places of your government, and by instant retaliation when any public officer has insulted you in the city's name by swerving in the slightest from the upright and full performance of his duty. It is you who have made this city the envy of the cities of the world. God will bless you for it—God will bless you for it. Why, when you approach the final resting-place the angels of heaven will gather at the gates and cry out:

"Here they come! Show them to the archangel's box, and turn the lime-light on them!"

CHINA AND THE PHILIPPINES

AT A DINNER GIVEN IN THE WALDORF-ASTORIA HOTEL, DECEMBER, 1900

Winston Spencer Churchill was introduced by Mr. Clemens.

FOR years I've been a self-appointed missionary to bring about the union of America and the motherland. They ought to be united. Behold America, the refuge of the oppressed from everywhere (who can pay fifty dollars' admission) —any one except a Chinaman—standing up for human rights everywhere, even helping China let people in free when she wants to collect fifty dollars upon them. And how unselfishly England has wrought for the open door for all! And how piously America has wrought for that open door in all cases where it was not her own!

Yes, as a missionary I've sung my songs of praise. And yet I think that England sinned when she got herself into a war in South Africa which she could have avoided, just as we sinned in getting into a similar war in the Philippines. Mr. Churchill, by his father, is an Englishman;

by his mother he is an American — no doubt a blend that makes the perfect man. England and America; yes, we are kin. And now that we are also kin in sin, there is nothing more to be desired. The harmony is complete, the blend is perfect.

THEORETICAL AND PRACTICAL MORALS

The New Vagabonds Club of London, made up of the leading younger literary men of the day, gave a dinner in honor of Mr. and Mrs. Clemens, July 8, 1899.

IT has always been difficult—leave that word difficult—not exceedingly difficult, but just difficult, nothing more than that, not the slightest shade to add to that—just difficult—to respond properly, in the right phraseology, when compliments are paid to me; but it is more than difficult when the compliments are paid to a better than I—my wife.

And while I am not here to testify against myself—I can't be expected to do so, a prisoner in your own country is not admitted to do so—as to which member of the family wrote my books, I could say in general that really I wrote the books myself. My wife puts the facts in, and they make it respectable. My modesty won't suffer while compliments are being paid to literature, and through literature to my family. I can't get enough of them.

THEORETICAL MORALS

I am curiously situated to-night. It so rarely happens that I am introduced by a humorist; I am generally introduced by a person of grave walk and carriage. That makes the proper background of gravity for brightness. I am going to alter to suit, and haply I may say some humorous things.

When you start with a blaze of sunshine and upburst of humor, when you begin with that, the proper office of humor is to reflect, to put you into that pensive mood of deep thought, to make you think of your sins, if you wish half an hour to fly. Humor makes me reflect now to-night, it sets the thinking machinery in motion. Always, when I am thinking, there come suggestions of what I am, and what we all are, and what we are coming to. A sermon comes from my lips always when I listen to a humorous speech.

I seize the opportunity to throw away frivolities, to say something to plant the seed, and make all better than when I came. In Mr. Grossmith's remarks there was a subtle something suggesting my favorite theory of the difference between theoretical morals and practical morals. I try to instil practical morals in the place of theatrical —I mean theoretical; but as an addendum—an annex—something added to theoretical morals.

When your chairman said it was the first time he had ever taken the chair, he did not mean that he had not taken lots of other things; he attended my first lecture and took notes. This indicated the man's disposition. There was nothing else flying round, so he took notes; he would have taken anything he could get.

I can bring a moral to bear here which shows the difference between theoretical morals and practical morals. Theoretical morals are the sort you get on your mother's knee, in good books, and from the pulpit. You gather them in your head, and not in your heart; they are theory without practice. Without the assistance of practice to perfect them, it is difficult to teach a child to "be honest, don't steal."

I will teach you how it should be done, lead you into temptation, teach you how to steal, so that you may recognize when you have stolen and feel the proper pangs. It is no good going round and bragging you have never taken the chair.

As by the fires of experience, so by commission of crime, you learn real morals. Commit all the crimes, familiarize yourself with all sins, take them in rotation (there are only two or three thousand of them), stick to it, commit two or three every day, and by-and-by you will be proof against them. When you are through you will be proof against all sins and morally perfect. You will be vaccinated against every possible commission of them. This is the only way.

I will read you a written statement upon the subject that I wrote three years ago to read to the Sabbath-schools. [Here the lecturer turned his pockets out, but without success.] No! I have left it at home. Still, it was a mere statement of fact, illustrating the value of practical morals produced by the commission of crime.

It was in my boyhood—just a statement of fact, reading is only more formal, merely facts, merely pathetic facts, which I can state so as to be understood. It relates to the first time I ever stole a watermelon; that is, I think it was the first time; anyway, it was right along there somewhere.

I stole it out of a farmer's wagon while he was waiting on another customer. "Stole" is a harsh term. I withdrew—I retired that watermelon. I carried it to a secluded corner of a lumber-yard. I broke it open. It was green—the greenest watermelon raised in the valley that year.

The minute I saw it was green I was sorry, and began to reflect—reflection is the beginning of reform. If you don't reflect when you commit a crime then that crime is of no use; it might just as well have been committed by some one else. You must reflect or the value is lost; you are not vaccinated against committing it again.

I began to reflect. I said to myself: "What ought a boy to do who has stolen a green watermelon? What would George Washington do, the father of his country, the only American who could not tell a lie? What would he do? There is only one right, high, noble thing for any boy to do who has stolen a watermelon of that class: he must make restitution; he must restore that stolen property to its rightful owner." I said I would do it when I made that good resolution. I felt it to be a noble, uplifting obligation. I rose up spiritually stronger and refreshed. I carried that watermelon back—what was left of it—and restored it to the farmer, and made him give me a ripe one in its place.

Now you see that this constant impact of crime upon crime protects you against further commission of crime. It builds you up. A man can't become morally perfect by stealing one or a thousand green watermelons, but every little helps.

I was at a great school yesterday (St. Paul's), where for four hundred years they have been busy with brains, and building up England by producing Pepys, Miltons, and Marlboroughs. Six hundred boys left to nothing in the world but theoretical morality. I wanted to become the professor of practical morality, but the high master was away, so I suppose I shall have to go on making my living the same old way—by adding practical to theoretical morality.

What are the glory that was Greece, the grandeur that was Rome, compared to the glory and grandeur and majesty of a perfected morality such as you see before you?

THEORETICAL MORALS

The New Vagabonds are old vagabonds (undergoing the old sort of reform). You drank my health; I hope I have not been unuseful. Take this system of morality to your hearts. Take it home to your neighbors and your graves, and I hope that it will be a long time before you arrive there.

LAYMAN'S SERMON

The Young Men's Christian Association asked Mr. Clemens to deliver a lay sermon at the Majestic Theatre, New York, March 4, 1906. More than five thousand young men tried to get into the theatre, and in a short time traffic was practically stopped in the adjacent streets. The police reserves had to be called out to thin the crowd. Doctor Fagnani had said something before about the police episode, and Mr. Clemens took it up.

I HAVE have been listening to what was said here, and there is in it a lesson of citizenship. You created the police, and you are responsible for them. One must pause, therefore, before criticising them too harshly. They are citizens, just as we are. A little of citizenship ought to be taught at the mother's knee and in the nursery. Citizenship is what makes a republic; monarchies can get along without it. What keeps a republic on its legs is good citizenship.

Organization is necessary in all things. It is even necessary in reform. I was an organization myself once—for twelve hours. I was in Chicago a few years ago about to depart for New York. There were with me Mr. Osgood, a publisher, and a stenographer. I picked out a state-room on a train, the principal feature of which was that it contained the privilege of smoking. The train had started but a short time when the conductor came in and said that there had been a mistake made, and asked that we vacate the apartment. I refused, but when I went out on the platform Osgood and the stenographer agreed to accept a section. They were too modest.

Now, I am not modest. I was born modest, but it didn't last. I asserted myself, insisted upon my rights, and finally the Pullman conductor and the train conductor capitulated, and I was left in possession.

I went into the dining-car the next morning for breakfast. Ordinarily I only care for coffee and rolls, but this particular morning I espied an important-looking man on the other side of the car eating broiled chicken. I asked for broiled chicken, and I was told by the waiter and later by the dining-car conductor that there was no broiled chicken. There must have been an argument, for the Pullman conductor came in and remarked: "If he wants broiled chicken, give it to him. If you haven't got it on the train, stop somewhere. It will be better for all concerned!" I got the chicken.

It is from experiences such as these that you get your education of life, and you string them into jewels or into tinware, as you may choose. I have received recently several letters asking my counsel or advice. The principal request is for some incident that may prove helpful to the young. There were a lot of incidents in my career to help me along — sometimes they helped me along faster than I wanted to go.

Here is such a request. It is a telegram from Joplin, Missouri, and it reads: "In what one of your works can we find the definition of a gentleman?"

I have not answered that telegram, either; I couldn't. It seems to me that if any man has just merciful and kindly instincts he would be a gentleman, for he would need nothing else in the world.

I received the other day a letter from my old friend, William Dean Howells—Howells, the head of American literature. No one is able to stand with him. He is an old, old friend of mine, and he writes me, "To-morrow I shall be sixty-nine years old." Why, I am surprised at Howells writing that! I have known him longer than that. I'm sorry to see a man trying to appear so young. Let's see. Howells says now, "I see you have been burying Patrick. I suppose he was old, too."

No, he was never old—Patrick. He came to us thirty-six years ago. He was my coachman on the morning that I drove my young bride to our new home. He was a young Irishman, slen-

der, tall, lithe, honest, truthful, and he never
changed in all his life. He really was with us but
twenty-five years, for he did not go with us to
Europe, but he never regarded that as separation.
As the children grew up he was their guide. He
was all honor, honesty, and affection. He was
with us in New Hampshire, with us last summer,
and his hair was just as black, his eyes were just
as blue, his form just as straight, and his heart
just as good as on the day we first met. In all
the long years Patrick never made a mistake. He
never needed an order, he never received a command. He knew. I have been asked for my idea
of an ideal gentleman, and I give it to you —
Patrick McAleer.

UNIVERSITY SETTLEMENT SOCIETY

*After the serious addresses were made, Seth Low
introduced Mr. Clemens at the Settlement House,
February 2, 1901.*

THE older we grow the greater becomes our
wonder at how much ignorance one can contain without bursting one's clothes. Ten days ago
I did not know anything about the University
Settlement except what I'd read in the pamphlets
sent me. Now, after being here and hearing
Mrs. Hewitt and Mrs. Thomas, it seems to me I
know of nothing like it at all. It's a charity that
carries no humiliation with it. Marvellous it is,
to think of schools where you don't have to drive
the children in but drive them out. It was not
so in my day.

Down-stairs just now I saw a dancing lesson
going on. You must pay a cent for a lesson.
You can't get it for nothing. That's the reason I
never learned to dance.

But it was the pawnbroker's shop you have
here that interested me mightily. I've known
something about pawnbrokers' shops in my time,

but here you have a wonderful plan. The ordinary pawnbroker charges thirty - six per cent. a year for a loan, and I've paid more myself, but here a man or woman in distress can obtain a loan for one per cent. a month! It's wonderful!

I've been interested in all I've heard to-day, especially in the romances recounted by Mrs. Thomas, which reminds me that I have a romance of my own in my autobiography, which I am building for the instruction of the world.

In San Francisco, many years ago, when I was a newspaper reporter (perhaps I should say I had been and was willing to be), a pawnbroker was taking care of what property I had. There was a friend of mine, a poet, out of a job, and he was having a hard time of it, too. There was passage in it, but I guess I've got to keep that for the autobiography.

Well, my friend the poet thought his life was a failure, and I told him I thought it was, and then he said he thought he ought to commit suicide, and I said "all right," which was disinterested advice to a friend in trouble; but, like all such advice, there was just a little bit of self-interest back of it, for if I could get a "scoop" on the other newspapers I could get a job.

The poet could be spared, and so, largely for his own good and partly for mine, I kept the thing in his mind, which was necessary, as would-be suicides are very changeable and hard to hold

141

to their purpose. He had a preference for a pistol, which was an extravagance, for we hadn't enough between us to hire a pistol. A fork would have been easier.

And so he concluded to drown himself, and I said it was an excellent idea—the only trouble being that he was so good a swimmer. So we went down to the beach. I went along to see that the thing was done right. Then something most romantic happened. There came in on the sea something that had been on its way for three years. It rolled in across the broad Pacific with a message that was full of meaning to that poor poet and cast itself at his feet. It was a life-preserver! This was a complication. And then I had an idea—he never had any, especially when he was going to write poetry; I suggested that we pawn the life-preserver and get a revolver.

The pawnbroker gave us an old derringer with a bullet as big as a hickory nut. When he heard that it was only a poet that was going to kill himself he did not quibble. Well, we succeeded in sending a bullet right through his head. It was a terrible moment when he placed that pistol against his forehead and stood for an instant. I said, "Oh, pull the trigger!" and he did, and cleaned out all the gray matter in his brains. It carried the poetic faculty away, and now he's a useful member of society.

Now, therefore, I realize that there's no more

beneficent institution than this penny fund of yours, and I want all the poets to know this. I did think about writing you a check, but now I think I'll send you a few copies of what one of your little members called *Strawberry Finn*.

PUBLIC EDUCATION ASSOCIATION

I DON'T suppose that I am called here as an expert on education, for that would show a lack of foresight on your part and a deliberate intention to remind me of my shortcomings.

As I sat here looking around for an idea it struck me that I was called for two reasons. One was to do good to me, a poor unfortunate traveller on the world's wide ocean, by giving me a knowledge of the nature and scope of your society and letting me know that others beside myself have been of some use in the world. The other reason that I can see is that you have called me to show by way of contrast what education can accomplish if administered in the right sort of doses.

Your worthy president said that the school pictures, which have received the admiration of the world at the Paris Exposition, have been sent to Russia, and this was a compliment from that Government—which is very surprising to me. Why, it is only an hour since I read a cablegram in the newspapers beginning "Russia Proposes to Retrench." I was not expecting such a thunderbolt, and I thought what a happy thing it will be for Russians when the retrenchment will bring home the thirty thousand Russian troops now in Manchuria, to live in peaceful pursuits. I thought this was what Germany should do also without delay, and that France and all the other nations in China should follow suit.

Why should not China be free from the foreigners, who are only making trouble on her soil? If they would only all go home, what a pleasant place China would be for the Chinese! We do not allow Chinamen to come here, and I say in all seriousness that it would be a graceful thing to let China decide who shall go there.

China never wanted foreigners any more than foreigners wanted Chinamen, and on this question I am with the Boxers every time. The Boxer is a patriot. He loves his country better than he does the countries of other people. I wish him success. The Boxer believes in driving us out of his country. I am a Boxer too, for I believe in driving him out of our country.

When I read the Russian despatch further my dream of world peace vanished. It said that the vast expense of maintaining the army had made it necessary to retrench, and so the Government had decided that to support the army it would be necessary to withdraw the appropriation from the public schools. This is a monstrous idea to us.

145

We believe that out of the public school grows the greatness of a nation.

It is curious to reflect how history repeats itself the world over. Why, I remember the same thing was done when I was a boy on the Mississippi River. There was a proposition in a township there to discontinue public schools because they were too expensive. An old farmer spoke up and said if they stopped the schools they would not save anything, because every time a school was closed a jail had to be built.

It's like feeding a dog on his own tail. He'll never get fat. I believe it is better to support schools than jails.

The work of your association is better and shows more wisdom than the Czar of Russia and all his people. This is not much of a compliment, but it's the best I've got in stock.

EDUCATION AND CITIZENSHIP

On the evening of May 14, 1908, the alumni of the College of the City of New York celebrated the opening of the new college buildings at a banquet in the Waldorf-Astoria. Mr. Clemens followed Mayor McClellan.

I AGREED when the Mayor said that there was not a man within hearing who did not agree that citizenship should be placed above everything else, even learning.

Have you ever thought about this? Is there a college in the whole country where there is a chair of good citizenship? There is a kind of bad citizenship which is taught in the schools, but no real good citizenship taught. There are some which teach insane citizenship, bastard citizenship, but that is all. Patriotism! Yes; but patriotism is usually the refuge of the scoundrel. He is the man who talks the loudest.

You can begin that chair of citizenship in the College of the City of New York. You can place it above mathematics and literature, and that is where it belongs.

We used to trust in God. I think it was in 1863 that some genius suggested that it be put upon the gold and silver coins which circulated among the rich. They didn't put it on the nickels and coppers because they didn't think the poor folks had any trust in God.

Good citizenship would teach accuracy of thinking and accuracy of statement. Now, that motto on the coin is an overstatement. Those Congressmen had no right to commit this whole country to a theological doctrine. But since they did, Congress ought to state what our creed should be.

There was never a nation in the world that put its whole trust in God. It is a statement made on insufficient evidence. Leaving out the gamblers, the burglars, and the plumbers, perhaps we do put our trust in God after a fashion. But, after all, it is an overstatement.

If the cholera or black plague should come to these shores, perhaps the bulk of the nation would pray to be delivered from it, but the rest would put their trust in the Health Board of the City of New York.

I read in the papers within the last day or two of a poor young girl who they said was a leper. Did the people in that populous section of the country where she was—did they put their trust in God? The girl was afflicted with the leprosy, a disease which cannot be communicated from one person to another.

Yet, instead of putting their trust in God, they harried that poor creature, shelterless and friendless, from place to place, exactly as they did in the Middle Ages, when they made lepers wear bells, so that people could be warned of their approach and avoid them. Perhaps those people in the Middle Ages thought they were putting their trust in God.

The President ordered the removal of that motto from the coin, and I thought that it was well. I thought that overstatement should not stay there. But I think it would better read, "Within certain judicious limitations we trust in God," and if there isn't enough room on the coin for this, why, enlarge the coin.

Now I want to tell a story about jumping at conclusions. It was told to me by Bram Stoker, and it concerns a christening. There was a little clergyman who was prone to jump at conclusions sometimes. One day he was invited to officiate at a christening. He went. There sat the relatives— intelligent-looking relatives they were. The little clergyman's instinct came to him to make a great speech. He was given to flights of oratory that way—a very dangerous thing, for often the wings which take one into clouds of oratorical enthusiasm are wax and melt up there, and down you come.

But the little clergyman couldn't resist. He took the child in his arms, and, holding it, looked at it a moment. It wasn't much of a child. It was little, like a sweet-potato. Then the little clergyman waited impressively, and then: "I see

11   149

in your countenances," he said, "disappointment of him. I see you are disappointed with this baby. Why? Because he is so little. My friends, if you had but the power of looking into the future you might see that great things may come of little things. There is the great ocean, holding the navies of the world, which comes from little drops of water no larger than a woman's tears. There are the great constellations in the sky, made up of little bits of stars. Oh, if you could consider his future you might see that he might become the greatest poet of the universe, the greatest warrior the world has ever known, greater than Cæsar, than Hannibal, than—er—er" (turning to the father)—"what's his name?"

The father hesitated, then whispered back: "His name? Well, his name is Mary Ann."

COURAGE

At a beefsteak dinner, given by artists, caricaturists, and humorists of New York City, April 18, 1908, Mr. Clemens, Mr. H. H. Rogers, and Mr. Patrick McCarren were the guests of honor. Each wore a white apron, and each made a short speech.

IN the matter of courage we all have our limits. There never was a hero who did not have his bounds. I suppose it may be said of Nelson and all the others whose courage has been advertised that there came times in their lives when their bravery knew it had come to its limit.

I have found mine a good many times. Sometimes this was expected—often it was unexpected. I know a man who is not afraid to sleep with a rattlesnake, but you could not get him to sleep with a safety-razor.

I never had the courage to talk across a long, narrow room I should be at the end of the room facing all the audience. If I attempt to talk across a room I find myself turning this way and that, and thus at alternate periods I have part of the audience behind me. You ought never to have any part of the audience behind you; you never can tell what they are going to do.

I'll sit down.

THE DINNER TO MR. CHOATE

At a Dinner Given in Honor of Ambassador
Joseph H. Choate at the Lotos Club,
November 24, 1901

*The speakers, among others, were: Senator Depew,
William Henry White, Speaker Thomas Reed, and
Mr. Choate. Mr. Clemens spoke, in part, as follows:*

THE greatness of this country rests on two
anecdotes. The first one is that of Washington and his hatchet, representing the foundation of true speaking, which is the characteristic
of our people. The second one is an old one, and
I've been waiting to hear it to-night; but as nobody has told it yet, I will tell it.

You've heard it before, and you'll hear it many,
many times more. It is an anecdote of our guest,
of the time when he was engaged as a young man
with a gentle Hebrew, in the process of skinning
the client. The main part in that business is the
collection of the bill for services in skinning the
man. "Services" is the term used in that craft
for the operation of that kind—diplomatic in its
nature.

Choate's—co-respondent—made out a bill for

$500 for his services, so called. But Choate told him he had better leave the matter to him, and the next day he collected the bill for the services and handed the Hebrew $5000, saying, "That's your half of the loot," and inducing that memorable response: "Almost thou persuadest me to be a Christian."

The deep-thinkers didn't merely laugh when that happened. They stopped to think, and said: "There's a rising man. He must be rescued from the law and consecrated to diplomacy. The commercial advantages of a great nation lie there in that man's keeping. We no longer require a man to take care of our moral character before the world. Washington and his anecdote have done that. We require a man to take care of our commercial prosperity."

Mr. Choate has carried that trait with him, and, as Mr. Carnegie has said, he has worked like a mole underground.

We see the result when American railroad iron is sold so cheap in England that the poorest family can have it. He has so beguiled that Cabinet of England.

He has been spreading the commerce of this nation, and has depressed English commerce in the same ratio. This was the principle underlying that anecdote, and the wise men saw it; the principle of give and take—give one and take ten—the principle of diplomacy.

ON STANLEY AND LIVINGSTONE

Mr. Clemens was entertained at dinner by the White-friars' Club, London, at the Mitre Tavern, on the evening of August 6, 1872. In reply to the toast in his honor he said:

GENTLEMEN,—I thank you very heartily indeed for this expression of kindness toward me. What I have done for England and civilization in the arduous affairs which I have engaged in (that is good: that is so smooth that I will say it again and again)—what I have done for England and civilization in the arduous part I have performed I have done with a single-hearted devotion and with no hope of reward. I am proud, I am very proud, that it was reserved for me to find Doctor Livingstone and for Mr. Stanley to get all the credit. I hunted for that man in Africa all over seventy-five or one hundred parishes, thousands and thousands of miles in the wilds and deserts all over the place, sometimes riding negroes and sometimes travelling by rail. I didn't mind the rail or anything else, so that I didn't come in for the tar and feathers. I found that man at Ujiji—a place you may remember if you have ever been there—and it was a very great satisfaction that I found him just in the nick of time. I found that poor old man deserted by his niggers and by his geographers, deserted by all of his kind except the gorillas— dejected, miserable, famishing, absolutely famishing—but he was eloquent. Just as I found him he had eaten his last elephant, and he said to me: "God knows where I shall get another." He had nothing to wear except his venerable and honorable naval suit, and nothing to eat but his diary.

But I said to him: "It is all right; I have discovered you, and Stanley will be here by the four-o'clock train and will discover you officially, and then we will turn to and have a reg'lar good time." I said: "Cheer up, for Stanley has got corn, ammunition, glass beads, hymn-books, whiskey, and everything which the human heart can desire; he has got all kinds of valuables, including telegraph-poles and a few cart-loads of money. By this time communication has been made with the land of Bibles and civilization, and property will advance." And then we surveyed all that country, from Ujiji, through Unanogo and other places, to Unyanyembe. I mention these names simply for your edification, nothing more—do not expect it—particularly as intelligence to the Royal Geographical Society. And then, having filled up the old man, we were all too full for utterance and departed. We have since then feasted on honors.

Stanley has received a snuff-box and I have received considerable snuff; he has got to write a book and gather in the rest of the credit, and I am going to levy on the copyright and to collect the money. Nothing comes amiss to me—cash or credit; but, seriously, I do feel that Stanley is the chief man and an illustrious one, and I do applaud him with all my heart. Whether he is an American or a Welshman by birth, or one, or both, matters not to me. So far as I am personally concerned, I am simply here to stay a few months, and to see English people and to learn English manners and customs, and to enjoy myself; so the simplest thing I can do is to thank you for the toast you have honored me with and for the remarks you have made, and to wish health and prosperity to the Whitefriars' Club, and to sink down to my accustomed level.

HENRY M. STANLEY

ADDRESS DELIVERED IN BOSTON, NOVEMBER, 1886

Mr. Clemens introduced Mr. Stanley.

LADIES AND GENTLEMEN, if any should ask, Why is it that you are here as introducer of the lecturer? I should answer that I happened to be around and was asked to perform this function. I was quite willing to do so, and, as there was no sort of need of an introduction, anyway, it could be necessary only that some person come forward for a moment and do an unnecessary thing, and this is quite in my line. Now, to introduce so illustrious a name as Henry M. Stanley by any detail of what the man has done is clear aside from my purpose; that would be stretching the unnecessary to an unconscionable degree. When I contrast what I have achieved in my measurably brief life with what he has achieved in his possibly briefer one, the effect is to sweep utterly away the ten-story edifice of my own self-appreciation and leave nothing behind but the cellar. When you compare these achievements of his with the achievements of really great men who

157

exist in history, the comparison, I believe, is in his favor. I am not here to disparage Columbus.

No, I won't do that; but when you come to regard the achievements of these two men, Columbus and Stanley, from the standpoint of the difficulties they encountered, the advantage is with Stanley and against Columbus. Now, Columbus started out to discover America. Well, he didn't need to do anything at all but sit in the cabin of his ship and hold his grip and sail straight on, and America would discover itself. Here it was, barring his passage the whole length and breadth of the South American continent, and he couldn't get by it. He'd got to discover it. But Stanley started out to find Doctor Livingstone, who was scattered abroad, as you may say, over the length and breadth of a vast slab of Africa as big as the United States.

It was a blind kind of search. He was the worst scattered of men. But I will throw the weight of this introduction upon one very peculiar feature of Mr. Stanley's character, and that is his indestructible Americanism—an Americanism which he is proud of. And in this day and time, when it is the custom to ape and imitate English methods and fashion, it is like a breath of fresh air to stand in the presence of this untainted American citizen who has been caressed and complimented by half of the crowned heads of Europe, who could clothe his body from his head to his heels with the orders and decorations lavished upon him. And yet, when the untitled myriads of his own country put out their hands in welcome to him and greet him, "Well done," through the Congress of the United States, that is the crown that is worth all the rest to him. He is a product of institutions which exist in no other country on earth—institutions that bring out all that is best and most heroic in a man. I introduce Henry M. Stanley.

DINNER TO MR. JEROME

A dinner to express their confidence in the integrity and good judgment of District-Attorney Jerome was given at Delmonico's by over three hundred of his admirers on the evening of May 7, 1909.

INDEED, that is very sudden. I was not informed that the verdict was going to depend upon my judgment, but that makes not the least difference in the world when you already know all about it. It is not any matter when you are called upon to express it; you can get up and do it, and my verdict has already been recorded in my heart and in my head as regards Mr. Jerome and his administration of the criminal affairs of this county.

I agree with everything Mr. Choate has said in his letter regarding Mr. Jerome; I agree with everything Mr. Shepard has said; and I agree with everything Mr. Jerome has said in his own commendation. And I thought Mr. Jerome was modest in that. If he had been talking about another officer of this county, he could have painted the joys and sorrows of office and his victories in even stronger language than he did.

DINNER TO MR. JEROME

I voted for Mr. Jerome in those old days, and I should like to vote for him again if he runs for any office. I moved out of New York, and that is the reason, I suppose, I cannot vote for him again. There may be some way, but I have not found it out. But now I am a farmer—a farmer up in Connecticut, and winning laurels. Those people already speak with such high favor, admiration, of my farming, and they say that I am the only man that has ever come to that region who could make two blades of grass grow where only three grew before.

Well, I cannot vote for him. You see that. As it stands now, I cannot. I am crippled in that way and to that extent, for I would ever so much like to do it. I am not a Congress, and I cannot distribute pensions, and I don't know any other legitimate way to buy a vote. But if I should think of any legitimate way, I shall make use of it, and then I shall vote for Mr. Jerome.

HENRY IRVING

The Dramatic and Literary Society of London gave a welcome-home dinner to Sir Henry Irving at the Savoy Hotel, London, June 9, 1900. In proposing the toast of "The Drama" Mr. Clemens said:

I FIND my task a very easy one. I have been a dramatist for thirty years. I have had an ambition in all that time to overdo the work of the Spaniard who said he left behind him four hundred dramas when he died. I leave behind me four hundred and fifteen, and am not yet dead.

The greatest of all the arts is to write a drama. It is a most difficult thing. It requires the highest talent possible and the rarest gifts. No, there is another talent that ranks with it—for anybody can write a drama—I had four hundred of them—but to get one accepted requires real ability. And I have never had that felicity yet.

But human nature is so constructed, we are so persistent, that when we know that we are born to a thing we do not care what the world thinks about it. We go on exploiting that talent year after year, as I have done. I shall go on writing dramas, and some day the impossible may happen, but I am not looking for it.

In writing plays the chief thing is novelty. The world grows tired of solid forms in all the arts. I struck a new idea myself years ago. I was not surprised at it. I was always expecting it would happen. A person who has suffered disappointment for many years loses confidence, and I thought I had better make inquiries before I exploited my new idea of doing a drama in the form of a dream, so I wrote to a great authority on knowledge of all kinds, and asked him whether it was new.

I could depend upon him. He lived in my dear home in America—that dear home, dearer to me through taxes. He sent me a list of plays in which that old device had been used, and he said that there was also a modern lot. He travelled back to China and to a play dated two thousand six hundred years before the Christian era. He said he would follow it up with a list of the previous plays of the kind, and in his innocence would have carried them back to the Flood.

That is the most discouraging thing that has ever happened to me in my dramatic career. I have done a world of good in a silent and private way, and have furnished Sir Henry Irving with plays and plays and plays. What has he achieved through that influence See where he stands now—on the summit of his art in two worlds—

and it was I who put him there—that partly put him there.

I need not enlarge upon the influence the drama has exerted upon civilization. It has made good morals entertaining. I am to be followed by Mr. Pinero. I conceive that we stand at the head of the profession. He has not written as many plays as I have, but he has had that God-given talent, which I lack, of working hem off on the manager. I couple his name with this toast, and add the hope that his influence will be supported in exercising his masterly handicraft in that great gift, and that he will long live to continue his fine work.

DINNER TO HAMILTON W. MABIE

ADDRESS DELIVERED APRIL 29, 1901

In introducing Mr. Clemens, Doctor Van Dyke said:
" The longer the speaking goes on to-night the more
I wonder how I got this job, and the only explanation
I can give for it is that it is the same kind of com-
pensation for the number of articles I have sent to
The Outlook, to be rejected by Hamilton W. Mabie.
There is one man here to-night that has a job cut out
for him that none of you would have had—a man
whose humor has put a girdle of light around the
globe, and whose sense of humor has been an example
for all five continents.   He is going to speak to you.
Gentlemen, you know him best as Mark Twain."

MR. CHAIRMAN AND GENTLEMEN,—This
man knows now how it feels to be the chief
guest, and if he has enjoyed it he is the first man I
have ever seen in that position that did enjoy it.
And I know, by side-remarks which he made to
me before his ordeal came upon him, that he was
feeling as some of the rest of us have felt under
the same circumstances.   He was afraid that he
would not do himself justice; but he did—to my
surprise.   It is a most serious thing to be a chief
guest on an occasion like this, and it is admirable,

it is fine. It is a great compliment to a man that he shall come out of it so gloriously as Mr. Mabie came out of it to-night—to my surprise. He did it well.

He appears to be editor of *The Outlook*, and notwithstanding that, I have every admiration, because when everything is said concerning *The Outlook*, after all one must admit that it is frank in its delinquencies, that it is outspoken in its departures from fact, that it is vigorous in its mistaken criticisms of men like me. I have lived in this world a long, long time, and I know you must not judge a man by the editorials that he puts in his paper. A man is always better than his printed opinions. A man always reserves to himself on the inside a purity and an honesty and a justice that are a credit to him, whereas the things that he prints are just the reverse.

Oh yes, you must not judge a man by what he writes in his paper. Even in an ordinary secular paper a man must observe some care about it; he must be better than the principles which he puts in print. And that is the case with Mr. Mabie. Why, to see what he writes about me and the missionaries you would think he did not have any principles. But that is Mr. Mabie in his public capacity. Mr. Mabie in his private capacity is just as clean a man as I am.

In this very room, a month or two ago, some people admired that portrait; some admired this, but the great majority fastened on that, and said, "There is a portrait that is a beautiful piece of art." When that portrait is a hundred years old it will suggest what were the manners and customs in our time. Just as they talk about Mr. Mabie to-night, in that enthusiastic way, pointing out the various virtues of the man and the grace of his spirit, and all that, so was that portrait talked about. They were enthusiastic, just as we men have been over the character and the work of Mr. Mabie. And when they were through they said that portrait, fine as it is, that work, beautiful as it is, that piece of humanity on that canvas, gracious and fine as it is, does not rise to those perfections that exist in the man himself. Come up, Mr. Alexander. [The reference was to James W. Alexander, who happened to be sitting beneath the portrait of himself on the wall.] Now, I should come up and show myself. But he cannot do it, he cannot do it. He was born that way, he was reared in that way. Let his modesty be an example, and I wish some of you had it, too. But that is just what I have been saying— that portrait, fine as it is, is not as fine as the man it represents, and all the things that have been said about Mr. Mabie, and certainly they have been very nobly worded and beautiful, still fall short of the real Mabie.

INTRODUCING NYE AND RILEY

James Whitcomb Riley and Edgar Wilson Nye (Bill Nye) were to give readings in Tremont Temple, Boston, November, 1888. Mr. Clemens was induced to introduce Messrs. Riley and Nye. His appearance on the platform was a surprise to the audience, and when they recognized him there was a tremendous demonstration.

I AM very glad indeed to introduce these young people to you, and at the same time get acquainted with them myself. I have seen them more than once for a moment, but have not had the privilege of knowing them personally as intimately as I wanted to. I saw them first, a great many years ago, when Mr. Barnum had them, and they were just fresh from Siam. The ligature was their best hold then, the literature became their best hold later, when one of them committed an indiscretion, and they had to cut the old bond to accommodate the sheriff.

In that old former time this one was Chang, that one was Eng. The sympathy existing between the two was most extraordinary; it was so fine, so strong, so subtle, that what the one ate the other digested; when one slept, the other snored; if one sold a thing, the other scooped the usufruct. This independent and yet dependent action was observable in all the details of their daily life—I mean this quaint and arbitrary distribution of originating cause and resulting effect between the two—between, I may say, this dynamo and the other always motor, or, in other words, that the one was always the creating force, the other always the utilizing force; no, no, for while it is true that within certain well-defined zones of activity the one was always dynamo and the other always motor, within certain other well-defined zones these positions became exactly reversed.

For instance, in moral matters Mr. Chang Riley was always dynamo, Mr. Eng Nye was always motor; for while Mr. Chang Riley had a high—in fact, an abnormally high and fine—moral sense, he had no machinery to work it with; whereas, Mr. Eng Nye, who hadn't any moral sense at all, and hasn't yet, was equipped with all the necessary plant for putting a noble deed through, if he could only get the inspiration on reasonable terms outside.

In intellectual matters, on the other hand, Mr. Eng Nye was always dynamo, Mr. Chang Riley was always motor; Mr. Eng Nye had a stately intellect, but couldn't make it go; Mr. Chang Riley hadn't, but could. That is to say, that while Mr. Chang Riley couldn't think things himself, he had a marvellous natural grace in setting them down and weaving them together when his pal furnished the raw material.

Thus, working together, they made a strong team; laboring together, they could do miracles; but break the circuit, and both were impotent. It has remained so to this day: they must travel together, hoe, and plant, and plough, and reap, and sell their public together, or there's no result.

I have made this explanation, this analysis, this vivisection, so to speak, in order that you may enjoy these delightful adventurers understandingly. When Mr. Eng Nye's deep and broad and limpid philosophies flow by in front of you, refreshing all the regions round about with their gracious floods, you will remember that it isn't his water; it's the other man's, and he is only working the pump. And when Mr. Chang Riley enchants your ear, and soothes your spirit, and touches your heart with the sweet and genuine music of his poetry—as sweet and as genuine as any that his friends, the birds and the bees, make about his other friends, the woods and the flowers— you will remember, while placing justice where justice is due, that it isn't his music, but the other man's—he is only turning the crank.

I beseech for these visitors a fair field, a single-minded, one-eyed umpire, and a score bulletin barren of goose-eggs if they earn it—and I judge they will and hope they will. Mr. James Whitcomb Chang Riley will now go to the bat.

DINNER TO WHITELAW REID

ADDRESS AT THE DINNER IN HONOR OF AMBASSADOR
REID, GIVEN BY THE PILGRIMS' CLUB OF
NEW YORK ON FEBRUARY 19, 1908

I AM very proud to respond to this toast, as it recalls the proudest day of my life. The delightful hospitality shown me at the time of my visit to Oxford I shall cherish until I die. In that long and distinguished career of mine I value that degree above all other honors. When the ship landed even the stevedores gathered on the shore and gave an English cheer. Nothing could surpass in my life the pleasure of those four weeks. No one could pass by me without taking my hand, even the policemen. I've been in all the principal capitals of Christendom in my life, and have always been an object of interest to policemen. Sometimes there was suspicion in their eyes, but not always. With their puissant hand they would hold up the commerce of the world to let me pass.

I noticed in the papers this afternoon a despatch from Washington, saying that Congress would immediately pass a bill restoring to our gold coinage the motto "In God We Trust." I'm glad of that; I'm glad of that. I was troubled when that motto was removed. Sure enough, the prosperities of the whole nation went down in a heap when we ceased to trust in God in that conspicuously advertised way. I knew there would be trouble. And if Pierpont Morgan hadn't stepped in—Bishop Lawrence may now add to his message to the old country that we are now trusting in God again. So we can discharge Mr. Morgan from his office with honor.

Mr. Reid said an hour or so ago something about my ruining my activities last summer. They are not ruined, they are renewed. I am stronger now—much stronger. I suppose that the spiritual uplift I received increased my physical power more than anything I ever had before. I was dancing last night at 12.30 o'clock.

Mr. Choate has mentioned Mr. Reid's predecessors. Mr. Choate's head is full of history, and some of it is true, too. I enjoyed hearing him tell about the list of the men who had the place before he did. He mentioned a long list of those predecessors, people I never heard of before, and elected five of them to the Presidency by his own vote. I'm glad and proud to find Mr. Reid in that high position, because he didn't look it when I knew him forty years ago. I was talking to Reid the other day, and he showed me my autograph on an old paper twenty years old. I didn't know

I had an autograph twenty years ago. Nobody ever asked me for it.

I remember a dinner I had long ago with Whitelaw Reid and John Hay at Reid's expense. I had another last summer when I was in London at the embassy that Choate blackguards so. I'd like to live there.

Some people say they couldn't live on the salary, but I could live on the salary and the nation together. Some of us don't appreciate what this country can do. There's John Hay, Reid, Choate, and me. This is the only country in the world where youth, talent, and energy can reach such heights. It shows what we could do without means, and what people can do with talent and energy when they find it in people like us.

When I first came to New York they were all struggling young men, and I am glad to see that they have got on in the world. I knew John Hay when I had no white hairs in my head and more hair than Reid has now. Those were days of joy and hope. Reid and Hay were on the staff of the *Tribune*. I went there once in that old building, and I looked all around, and I finally found a door ajar and looked in. It wasn't Reid or Hay there, but it was Horace Greeley. Those were in the days when Horace Greeley was a king. That was the first time I ever saw him and the last.

I was admiring him when he stopped and seemed to realize that there was a fine presence there somewhere. He tried to smile, but he was out of smiles. He looked at me a moment, and said: "What in H— do you want?"

He began with that word "H." That's a long word and a profane word. I don't remember what the word was now, but I recognized the power of it. I had never used that language myself, but at that moment I was converted. It has been a great refuge for me in time of trouble. If a man doesn't know that language he can't express himself on strenuous occasions. When you have that word at your command let trouble come.

But later Hay rose, and you know what summit Whitelaw Reid has reached, and you see me. Those two men have regulated troubles of nations and conferred peace upon mankind. And in my humble way, of which I am quite vain, I was the principal moral force in all those great international movements. These great men illustrated what I say. Look at us great people—we all come from the dregs of society. That's what can be done in this country. That's what this country does for you.

Choate here—he hasn't got anything to say, but he says it just the same, and he can do it so felicitously, too. I said long ago he was the handsomest man America ever produced. May the progress of civilization always rest on such distinguished men as it has in the past!

ROGERS AND RAILROADS

At a Banquet Given Mr. H. H. Rogers by the
Business Men of Norfolk, Va., Celebrat-
ing the Opening of the Virginian
Railway, April, 3, 1909

Toastmaster:

"I have often thought that when the time comes,
which must come to all of us, when we reach that
Great Way in the Great Beyond, and the question is
propounded, 'What have you done to gain admission
into this great realm?' if the answer could be sincerely made, 'I have made men laugh,' it would be
the surest passport to a welcome entrance. We have
here to-night one who has made millions laugh—not
the loud laughter that bespeaks the vacant mind, but
the laugh of intelligent mirth that helps the human
heart and the human mind. I refer, of course, to
Doctor Clemens. I was going to say Mark Twain,
his literary title, which is a household phrase in more
homes than that of any other man, and you know
him best by that dear old title."

I THANK you, Mr. Toastmaster, for the compliment which you have paid me, and I am sure I
would rather have made people laugh than cry,
yet in my time I have made some of them cry;
and before I stop entirely I hope to make some

more of them cry. I like compliments. I deal in them myself. I have listened with the greatest pleasure to the compliments which the chairman has paid to Mr. Rogers and that road of his to-night, and I hope some of them are deserved.

It is no small distinction to a man like that to sit here before an intelligent crowd like this and to be classed with Napoleon and Cæsar. Why didn't he say that this was the proudest day of his life? Napoleon and Cæsar are dead, and they can't be here to defend themselves. But I'm here!

The chairman said, and very truly, that the most lasting thing in the hands of man are the roads which Cæsar built, and it is true that he built a lot of them; and they are there yet.

Yes, Cæsar built a lot of roads in England, and you can find them. But Rogers has only built one road, and he hasn't finished that yet. I like to hear my old friend complimented, but I don't like to hear it overdone.

I didn't go around to-day with the others to see what he is doing. I will do that in a quiet time, when there is not anything going on, and when I shall not be called upon to deliver intemperate compliments on a railroad in which I own no stock.

They proposed that I go along with the committee and help inspect that dump down yonder.

I didn't go. I saw that dump. I saw that thing when I was coming in on the steamer, and I didn't go because I was diffident, sentimentally diffident, about going and looking at that thing again—that great, long, bony thing; it looked just like Mr. Rogers's foot.

The chairman says Mr. Rogers is full of practical wisdom, and he is. It is intimated here that he is a very ingenious man, and he is a very competent financier. Maybe he is now, but it was not always so. I know lots of private things in his life which people don't know, and I know how he started; and it was not a very good start. I could have done better myself. The first time he crossed the Atlantic he had just made the first little strike in oil, and he was so young he did not like to ask questions. He did not like to appear ignorant. To this day he don't like to appear ignorant, but he can look as ignorant as anybody. On board the ship they were betting on the run of the ship, betting a couple of shillings, or half a crown, and they proposed that this youth from the oil regions should bet on the run of the ship. He did not like to ask what a half-crown was, and he didn't know; but rather than be ashamed of himself he did bet half a crown on the run of the ship, and in bed he could not sleep. He wondered if he could afford that outlay in case he lost. He kept wondering over it, and said to himself: "A king's crown must be worth

$20,000, so half a crown would cost $10,000."
He could not afford to bet away $10,000 on the
run of the ship, so he went up to the stakeholder
and gave him $150 to let him off.

I like to hear Mr. Rogers complimented. I am
not stingy in compliments to him myself. Why,
I did it to-day when I sent his wife a telegram to
comfort her. That is the kind of person I am.
I knew she would be uneasy about him. I knew
she would be solicitous about what he might do
down here, so I did it to quiet her and to comfort
her. I said he was doing well for a person out of
practice. There is nothing like it. He is like I
used to be. There were times when I was careless—careless in my dress when I got older. You
know how uncomfortable your wife can get when
you are going away without her superintendence.
Once when my wife could not go with me (she
always went with me when she could—I always
did meet that kind of luck), I was going to Wash-
ton once, a long time ago, in Mr. Cleveland's first
administration, and she could not go; but, in her
anxiety that I should not desecrate the house,
she made preparation. She knew that there was
to be a reception of those authors at the White
House at seven o'clock in the evening. She said,
"If I should tell you now what I want to ask of
you, you would forget it before you get to Washington, and, therefore, I have written it on a
card, and you will find it in your dress - vest

178

pocket when you are dressing at the Arlington—when you are dressing to see the President." I never thought of it again until I was dressing, and I felt in that pocket and took it out, and it said, in a kind of imploring way, "Don't wear your arctics in the White House."

You complimented Mr. Rogers on his energy, his foresightedness, complimented him in various ways, and he has deserved those compliments, although I say it myself; and I enjoy them all. There is one side of Mr. Rogers that has not been mentioned. If you will leave that to me I will touch upon that. There was a note in an editorial in one of the Norfolk papers this morning that touched upon that very thing, that hidden side of Mr. Rogers, where it spoke of Helen Keller and her affection for Mr. Rogers, to whom she dedicated her life book. And she has a right to feel that way, because, without the public knowing anything about it, he rescued, if I may use that term, that marvellous girl, that wonderful Southern girl, that girl who was stone deaf, blind, and dumb from scarlet - fever when she was a baby eighteen months old; and who now is as well and thoroughly educated as any woman on this planet at twenty-nine years of age. She is the most marvellous person of her sex that has existed on this earth since Joan of Arc.

That is not all Mr. Rogers has done; but you never see that side of his character, because it is never protruding; but he lends a helping hand daily out of that generous heart of his. You never hear of it. He is supposed to be a moon which has one side dark and the other bright. But the other side, though you don't see it, is not dark; it is bright, and its rays penetrate, and others do see it who are not God.

I would take this opportunity to tell something that I have never been allowed to tell by Mr. Rogers, either by my mouth or in print, and if I don't look at him I can tell it now.

In 1893, when the publishing company of Charles L. Webster, of which I was financial agent, failed, it left me heavily in debt. If you will remember what commerce was at that time you will recall that you could not sell anything, and could not buy anything, and I was on my back; my books were not worth anything at all, and I could not give away my copyrights. Mr. Rogers had long enough vision ahead to say, "Your books have supported you before, and after the panic is over they will support you again," and that was a correct proposition. He saved my copyrights, and saved me from financial ruin. He it was who arranged with my creditors to allow me to roam the face of the earth for four years and persecute the nations thereof with lectures, promising that at the end of four years I would pay dollar for dollar. That arrangement was made; otherwise I would now be living out-of-doors under an umbrella, and a borrowed one at that.

You see his white mustache and his head trying to get white (he is always trying to look like me—I don't blame him for that). These are only emblematic of his character, and that is all. I say, without exception, hair and all, he is the whitest man I have ever known.

13

THE OLD-FASHIONED PRINTER

ADDRESS AT THE TYPOTHETÆ DINNER GIVEN AT DEL-
MONICO'S, JANUARY 18, 1886, COMMEMORATING
THE BIRTHDAY OF BENJAMIN FRANKLIN

*Mr. Clemens responded to the toast " The Composi-
tor."*

THE chairman's historical reminiscences of
Gutenberg have caused me to fall into reminiscences, for I myself am something of an antiquity. All things change in the procession of
years, and it may be that I am among strangers.
It may be that the printer of to-day is not the
printer of thirty-five years ago. I was no stranger
to him. I knew him well. I built his fire for
him in the winter mornings; I brought his water
from the village pump; I swept out his office; I
picked up his type from under his stand; and,
if he were there to see, I put the good type in his
case and the broken ones among the "hell matter"; and if he wasn't there to see, I dumped it
all with the "pi" on the imposing-stone—for that
was the furtive fashion of the cub, and I was a
cub. I wetted down the paper Saturdays, I

turned it Sundays—for this was a country weekly; I rolled, I washed the rollers, I washed the forms, I folded the papers, I carried them around at dawn Thursday mornings. The carrier was then an object of interest to all the dogs in town. If I had saved up all the bites I ever received, I could keep M. Pasteur busy for a year. I enveloped the papers that were for the mail—we had a hundred town subscribers and three hundred and fifty country ones; the town subscribers paid in groceries and the country ones in cabbages and cord-wood—when they paid at all, which was merely sometimes, and then we always stated the fact in the paper, and gave them a puff; and if we forgot it they stopped the paper. Every man on the town list helped edit the thing—that is, he gave orders as to how it was to be edited; dictated its opinions, marked out its course for it, and every time the boss failed to connect he stopped his paper. We were just infested with critics, and we tried to satisfy them all over. We had one subscriber who paid cash, and he was more trouble than all the rest. He bought us once a year, body and soul, for two dollars. He used to modify our politics every which way, and he made us change our religion four times in five years. If we ever tried to reason with him, he would threaten to stop his paper, and, of course, that meant bankruptcy and destruction. That man used to write articles a column and a

half long, leaded long primer, and sign them
"Junius," or "Veritas," or "Vox Populi," or some
other high-sounding rot; and then, after it was
set up, he would come in and say he had changed
his mind—which was a gilded figure of speech,
because he hadn't any—and order it to be left out.
We couldn't afford "bogus" in that office, so we
always took the leads out, altered the signature,
credited the article to the rival paper in the next
village, and put it in. Well, we did have one or
two kinds of "bogus." Whenever there was a
barbecue, or a circus, or a baptizing, we knocked
off for half a day, and then to make up for short
matter we would "turn over ads"—turn over the
whole page and duplicate it. The other "bogus"
was deep philosophical stuff, which we judged
nobody ever read; so we kept a galley of it standing, and kept on slapping the same old batches
of it in, every now and then, till it got dangerous.
Also, in the early days of the telegraph we used to
economize on the news. We picked out the items
that were pointless and barren of information
and stood them on a galley, and changed the dates
and localities, and used them over and over again
till the public interest in them was worn to the
bone. We marked the ads, but we seldom paid
any attention to the marks afterward; so the
life of a "td" ad and a "tf" ad was equally
eternal. I have seen a "td" notice of a sheriff's
sale still booming serenely along two years after

the sale was over, the sheriff dead, and the whole circumstance become ancient history. Most of the yearly ads were patent-medicine stereotypes, and we used to fence with them.

I can see that printing-office of prehistoric times yet, with its horse bills on the walls, its "d" boxes clogged with tallow, because we always stood the candle in the "k" box nights, its towel, which was not considered soiled until it could stand alone, and other signs and symbols that marked the establishment of that kind in the Mississippi Valley; and I can see, also, the tramping "jour," who flitted by in the summer and tarried a day, with his wallet stuffed with one shirt and a hatful of handbills; for if he couldn't get any type to set he would do a temperance lecture. His way of life was simple, his needs not complex; all he wanted was plate and bed and money enough to get drunk on, and he was satisfied. But it may be, as I have said, that I am among strangers, and sing the glories of a forgotten age to unfamiliar ears, so I will "make even" and stop.

SOCIETY OF AMERICAN AUTHORS

On November 15, 1900, the society gave a reception to Mr. Clemens, who came with his wife and daughter. So many members surrounded the guests that Mr. Clemens asked: "Is this genuine popularity or is it all a part of a prearranged programme?"

MR. CHAIRMAN, LADIES AND GENTLE-MEN, — It seems a most difficult thing for any man to say anything about me that is not complimentary. I don't know what the charm is about me which makes it impossible for a person to say a harsh thing about me and say it heartily, as if he was glad to say it.

If this thing keeps on it will make me believe that I am what these kind chairmen say of me. In introducing me, Judge Ransom spoke of my modesty as if he was envious of me. I would like to have one man come out flat-footed and say something harsh and disparaging of me, even if it were true. I thought at one time, as the learned Judge was speaking, that I had found that man; but he wound up, like all the others, by saying complimentary things.

I am constructed like everybody else, and enjoy a compliment as well as any other fool, but I do like to have the other side presented. And there is another side. I have a wicked side. Estimable friends who know all about it would tell you and take a certain delight in telling you things that I have done, and things further that I have not repented.

The real life that I live, and the real life that I suppose all of you live, is a life of interior sin. That is what makes life valuable and pleasant. To lead a life of undiscovered sin! That is true joy.

Judge Ransom seems to have all the virtues that he ascribes to me. But, oh my! if you could throw an X-ray through him. We are a pair. I have made a life-study of trying to appear to be what he seems to think I am. Everybody believes that I am a monument of all the virtues, but it is nothing of the sort. I am living two lives, and it keeps me pretty busy.

Some day there will be a chairman who will forget some of these merits of mine, and then he will make a speech.

I have more personal vanity than modesty, and twice as much veracity as the two put together.

When that fearless and forgetful chairman is found there will be another story told. At the Press Club recently I thought that I had found him. He started in in the way that I knew I should be painted with all sincerity, and was leading to things that would not be to my credit; but when he said that he never read a book of mine I knew at once that he was a liar, because he never could have had all the wit and intelligence with which he was blessed unless he had read my works as a basis.

I like compliments. I like to go home and tell them all over again to the members of my family. They don't believe them, but I like to tell them in the home circle, all the same. I like to dream of them if I can.

I thank everybody for their compliments, but I don't think that I am praised any more than I am entitled to be.

READING-ROOM OPENING

On October 13, 1900, Mr. Clemens made his last address preceding his departure for America at Kensal Rise, London.

I FORMALLY declare this reading-room open, and I think that the legislature should not compel a community to provide itself with intelligent food, but give it the privilege of providing it if the community so desires.

If the community is anxious to have a reading-room it would put its hand in its pocket and bring out the penny tax. I think it a proof of the healthy, moral, financial, and mental condition of the community if it taxes itself for its mental food.

A reading-room is the proper introduction to a library, leading up through the newspapers and magazines to other literature. What would we do without newspapers?

Look at the rapid manner in which the news of the Galveston disaster was made known to the entire world. This reminds me of an episode which occurred fifteen years ago when I was at church in Hartford, Connecticut.

The clergyman decided to make a collection for the survivors, if any. He did not include me among the leading citizens who took the plates around for collection. I complained to the governor of his lack of financial trust in me, and he replied: "I would trust you myself—if you had a bell-punch."

You have paid me many compliments, and I like to listen to compliments. I indorse all your chairman has said to you about the union of England and America. He also alluded to my name, of which I am rather fond.

A little girl wrote me from New Zealand in a letter I received yesterday, stating that her father said my proper name was not Mark Twain but Samuel Clemens, but that she knew better, because Clemens was the name of the man who sold the patent medicine, and his name was not Mark. She was sure it was Mark Twain, because Mark is in the Bible and Twain is in the Bible.

I was very glad to get that expression of confidence in my origin, and as I now know my name to be a scriptural one, I am not without hopes of making it worthy.

LITERATURE

ADDRESS AT THE ROYAL LITERARY FUND BANQUET,
LONDON, MAY 4, 1900

*Anthony Hope introduced Mr. Clemens to make the
response to the toast "Literature."*

MR. HOPE has been able to deal adequately
with this toast without assistance from me.
Still, I was born generous. If he had advanced
any theories that needed refutation or correction
I would have attended to them, and if he had made
any statements stronger than those which he is in
the habit of making I would have dealt with
them.

In fact, I was surprised at the mildness of his
statements. I could not have made such statements if I had preferred to, because to exaggerate
is the only way I can approximate to the truth.
You cannot have a theory without principles.
Principles is another name for prejudices. I have
no prejudices in politics, religion, literature, or
anything else.

I am now on my way to my own country to
run for the presidency because there are not yet

enough candidates in the field, and those who have entered are too much hampered by their own principles, which are prejudices.

I propose to go there to purify the political atmosphere. I am in favor of everything everybody is in favor of. What you should do is to satisfy the whole nation, not half of it, for then you would only be half a President.

There could not be a broader platform than mine. I am in favor of anything and everything—of temperance and intemperance, morality and qualified immorality, gold standard and free silver.

I have tried all sorts of things, and that is why I want to try the great position of ruler of a country. I have been in turn reporter, editor, publisher, author, lawyer, burglar. I have worked my way up, and wish to continue to do so.

I read to-day in a magazine article that Christendom issued last year fifty-five thousand new books. Consider what that means! Fifty-five thousand new books meant fifty-four thousand new authors. We are going to have them all on our hands to take care of sooner or later. Therefore, double your subscriptions to the literary fund!

DISAPPEARANCE OF LITERATURE

Address at the Dinner of the Nineteenth Century Club, at Sherry's, New York, November 20, 1900

Mr. Clemens spoke to the toast "The Disappearance of Literature." Doctor Gould presided, and in introducing Mr. Clemens said that he (the speaker), when in Germany, had to do a lot of apologizing for a certain literary man who was taking what the Germans thought undue liberties with their language.

IT wasn't necessary for your chairman to apologize for me in Germany. It wasn't necessary at all. Instead of that he ought to have impressed upon those poor benighted Teutons the service I rendered them. Their language had needed untangling for a good many years. Nobody else seemed to want to take the job, and so I took it, and I flatter myself that I made a pretty good job of it. The Germans have an inhuman way of cutting up their verbs. Now a verb has a hard time enough of it in this world when it's all together. It's downright inhuman to split it up. But that's just what those Germans do. They take part of a verb and put it down here, like a

193

stake, and they take the other part of it and put it away over yonder like another stake, and between these two limits they just shovel in German. I maintain that there is no necessity for apologizing for a man who helped in a small way to stop such mutilation.

We have heard a discussion to-night on the disappearance of literature. That's no new thing. That's what certain kinds of literature have been doing for several years. The fact is, my friends, that the fashion in literature changes, and the literary tailors have to change their cuts or go out of business. Professor Winchester here, if I remember fairly correctly what he said, remarked that few, if any, of the novels produced to-day would live as long as the novels of Walter Scott. That may be his notion. Maybe he is right; but so far as I am concerned, I don't care if they don't.

Professor Winchester also said something about there being no modern epics like *Paradise Lost.* I guess he's right. He talked as if he was pretty familiar with that piece of literary work, and nobody would suppose that he never had read it. I don't believe any of you have ever read *Paradise Lost,* and you don't want to. That's something that you just want to take on trust. It's a classic, just as Professor Winchester says, and it meets his definition of a classic—something that everybody wants to have read and nobody wants to read.

Professor Trent also had a good deal to say about the disappearance of literature. He said that Scott would oulive all his critics. I guess that's true. The fact of the business is, you've got to be one of two ages to appreciate Scott. When you're eighteen you can read *Ivanhoe*, and you want to wait until you are ninety to read some of the rest. It takes a pretty well-regulated, abstemious critic to live ninety years.

But as much as these two gentlemen have talked about the disappearance of literature, they didn't say anything about my books. Maybe they think they've disappeared. If they do, that just shows their ignorance on the general subject of literature. I am not as young as I was several years ago, and maybe I'm not so fashionable, but I'd be willing to take my chances with Mr. Scott to-morrow morning in selling a piece of literature to the Century Publishing Company. And I haven't got much of a pull here, either. I often think that the highest compliment ever paid to my poor efforts was paid by Darwin through President Eliot, of Harvard College. At least, Eliot said it was a compliment, and I always take the opinion of great men like college presidents on all such subjects as that.

I went out to Cambridge one day a few years ago and called on President Eliot. In the course of the conversation he said that he had just returned from England, and that he was very much touched by what he considered the high compliment Darwin was paying to my books, and he went on to tell me something like this:

"Do you know that there is one room in Darwin's house, his bedroom, where the housemaid is never allowed to touch two things? One is a plant he is growing and studying while it grows" (it was one of those insect-devouring plants which consumed bugs and beetles and things for the particular delectation of Mr. Darwin) "and the other some books that lie on the night table at the head of his bed. They are your books, Mr. Clemens, and Mr. Darwin reads them every night to lull him to sleep."

My friends, I thoroughly appreciated that compliment, and considered it the highest one that was ever paid to me. To be the means of soothing to sleep a brain teeming with bugs and squirming things like Darwin's was something that I had never hoped for, and now that he is dead I never hope to be able to do it again.

THE NEW YORK PRESS CLUB DINNER

At the Annual Dinner, November 13, 1900

Col. William L. Brown, the former editor of the Daily News, *as president of the club, introduced Mr. Clemens as the principal ornament of American literature.*

I MUST say that I have already begun to regret that I left my gun at home. I've said so many times when a chairman has distressed me with just such compliments that the next time such a thing occurs I will certainly use a gun on that chairman. It is my privilege to compliment him in return. You behold before you a very, very old man. A cursory glance at him would deceive the most penetrating. His features seem to reveal a person dead to all honorable instincts—they seem to bear the traces of all the known crimes, instead of the marks of a life spent for the most part, and now altogether, in the Sunday-school—of a life that may well stand as an example to all generations that have risen or will riz—I mean to say, will rise. His private character is altogether suggestive of virtues which to all appearances he has not. If you examine his past history you will find it as deceptive as his features, because it is marked all over with waywardness and misdemeanor—mere effects of a great spirit upon a weak body—mere accidents of a great career. In his heart he cherishes every virtue on the list of virtues, and he practises them all—secretly—always secretly. You all know him so well that there is no need for him to be introduced here. Gentlemen, Colonel Brown.

THE ALPHABET AND SIMPLIFIED SPELLING

Address at the Dinner Given to Mr. Carnegie at the Dedication of the New York Engineers' Club, December 9, 1907

Mr. Clemens was introduced by the president of the club, who, quoting from the Mark Twain autobiography, recalled the day when the distinguished writer came to New York with $3 in small change in his pockets and a $10 bill sewed in his clothes.

IT seems to me that I was around here in the neighborhood of the Public Library about fifty or sixty years ago. I don't deny the circumstance, although I don't see how you got it out of my autobiography, which was not to be printed until I am dead, unless I'm dead now. I had that $3 in change, and I remember well the $10 which was sewed in my coat. I have prospered since. Now I have plenty of money and a disposition to squander it, but I can't. One of those trust companies is taking care of it.

Now, as this is probably the last time that I shall be out after nightfall this winter, I must say that I have come here with a mission, and I would make my errand of value.

Many compliments have been paid to Mr. Carnegie to-night. I was expecting them. They are very gratifying to me.

I have been a guest of honor myself, and I know what Mr. Carnegie is experiencing now. It is embarrassing to get compliments and compliments and only compliments, particularly when he knows as well as the rest of us that on the other side of him there are all sorts of things worthy of our condemnation.

Just look at Mr. Carnegie's face. It is fairly scintillating with fictitious innocence. You would think, looking at him, that he had never committed a crime in his life. But no — look at his pestiferous simplified spelling. You can't any of you imagine what a crime that has been. Torquemada was nothing to Mr. Carnegie. That old fellow shed some blood in the Inquisition, but Mr. Carnegie has brought destruction to the entire race. I know he didn't mean it to be a crime, but it was, just the same. He's got us all so we can't spell anything.

The trouble with him is that he attacked orthography at the wrong end. He meant well, but he attacked the symptoms and not the cause of the disease. He ought to have gone to work on the alphabet. There's not a vowel in it with a definite value, and not a consonant that you can hitch anything to. Look at the "h's" distributed all around. There's "gherkin." What are you going to do with the "h" in that? What the devil's the use of "h" in gherkin, I'd like to know. It's one thing I admire the English for: they just don't mind anything about them at all.

But look at the "pneumatics" and the "pneumonias" and the rest of them. A real reform would settle them once and for all, and wind up by giving us an alphabet that we wouldn't have to spell with at all, instead of this present silly alphabet, which I fancy was invented by a drunken thief. Why, there isn't a man who doesn't have to throw out about fifteen hundred words a day when he writes his letters because he can't spell them! It's like trying to do a St. Vitus's dance with wooden legs.

Now I'll bet there isn't a man here who can spell "pterodactyl," not even the prisoner at the bar. I'd like to hear him try once—but not in public, for it's too near Sunday, when all extravagant histrionic entertainments are barred. I'd like to hear him try in private, and when he got through trying to spell "pterodactyl" you wouldn't know whether it was a fish or a beast or a bird, and whether it flew on its legs or walked with its wings. The chances are that he would give it tusks and make it lay eggs.

Let's get Mr. Carnegie to reform the alphabet, and we'll pray for him—if he'll take the risk.

If we had adequate, competent vowels, with a system of accents, giving to each vowel its own soul and value, so every shade of that vowel would be shown in its accent, there is not a word in any tongue that we could not spell accurately. That would be competent, adequate, simplified spelling, in contrast to the clipping, the hair punching, the carbuncles, and the cancers which go by the name of simplified spelling. If I ask you what b-o-w spells you can't tell me unless you know which b-o-w I mean, and it is the same with r-o-w, b-o-r-e, and the whole family of words which were born out of lawful wedlock and don't know their own origin.

Now, if we had an alphabet that was adequate and competent, instead of inadequate and incompetent, things would be different. Spelling reform has only made it bald-headed and unsightly. There is the whole tribe of them, "row" and "read" and "lead"—a whole family who don't know who they are. I ask you to pronounce s-o-w, and you ask me what kind of a one.

If we had a sane, determinate alphabet, instead of a hospital of comminuted eunuchs, you would know whether one referred to the act of a man casting the seed over the ploughed land or whether one wished to recall the lady hog and the future ham.

It's a rotten alphabet. I appoint Mr. Carnegie to get after it, and leave simplified spelling alone.

202

SIMPLIFIED SPELLING

Simplified spelling brought about sun-spots, the San Francisco earthquake, and the recent business depression, which we would never have had if spelling had been left all alone.

Now, I hope I have soothed Mr. Carnegie and made him more comfortable than he would have been had he received only compliment after compliment, and I wish to say to him that simplified spelling is all right, but, like chastity, you can carry it too far.

SPELLING AND PICTURES

ADDRESS AT THE ANNUAL DINNER OF THE ASSO-
CIATED PRESS, AT THE WALDORF-ASTORIA,
SEPTEMBER 18, 1906

I AM here to make an appeal to the nations in
behalf of the simplified spelling. I have come
here because they cannot all be reached except
through you. There are only two forces that can
carry light to all the corners of the globe—only
two—the sun in the heavens and the Associated
Press down here. I may seem to be flattering
the sun, but I do not mean it so; I am meaning
only to be just and fair all around. You speak
with a million voices; no one can reach so many
races, so many hearts and intellects, as you—except Rudyard Kipling, and he cannot do it without
your help. If the Associated Press will adopt and
use our simplified forms, and thus spread them to
the ends of the earth, covering the whole spacious
planet with them as with a garden of flowers, our
difficulties are at an end.

Every day of the three hundred and sixty-five
the only pages of the world's countless newspapers
that are read by all the human beings and angels

and devils that can read, are these pages that are built out of Associated Press despatches. And so I beg you, I beseech you — oh, I implore you to spell them in our simplified forms. Do this daily, constantly, persistently, for three months— only three months—it is all I ask. The infallible result?—victory, victory all down the line. For by that time all eyes here and above and below will have become adjusted to the change and in love with it, and the present clumsy and ragged forms will be grotesque to the eye and revolting to the soul. And we shall be rid of phthisis and phthisic and pneumonia and pneumatics, and diphtheria and pterodactyl, and all those other insane words which no man addicted to the simple Christian life can try to spell and not lose some of the bloom of his piety in the demoralizing attempt. Do not doubt it. We are chameleons, and our partialities and prejudices change places with an easy and blessed facility, and we are soon wonted to the change and happy in it. We do not regret our old, yellow fangs and snags and tushes after we have worn nice, fresh, uniform store teeth a while.

Do I seem to be seeking the good of the world? That is the idea. It is my public attitude; privately I am merely seeking my own profit. We all do it, but it is sound and it is virtuous, for no public interest is anything other or nobler than a massed accumulation of private interests. In

1883, when the simplified-spelling movement first tried to make a noise, I was indifferent to it; more —I even irreverently scoffed at it. What I needed was an object-lesson, you see. It is the only way to teach some people. Very well, I got it. At that time I was scrambling along, earning the family's bread on magazine work at seven cents a word, compound words at single rates, just as it is in the dark present. I was the property of a magazine, a seven-cent slave under a boiler-iron contract. One day there came a note from the editor requiring me to write ten pages on this revolting text: "Considerations concerning the alleged subterranean holophotal extemporaneousness of the conchyliaceous superimbrication of the Ornithorhyncus, as foreshadowed by the unintelligibility of its plesiosaurian anisodactylous aspects."

Ten pages of that. Each and every word a seventeen-jointed vestibuled railroad train. Seven cents a word. I saw starvation staring the family in the face. I went to the editor, and I took a stenographer along so as to have the interview down in black and white, for no magazine editor can ever remember any part of a business talk except the part that's got graft in it for him and the magazine. I said, "Read that text, Jackson, and let it go on the record; read it out loud." He read it: "Considerations concerning the alleged subterranean holophotal extemporaneousness of the conchyliaceous superimbrication of the Ornithorhyncus, as foreshadowed by the unintelligibility of its plesiosaurian anisodactylous aspects."

I said, "You want ten pages of those rumbling, great, long, summer thunderpeals, and you expect to get them at seven cents a peal?"

He said, "A word's a word, and seven cents is the contract; what are you going to do about it?"

I said, "Jackson, this is cold-blooded oppression. What's an average English word?"

He said, "Six letters."

I said, "Nothing of the kind; that's French, and includes the spaces between the words; an average English word is four letters and a half. By hard, honest labor I've dug all the large words out of my vocabulary and shaved it down till the average is three letters and a half. I can put one thousand and two hundred words on your page, and there's not another man alive that can come within two hundred of it. My page is worth eighty-four dollars to me. It takes exactly as long to fill your magazine page with long words as it does with short ones—four hours. Now, then, look at the criminal injustice of this requirement of yours. I am careful, I am economical of my time and labor. For the family's sake I've got to be so. So I never write 'metropolis' for seven cents, because I can get the same money for 'city.' I never write 'policeman,' because I can get the same price for 'cop.' And so on and so on. I never write 'valetudinarian' at all, for not even hunger and wretchedness can humble me to the point where I will do a word like that for seven cents; I wouldn't do it for fifteen. Examine your obscene text, please; count the words.''

He counted and said it was twenty-four. I asked him to count the letters. He made it two hundred and three.

I said, ''Now, I hope you see the whole size of your crime. With my vocabulary I would make sixty words out of those two hundred and five letters, and get four dollars and twenty cents for it; whereas for your inhuman twenty-four I would get only one dollar and sixty-eight cents. Ten pages of these sky-scrapers of yours would pay me only about three hundred dollars; in my simplified vocabulary the same space and the same labor would pay me eight hundred and forty dollars. I do not wish to work upon this scandalous job by the piece. I want to be hired by the year.'' He coldly refused. I said:

''Then for the sake of the family, if you have no feeling for me, you ought at least to allow me overtime on that word extemporaneousness.'' Again he coldly refused. I seldom say a harsh word to any one, but I was not master of myself then, and I spoke right out and called him an anisodactylous plesiosaurian conchyliaceous Ornithorhyncus, and rotten to the heart with holophotal subterranean extemporaneousness. God forgive me for that wanton crime; he lived only two hours.

From that day to this I have been a devoted and hard-working member of the heaven-born institution, the International Association for the Prevention of Cruelty to Authors, and now I am laboring with Carnegie's Simplified Committee, and with my heart in the work. . . .

Now then, let us look at this mighty question reasonably, rationally, sanely—yes, and calmly, not excitedly. What is the real function, the essential function, the supreme function, of language? Isn't it merely to convey ideas and emotions? Certainly. Then if we can do it with words of fonetic brevity and compactness, why keep the present cumbersome forms? But can we? Yes. I hold in my hand the proof of it. Here is a letter written by a woman, right out of her heart of hearts. I think she never saw a spelling-book in her life. The spelling is her own. There isn't a waste letter in it anywhere. It reduces the fonetics to the last gasp—it squeezes the surplusage out of every word—there's no spelling that can begin with it on this planet outside of the White House. And as for the punctuation, there isn't any. It is all one sentence, eagerly and breathlessly uttered, without break or pause in it anywhere. The letter is absolutely genuine— I have the proofs of that in my possession. I can't stop to spell the words for you, but you can take the letter presently and comfort your eyes with it. I will read the letter:

"Miss ——— dear freind I took some Close into the armerry and give them to you to Send too the suffrers out to California and i Hate to truble you but i got to have one of them Back it was a black oll wolle Shevyott With a jacket to Mach trimed Kind of Fancy no 38 Burst measure and passy menterry acrost the front And the color i woodent Trubble you but it belonged to my brothers wife and she is Mad about it i thoght she was willin but she want she says she want done with it and she was going to Wear it a Spell longer she ant so free harted as what i am and she Has got more to do with Than i have having a Husband to Work and slave For her i gess you remember Me I am shot and stout and light complected i torked with you quite a spell about the suffrars and said it was orful about that erth quake I shoodent wondar if they had another one rite off seeine general Condision of the country is Kind of Explossive i hate to take that Black dress away from the suffrars but i will hunt round And see if i can get another One if i can i will call to the armerry for it if you will jest lay it asside so no more at present from your True freind
i liked your
appearance very Much"

Now you see what simplified spelling can do.

It can convey any fact you need to convey; and it can pour out emotions like a sewer. I beg you, I beseech you, to adopt our spelling, and print all your despatches in it.

Now I wish to say just one entirely serious word:

I have reached a time of life, seventy years and a half, where none of the concerns of this world have much interest for me personally. I think I can speak dispassionately upon this matter, because in the little while that I have got to remain here I can get along very well with these old-fashioned forms, and I don't propose to make any trouble about it at all. I shall soon be where they won't care how I spell so long as I keep the Sabbath.

There are eighty-two millions of us people that use this orthography, and it ought to be simplified in our behalf, but it is kept in its present condition to satisfy one million people who like to have their literature in the old form. That looks to me to be rather selfish, and we keep the forms as they are while we have got one million people coming in here from foreign countries every year and they have got to struggle with this orthography of ours, and it keeps them back and damages their citizenship for years until they learn to spell the language, if they ever do learn. This is merely sentimental argument.

People say it is the spelling of Chaucer and

Spenser and Shakespeare and a lot of other people who do not know how to spell anyway, and it has been transmitted to us and we preserved it and wish to preserve it because of its ancient and hallowed associations.

Now, I don't see that there is any real argument about that. If that argument is good, then it would be a good argument not to banish the flies and the cockroaches from hospitals because they have been there so long that the patients have got used to them and they feel a tenderness for them on account of the associations. Why, it is like preserving a cancer in a family because it is a family cancer, and we are bound to it by the test of affection and reverence and old, mouldy antiquity.

I think that this declaration to improve this orthography of ours is our family cancer, and I wish we could reconcile ourselves to have it cut out and let the family cancer go.

Now, you see before you the wreck and ruin of what was once a young person like yourselves. I am exhausted by the heat of the day. I must take what is left of this wreck and run out of your presence and carry it away to my home and spread it out there and sleep the sleep of the righteous. There is nothing much left of me but my age and my righteousness, but I leave with you my love and my blessing, and may you always keep your youth.

BOOKS AND BURGLARS

ADDRESS TO THE REDDING (CONN.) LIBRARY ASSO-
CIATION, OCTOBER 28, 1908

SUPPOSE this library had been in operation a few weeks ago, and the burglars who happened along and broke into my house—taking a lot of things they didn't need, and for that matter which I didn't need—had first made entry into this institution.

Picture them seated here on the floor, poring by the light of their dark-lanterns over some of the books they found, and thus absorbing moral truths and getting a moral uplift. The whole course of their lives would have been changed. As it was, they kept straight on in their immoral way and were sent to jail.

For all we know, they may next be sent to Congress.

And, speaking of burglars, let us not speak of them too harshly. Now, I have known so many burglars—not exactly known, but so many of them have come near me in my various dwelling-places, that I am disposed to allow them credit for whatever good qualities they possess.

15   213

Chief among these, and, indeed, the only one I just now think of, is their great care while doing business to avoid disturbing people's sleep.

Noiseless as they may be while at work, however, the effect of their visitation is to murder sleep later on.

Now we are prepared for these visitors. All sorts of alarm devices have been put in the house, and the ground for half a mile around it has been electrified. The burglar who steps within this danger zone will set loose a bedlam of sounds, and spring into readiness for action our elaborate system of defences. As for the fate of the trespasser, do not seek to know that. He will never be heard of more.

AUTHORS' CLUB

ADDRESS AT THE DINNER GIVEN IN HONOR OF MR. CLEMENS, LONDON, JUNE, 1899

Mr. Clemens was introduced by Sir Walter Besant.

IT does not embarrass me to hear my books praised so much. It only pleases and delights me. I have not gone beyond the age when embarrassment is possible, but I have reached the age when I know how to conceal it. It is such a satisfaction to me to hear Sir Walter Besant, who is much more capable than I to judge of my work, deliver a judgment which is such a contentment to my spirit.

Well, I have thought well of the books myself, but I think more of them now. It charms me also to hear Sir Spencer Walpole deliver a similar judgment, and I shall treasure his remarks also. I shall not discount the praises in any possible way. When I report them to my family they shall lose nothing. There are, however, certain heredities which come down to us which our writings of the present day may be traced to. I, for instance, read the *Walpole Letters* when I was a boy. I absorbed them, gathered in their grace, wit, and humor, and put them away to be used by-and-by. One does that so unconsciously with things one really likes. I am reminded now of what use those letters have been to me.

They must not claim credit in America for what was really written in another form so long ago. They must only claim that I trimmed this, that, and the other, and so changed their appearance as to make them seem to be original. You now see what modesty I have in stock. But it has taken long practice to get it there.

But I must not stand here talking. I merely meant to get up and give my thanks for the pleasant things that preceding speakers have said of me. I wish also to extend my thanks to the Authors' Club for constituting me a member, at a reasonable price per year, and for giving me the benefit of your legal adviser.

I believe you keep a lawyer. I have always kept a lawyer, too, though I have never made anything out of him. It is service to an author to have a lawyer. There is something so disagreeable in having a personal contact with a publisher. So it is better to work through a lawyer—and lose your case. I understand that the publishers have been meeting together also like us. I don't know what for, but possibly they are devising new and mysterious ways for remunerating authors. I only wish now to thank you for electing me a member of this club—I believe I have paid my dues—and to thank you again for the pleasant things you have said of me.

Last February, when Rudyard Kipling was ill in America, the sympathy which was poured out to him was genuine and sincere, and I believe that which cost Kipling so much will bring England and America closer together. I have been proud and pleased to see this growing affection and respect between the two countries. I hope it will continue to grow, and, please God, it will continue to grow. I trust we authors will leave to posterity, if we have nothing else to leave, a friendship between England and America that will count for much. I will now confess that I have been engaged for the past eight days in compiling a publication. I have brought it here to lay at your feet. I do not ask your indulgence in presenting it, but for your applause.

Here it is: "Since England and America may be joined together in Kipling, may they not be severed in 'Twain.'"

BOOKSELLERS

Address at banquet on Wednesday evening, May 20, 1908, of the American Booksellers' Association, which included most of the leading booksellers of America, held at the rooms of the Aldine Association, New York.

THIS annual gathering of booksellers from all over America comes together ostensibly to eat and drink, but really to discuss business; therefore I am required to talk shop. I am required to furnish a statement of the indebtedness under which I lie to you gentlemen for your help in enabling me to earn my living. For something over forty years I have acquired my bread by print, beginning with *The Innocents Abroad*, followed at intervals of a year or so by *Roughing It*, *Tom Sawyer*, *Gilded Age*, and so on. For thirty-six years my books were sold by subscription. You are not interested in those years, but only in the four which have since followed. The books passed into the hands of my present publishers at the beginning of 1904, and you then became the providers of my diet. I think I may say, without flattering you, that you have done exceedingly well by me. Exceedingly well is not too strong a phrase, since the official statistics show that in four years you have sold twice as many volumes of my venerable books as my contract with my publishers bound you and them to sell in five years. To your sorrow you are aware that frequently, much too frequently, when a book gets to be five or ten years old its annual sale shrinks to two or three hundred copies, and after an added ten or twenty years ceases to sell. But you sell thousands of my moss-backed old books every year—the youngest of them being books that range from fifteen to twenty-seven years old, and the oldest reaching back to thirty-five and forty.

By the terms of my contract my publishers had to account to me for 50,000 volumes per year for five years, and pay me for them whether they sold them or not. It is at this point that you gentlemen come in, for it was your business to unload 250,000 volumes upon the public in five years if you possibly could. Have you succeeded? Yes, you have—and more. For in four years, with a year still to spare, you have sold the 250,000 volumes, and 240,000 besides.

Your sales have increased each year. In the first year you sold 90,328; in the second year, 104,851; in the third, 133,975; in the fourth year—which was last year—you sold 160,000. The aggregate for the four years is 500,000 volumes, lacking 11,000.

Of the oldest book, *The Innocents Abroad,*—now forty years old—you sold upward of 46,000 copies in the four years; of *Roughing It*—now thirty-eight years old, I think—you sold 40,334; of *Tom Sawyer*, 41,000. And so on.

And there is one thing that is peculiarly gratifying to me: the *Personal Recollections of Joan of Arc* is a serious book; I wrote it for love, and never expected it to sell, but you have pleasantly disappointed me in that matter. In your hands its sale has increased each year. In 1904 you sold 1726 copies; in 1905, 2445; in 1906, 5381; and last year, 6574.

"MARK TWAIN'S FIRST APPEARANCE"

On October 5, 1906, Mr. Clemens, following a musical recital by his daughter in Norfolk, Conn., addressed her audience on the subject of stage-fright. He thanked the people for making things as easy as possible for his daughter's American début as a contralto, and then told of his first experience before the public.

MY heart goes out in sympathy to any one who is making his first appearance before an audience of human beings. By a direct process of memory I go back forty years, less one month— for I'm older than I look.

I recall the occasion of my first appearance. San Francisco knew me then only as a reporter, and I was to make my bow to San Francisco as a lecturer. I knew that nothing short of compulsion would get me to the theatre. So I bound myself by a hard-and-fast contract so that I could not escape. I got to the theatre forty-five minutes before the hour set for the lecture. My knees were shaking so that I didn't know whether I could stand up. If there is an awful, horrible malady in the world, it is stage-fright—and seasickness. They are a pair. I had stage - fright then for the first and last time. I was only sea-sick once, too. It was on a little ship on which there were two hundred other passengers. I—was—sick. I was so sick that there wasn't any left for those other two hundred passengers.

It was dark and lonely behind the scenes in that theatre, and I peeked through the little peek-holes they have in theatre curtains and looked into the big auditorium. That was dark and empty, too. By-and-by it lighted up, and the audience began to arrive.

I had got a number of friends of mine, stalwart men, to sprinkle themselves through the audience armed with big clubs. Every time I said anything they could possibly guess I intended to be funny they were to pound those clubs on the floor. Then there was a kind lady in a box up there, also a good friend of mine, the wife of the Governor. She was to watch me intently, and whenever I glanced toward her she was going to deliver a gubernatorial laugh that would lead the whole audience into applause.

At last I began. I had the manuscript tucked under a United States flag in front of me where I could get at it in case of need. But I managed to get started without it. I walked up and down —I was young in those days and needed the ex-ercise—and talked and talked.

Right in the middle of the speech I had placed a gem. I had put in a moving, pathetic part which was to get at the hearts and souls of my hearers. When I delivered it they did just what I hoped and expected. They sat silent and awed. I had touched them. Then I happened to glance up at the box where the Governor's wife was—you know what happened.

Well, after the first agonizing five minutes, my stage-fright left me, never to return. I know if I was going to be hanged I could get up and make a good showing, and I intend to. But I shall never forget my feelings before the agony left me, and I got up here to thank you for her for helping my daughter, by your kindness, to live through her first appearance. And I want to thank you for your appreciation of her singing, which is, by-the-way, hereditary.

MORALS AND MEMORY

Mr. Clemens was the guest of honor at a reception held at Barnard College (Columbia University), March 7, 1906, by the Barnard Union. One of the young ladies presented Mr. Clemens, and thanked him for his amiability in coming to make them an address. She closed with the expression of the great joy it gave her fellow-collegians, "because we all love you."

IF any one here loves me, she has my sincere thanks. Nay, if any one here is so good as to love me—why, I'll be a brother to her. She shall have my sincere, warm, unsullied affection When I was coming up in the car with the very kind young lady who was delegated to show me the way, she asked me what I was going to talk about. And I said I wasn't sure. I said I had some illustrations, and I was going to bring them in. I said I was certain to give those illustrations, but that I hadn't the faintest notion what they were going to illustrate.

Now, I've been thinking it over in this forest glade [indicating the woods of Arcady on the scene setting], and I've decided to work them in with something about morals and the caprices of memory. That seems to me to be a pretty good subject. You see, everybody has a memory and it's pretty sure to have caprices. And, of course, everybody has morals.

It's my opinion that every one I know has morals, though I wouldn't like to ask. I know I have. But I'd rather teach them than practice them any day. "Give them to others"— that's my motto. Then you never have any use for them when you're left without. Now, speaking of the caprices of memory in general, and of mine in particular, it's strange to think of all the tricks this little mental process plays on us. Here we're endowed with a faculty of mind that ought to be more supremely serviceable to us than them all. And what happens? This memory of ours stores up a perfect record of the most useless facts and anecdotes and experiences. And all the things that we ought to know—that we need to know—that we'd profit by knowing—it casts aside with the careless indifference of a girl refusing her true lover. It's terrible to think of this phenomenon. I tremble in all my members when I consider all the really valuable things that I've forgotten in seventy years— when I meditate upon the caprices of my memory.

There's a bird out in California that is one perfect symbol of the human memory. I've forgotten the bird's name (just because it would be valuable for me to know it—to recall it to your own minds, perhaps).

But this fool of a creature goes around collecting the most ridiculous things you can imagine and storing them up. He never selects a thing that could ever prove of the slightest help to him; but he goes about gathering iron forks, and spoons, and tin cans, and broken mouse-traps —all sorts of rubbish that is difficult for him to carry and yet be any use when he gets it. Why, that bird will go by a gold watch to bring back one of those patent cake-pans.

Now, my mind is just like that, and my mind isn't very different from yours—and so our minds are just like that bird. We pass by what would be of inestimable value to us, and pack our memories with the most trivial odds and ends that never by any chance, under any circumstances whatsoever, could be of the slightest use to any one.

Now, things that I have remembered are constantly popping into my head. And I am repeatedly startled by the vividness with which they recur to me after the lapse of years and their utter uselessness in being remembered at all.

I was thinking over some on my way up here. They were the illustrations I spoke about to the young lady on the way up. And I've come to the conclusion, curious though it is, that I can use every one of these freaks of memory to teach you all a lesson. I'm convinced that each one has its moral. And I think it's my duty to hand the moral on to you.

Now, I recall that when I was a boy I was a good boy—I was a very good boy. Why, I was the best boy in my school. I was the best boy in that little Mississippi town where I lived. The population was only about twenty million. You may not believe it, but I was the best boy in that State—and in the United States, for that matter.

But I don't know why I never heard any one say that but myself. I always recognized it. But even those nearest and dearest to me couldn't seem to see it. My mother, especially, seemed to think there was something wrong with that estimate. And she never got over that prejudice.

Now, when my mother got to be eighty-five years old her memory failed her. She forgot little threads that hold life's patches of meaning together. She was living out West then, and I went on to visit her.

I hadn't seen my mother in a year or so. And when I got there she knew my face; knew I was married; knew I had a family, and that I was living with them. But she couldn't, for the life of her, tell my name or who I was. So I told her I was her boy.

"But you don't live with me," she said.

"No," said I, "I'm living in Rochester."

"What are you doing there?"

"Going to school."

"Large school?"

"Very large."

"All boys?"

"All boys."

"And how do you stand?" said my mother.

"I'm the best boy in that school," I answered.

"Well," said my mother, with a return of her old fire, "I'd like to know what the other boys are like."

Now, one point in this story is the fact that my mother's mind went back to my school days, and remembered my little youthful self-prejudice when she'd forgotten everything else about me.

The other point is the moral. There's one there that you will find if you search for it.

Now, here's something else I remember. It's about the first time I ever stole a watermelon. "Stole" is a strong word. Stole? Stole? No, I don't mean that. It was the first time I ever withdrew a watermelon. It was the first time I ever extracted a watermelon. That is exactly the word I want—"extracted." It is definite. It is precise. It perfectly conveys my idea. Its use in dentistry connotes the delicate shade of meaning I am looking for. You know we never extract our own teeth.

And it was not my watermelon that I extracted. I extracted that watermelon from a farmer's wagon while he was inside negotiating with another customer. I carried that watermelon to one of the secluded recesses of the lumber-yard, and there I broke it open.

It was a green watermelon.

Well, do you know when I saw that I began to feel sorry—sorry—sorry. It seemed to me that I had done wrong. I reflected deeply. I reflected that I was young—I think I was just eleven. But I knew that though immature I did not lack moral advancement. I knew what a boy ought to do who had extracted a watermelon—like that.

I considered George Washington, and what action he would have taken under similar circumstances. Then I knew there was just one thing to make me feel right inside, and that was—Restitution.

So I said to myself: "I will do that. I will take that green watermelon back where I got it from." And the minute I had said it I felt that great moral uplift that comes to you when you've made a noble resolution.

So I gathered up the biggest fragments, and I carried them back to the farmer's wagon, and I restored the watermelon—what was left of it. And I made him give me a good one in place of it, too.

And I told him he ought to be ashamed of himself going around working off his worthless, old, green watermelons on trusting purchasers who had to rely on him. How could they tell from the outside whether the melons were good or not? That was his business. And if he didn't reform, I told him I'd see that he didn't get any more of my trade—nor anybody else's I knew, if I could help it.

You know that man was as contrite as a revivalist's last convert. He said he was all broken up to think I'd gotten a green watermelon. He promised me he would never carry another green watermelon if he starved for it. And he drove off—a better man.

Now, do you see what I did for that man? He was on a downward path, and I rescued him. But all I got out of it was a watermelon.

Yet I'd rather have that memory—just that memory of the good I did for that depraved farmer—than all the material gain you can think of. Look at the lesson he got! I never got anything like that from it. But I ought to be satisfied. I was only eleven years old, but I secured everlasting benefit to other people.

The moral in this is perfectly clear, and I think there's one in the next memory I'm going to tell you about.

To go back to my childhood, there's another little incident that comes to me from which you can draw even another moral. It's about one of the times I went fishing. You see, in our house there was a sort of family prejudice against going fishing if you hadn't permission. But it would frequently be bad judgment to ask. So I went fishing secretly, as it were—way up the Mississippi. It was an exquisitely happy trip, I recall, with a very pleasant sensation.

Well, while I was away there was a tragedy in our town. A stranger, stopping over on his way East from California, was stabbed to death in an unseemly brawl.

Now, my father was justice of the peace, and because he was justice of the peace he was coroner; and since he was coroner he was also constable; and being constable he was sheriff; and out of consideration for his holding the office of sheriff he was likewise county clerk and a dozen other officials I don't think of just this minute.

I thought he had power of life or death, only he didn't use it over other boys. He was sort of an austere man. Somehow I didn't like being round him when I'd done anything he disapproved of. So that's the reason I wasn't often around.

Well, when this gentleman got knifed they communicated with the proper authority, the coroner, and they laid the corpse out in the coroner's office—our front sitting-room—in preparation for the inquest the next morning.

About 9 or 10 o'clock I got back from fishing. It was a little too late for me to be received by my folks, so I took my shoes off and slipped noiselessly up the back way to the sitting-room. I was very tired, and I didn't wish to disturb my people. So I groped my way to the sofa and lay down.

Now, I didn't know anything of what had happened during my absence. But I was sort of nervous on my own account—afraid of being caught, and rather dubious about the morning affair. And I had been lying there a few moments when my eyes gradually got used to the darkness, and I became aware of something on the other side of the room.

It was something foreign to the apartment. It had an uncanny appearance. And I sat up looking very hard, and wondering what in heaven this long, formless, vicious-looking thing might be.

First I thought I'd go and see. Then I thought, "Never mind that."

Mind you, I had no cowardly sensations whatever, but it didn't seem exactly prudent to investigate. But I somehow couldn't keep my eyes off the thing. And the more I looked at it the more disagreeably it grew on me. But I was resolved to play the man. So I decided to turn over and count a hundred, and let the patch of moonlight creep up and show me what the dickens it was.

Well, I turned over and tried to count, but I couldn't keep my mind on it. I kept thinking of that grewsome mass. I was losing count all the time, and going back and beginning over again. Oh no; I wasn't frightened—just annoyed. But by the time I'd gotten to the century mark I turned cautiously over and opened my eyes with great fortitude.

The moonlight revealed to me a marble-white human hand. Well, maybe I wasn't embarrassed! But then that changed to a creepy feeling again, and I thought I'd try the counting again. I don't know how many hours or weeks it was that I lay there counting hard. But the moonlight crept up that white arm, and it showed me a lead face and a terrible wound over the heart.

I could scarcely say that I was terror-stricken or anything like that. But somehow his eyes interested me so that I went right out of the window. I didn't need the sash. But it seemed easier to take it than leave it behind.

Now, let that teach you a lesson—I don't know just what it is. But at seventy years old I find that memory of peculiar value to me. I have been unconsciously guided by it all these years. Things that seemed pigeon-holed and remote are a perpetual influence. Yes, you're taught in so many ways. And you're so felicitously taught when you don't know it.

Here's something else that taught me a good deal.

When I was seventeen I was very bashful, and a sixteen-year-old girl came to stay a week with us. She was a peach, and I was seized with a happiness not of this world.

One evening my mother suggested that, to entertain her, I take her to the theatre. I didn't really like to, because I was seventeen and sensitive about appearing in the streets with a girl. I couldn't see my way to enjoying my delight in public. But we went.

I didn't feel very happy. I couldn't seem to keep my mind on the play. I became conscious, after a while, that that was due less to my lovely company than my boots. They were sweet to look upon, as smooth as skin, but fitted ten times as close. I got oblivious to the play and the girl and the other people and everything but my boots until—I hitched one partly off. The sensation was sensuously perfect. I couldn't help it. I had to get the other off, partly. Then I was obliged to get them off altogether, except that I kept my feet in the legs so they couldn't get away.

From that time I enjoyed the play. But the first thing I knew the curtain came down, like that, without my notice, and I hadn't any boots on. What's more, they wouldn't go on. I tugged strenuously. And the people in our row got up and fussed and said things until the peach and I simply had to move on.

We moved—the girl on one arm and the boots under the other.

We walked home that way, sixteen blocks, with

a retinue a mile long. Every time we passed a
lamp-post death gripped me at the throat. But
we got home—and I had on white socks.

If I live to be nine hundred and ninety-nine
years old I don't suppose I could ever forget that
walk. I remember it about as keenly as the
chagrin I suffered on another occasion.

At one time in our domestic history we had a
colored butler who had a failing. He could never
remember to ask people who came to the door
to state their business. So I used to suffer a good
many calls unnecessarily.

One morning when I was especially busy he
brought me a card engraved with a name I did
not know. So I said, "What does he wish to see
me for?" and Sylvester said, "Ah couldn't ask
him, sah; he wuz a genlmun." "Return instantly," I thundered, " and inquire his mission.
Ask him what's his game." Well, Sylvester returned with the announcement that he had light-
ning-rods to sell. "Indeed," said I, "things are
coming to a fine pass when lightning-rod agents
send up engraved cards." "He has pictures,"
added Sylvester. "Pictures, indeed! He may be
peddling etchings. Has he a Russia leather case?"
But Sylvester was too frightened to remember.
I said, "I am going down to make it hot for that
upstart!"

I went down the stairs, working up my temper
all the way. When I got to the parlor I was in a

235

fine frenzy concealed beneath a veneer of frigid courtesy. And when I looked in the door, sure enough he had a Russia leather case in his hand. But I didn't happen to notice that it was our Russia leather case.

And if you'd believe me, that man was sitting with a whole gallery of etchings spread out before him. But I didn't happen to notice that they were our etchings, spread out by some member of my family for some unguessed purpose.

Very curtly I asked the gentleman his business. With a surprised, timid manner he faltered that he had met my wife and daughter at Onteora, and they had asked him to call. Fine lie, I thought, and I froze him.

He seemed to be kind of nonplussed, and sat there fingering the etchings in the case until I told him he needn't bother, because we had those. That pleased him so much that he leaned over, in an embarrassed way, to pick up another from the floor. But I stopped him. I said, "We've got that, too." He seemed pitifully amazed, but I was congratulating myself on my great success.

Finally the gentleman asked where Mr. Winton lived; he'd met him in the mountains, too. So I said I'd show him gladly. And I did on the spot. And when he was gone I felt queer, because there were all his etchings spread out on the floor.

Well, my wife came in and asked me who had been in. I showed her the card, and told her all exultantly. To my dismay she nearly fainted. She told me he had been a most kind friend to them in the country, and had forgotten to tell me that he was expected our way. And she pushed me out of the door, and commanded me to get over to the Wintons in a hurry and get him back.

I came into the drawing-room, where Mrs. Winton was sitting up very stiff in a chair, beating me at my own game. Well, I began to put another light on things. Before many seconds Mrs. Winton saw it was time to change her temperature. In five minutes I had asked the man to luncheon, and she to dinner, and so on.

We made that fellow change his trip and stay a week, and we gave him the time of his life. Why, I don't believe we let him get sober the whole time.

I trust that you will carry away some good thought from these lessons I have given you, and that the memory of them will inspire you to higher things, and elevate you to plans far above the old—and—and—

And I tell you one thing, young ladies: I've had a better time with you to-day than with that peach fifty-three years ago.

QUEEN VICTORIA

ADDRESS TO THE BRITISH SCHOOLS AND UNIVERSITIES
CLUB, AT DELMONICO'S, MONDAY, MAY 25,
1908, IN HONOR OF QUEEN VIC-
TORIA'S BIRTHDAY

*Mr. Clemens told the story of his duel with a rival
editor: how he practised firing at a barn door and
failed to hit it, but a friend of his took off the head of
a little bird at thirty-five yards and attributed the shot
to Mark Twain. The duel did not take place. Mr.
Clemens continued as follows:*

IT also happened that I was the means of stopping duelling in Nevada, for a law was passed
sending all duellists to jail for two years, and
the Governor, hearing of my marksmanship, said
that if he got me I should go to prison for the full
term. That's why I left Nevada, and I have not
been there since.

You do me a high honor, indeed, in selecting me
to speak of my country in this commemoration
of the birthday of that noble lady whose life was
consecrated to the virtues and the humanities and
to the promotion of lofty ideals, and was a model
upon which many a humbler life was formed and

made beautiful while she lived, and upon which many such lives will still be formed in the generations that are to come—a life which finds its just image in the star which falls out of its place in the sky and out of existence, but whose light still streams with unfaded lustre across the abysses of space long after its fires have been extinguished at their source.

As a woman the Queen was all that the most exacting standards could require. As a far-reaching and effective beneficent moral force she had no peer in her time among either monarchs or commoners. As a monarch she was without reproach in her great office. We may not venture, perhaps, to say so sweeping a thing as this in cold blood about any monarch that preceded her upon either her own throne or upon any other. It is a colossal eulogy, but it is justified.

In those qualities of the heart which beget affection in all sorts and conditions of men she was rich, surprisingly rich, and for this she will still be remembered and revered in the far-off ages when the political glories of her reign shall have faded from vital history and fallen to a place in that scrap-heap of unverifiable odds and ends which we call tradition. Which is to say, in briefer phrase, that her name will live always. And with it her character—a fame rare in the history of thrones, dominions, principalities, and powers, since it will not rest upon harvested selfish and sordid ambitions, but upon love, earned and freely vouchsafed. She mended broken hearts where she could, but she broke none.

What she did for us in America in our time of storm and stress we shall not forget, and whenever we call it to mind we shall always remember the wise and righteous mind that guided her in it and sustained and supported her—Prince Albert's. We need not talk any idle talk here to-night about either possible or impossible war between the two countries; there will be no war while we remain sane and the son of Victoria and Albert sits upon the throne. In conclusion, I believe I may justly claim to utter the voice of my country in saying that we hold him in deep honor, and also in cordially wishing him a long life and a happy reign.

JOAN OF ARC

ADDRESS AT THE DINNER OF THE SOCIETY OF ILLUS-
TRATORS, GIVEN AT THE ALDINE ASSOCIA-
TION CLUB, DECEMBER 22, 1905

*Just before Mr. Clemens made his speech, a young
woman attired as Joan of Arc, with a page bearing
her flag of battle, courtesied reverently and tendered Mr.
Clemens a laurel wreath on a satin pillow. He tried
to speak, but his voice failed from excess of emotion.
" I thank you!" he finally exclaimed, and, pulling himself together, he began his speech.*

NOW there is an illustration [pointing to the
retreating Joan of Arc]. That is exactly
what I wanted—precisely what I wanted—when I
was describing to myself Joan of Arc, after studying her history and her character for twelve years
diligently.

That was the product—not the conventional
Joan of Arc. Wherever you find the conventional
Joan of Arc in history she is an offence to anybody
who knows the story of that wonderful girl.

Why, she was—she was almost supreme in
several details. She had a marvellous intellect;
she had a great heart, had a noble spirit, was abso-

241

lutely pure in her character, her feeling, her language, her words, her everything—she was only eighteen years old.

Now put that heart into such a breast—eighteen years old—and give it that masterly intellect which showed in the face, and furnish it with that almost god-like spirit, and what are you going to have? The conventional Joan of Arc? Not by any means. That is impossible. I cannot comprehend any such thing as that.

You must have a creature like that young and fair and beautiful girl we just saw. And her spirit must look out of the eyes. The figure should be—the figure should be in harmony with all that, but, oh, what we get in the conventional picture, and it is always the conventional picture!

I hope you will allow me to say that your guild, when you take the conventional, you have got it at second-hand. Certainly, if you had studied and studied, then you might have something else as a result, but when you have the common convention you stick to that.

You cannot prevail upon the artist to do it; he always gives you a Joan of Arc—that lovely creature that started a great career at thirteen, but whose greatness arrived when she was eighteen; and merely because she was a girl he cannot see the divinity in her, and so he paints a peasant, a coarse and lubberly figure—the figure of a cotton-bale, and he clothes that in the coarsest raiment of the peasant region—just like a fish-woman, her hair cropped short like a Russian peasant, and that face of hers, which should be beautiful and which should radiate all the glories which are in the spirit and in her heart—that expression in that face is always just the fixed expression of a ham.

But now Mr. Beard has intimated a moment ago, and so has Sir Purdon-Clarke also, that the artist, the illustrator, does not often get the idea of the man whose book he is illustrating. Here is a very remarkable instance of the other thing in Mr. Beard, who illustrated a book of mine. You may never have heard of it. I will tell you about it now—*A Yankee in King Arthur's Court*.

Now, Beard got everything that I put into that book and a little more besides. Those pictures of Beard's in that book—oh, from the first page to the last is one vast sardonic laugh at the trivialities, the servilities of our poor human race, and also at the professions and the insolence of priest-craft and kingcraft—those creatures that make slaves of themselves and have not the manliness to shake it off. Beard put it all in that book. I meant it to be there. I put a lot of it there and Beard put the rest.

That publisher of mine in Hartford had an eye for the pennies, and he saved them. He did not waste any on the illustrations. He had a very good artist—Williams—who had never taken a lesson in drawing. Everything he did was original. The publisher hired the cheapest wood-engraver he could find, and in my early books you can see a trace of that. You can see that if Williams had had a chance he would have made some very good pictures. He had a good heart and good intentions.

I had a character in the first book he illustrated —*The Innocents Abroad.* That was a boy seventeen or eighteen years old —Jack Van Nostrand —a New York boy, who, to my mind, was a very remarkable creature. He and I tried to get Williams to understand that boy, and make a picture of Jack that would be worthy of Jack.

Jack was a most singular combination. He was born and reared in New York here. He was as delicate in his feelings, as clean and pure and refined in his feelings as any lovely girl that ever was, but whenever he expressed a feeling he did it in Bowery slang, and it was a most curious combination—that delicacy of his and that apparent coarseness. There was no coarseness inside of Jack at all, and Jack, in the course of seventeen or eighteen years, had acquired a capital of ignorance that was marvellous—ignorance of various things, not of all things. For instance, he did not know anything about the Bible. He had never been in Sunday-school. Jack got more out of the Holy Land than anybody else, because the others knew what they were expecting, but it was a land of surprises to him.

I said in the book that we found him watching a turtle on a log, stoning that turtle, and he was stoning that turtle because he had read that "The song of the turtle was heard in the land," and this turtle wouldn't sing. It sounded absurd, but it was charged on Jack as a fact, and as he went along through that country he had a proper foil in an old rebel colonel, who was superintendent and head engineer in a large Sunday-school in Wheeling, West Virginia. That man was full of enthusiasm wherever he went, and would stand and deliver himself of speeches, and Jack would listen to those speeches of the colonel and wonder.

Jack had made a trip as a child almost across this continent in the first overland stage-coach. That man's name who ran that line of stages— well, I declare that name is gone. Well, names will go.

Halliday—ah, that's the name—Ben Halliday, your uncle [turning to Mr. Carnegie]. That was the fellow — Ben Halliday — and Jack was full of admiration at the prodigious speed that that line of stages made—and it was good speed—one hundred and twenty-five miles a day, going day and night, and it was the event of Jack's life, and there at the Fords of the Jordan the colonel was inspired to a speech (he was always making a speech), so he called us up to

17   245

him. He called up five sinners and three saints. It has been only lately that Mr. Carnegie beatified me. And he said: "Here are the Fords of the Jordan—a monumental place. At this very point, when Moses brought the children of Israel through—he brought the children of Israel from Egypt through the desert you see there—he guarded them through that desert patiently, patiently during forty years, and brought them to this spot safe and sound. There you see— there is the scene of what Moses did."

And Jack said: "Moses who?"

"Oh," he says, "Jack, you ought not to ask that! Moses, the great law-giver! Moses, the great patriot! Moses, the great warrior! Moses, the great guide, who, as I tell you, brought these people through these three hundred miles of sand in forty years, and landed them safe and sound."

Jack said: "There's nothin' in that three hundred miles in forty years. Ben Halliday would have snaked 'em through in thirty-six hours."

Well, I was speaking of Jack's innocence, and it was beautiful. Jack was not ignorant on all subjects. That boy was a deep student in the history of Anglo-Saxon liberty, and he was a patriot all the way through to the marrow. There was a subject that interested him all the time. Other subjects were of no concern to Jack, but that quaint, inscrutable innocence of his I could not get Williams to put into the picture.

Yes, Williams wanted to do it. He said: "I will make him as innocent as a virgin." He thought a moment, and then said, "I will make him as innocent as an unborn virgin," which covered the ground.

I was reminded of Jack because I came across a letter to-day which is over thirty years old that Jack wrote. Jack was doomed to consumption. He was very long and slim, poor creature, and in a year or two after he got back from that excursion to the Holy Land he went on a ride on horseback through Colorado, and he did not last but a year or two.

He wrote this letter, not to me, but to a friend of mine, and he said: "I have ridden horseback" —this was three years after—"I have ridden horseback four hundred miles through a desert country where you never see anything but cattle now and then, and now and then a cattle station— ten miles apart, twenty miles apart. Now you tell Clemens that in all that stretch of four hundred miles I have seen only two books—the Bible and *Innocents Abroad*. Tell Clemens the Bible was in a very good condition."

I say that he had studied, and he had, the real Saxon liberty, the acquirement of our liberty, and Jack used to repeat some verses—I don't know where they came from, but I thought of them to-day when I saw that letter—that that boy could have been talking of himself in those quoted lines from that unknown poet:

"For he had sat at Sidney's feet
  And walked with him in plain apart,
And through the centuries heard the beat
  Of Freedom's march through Cromwell's heart."

And he was that kind of a boy. He should have lived, and yet he should not have lived, because he died at that early age—he couldn't have been more than twenty—he had seen all there was to see in the world that was worth the trouble of living in it; he had seen all of this world that is valuable; he had seen all of this world that was illusion, and illusion is the only valuable thing in it. He had arrived at that point where presently the illusions would cease and he would have entered upon the realities of life, and God help the man that has arrived at that point.

ACCIDENT INSURANCE—ETC.

Delivered in Hartford, at a Dinner to Cornelius
Walford, of London

GENTLEMEN,—I am glad, indeed, to assist
in welcoming the distinguished guest of this
occasion to a city whose fame as an insurance
centre has extended to all lands, and given us the
name of being a quadruple band of brothers working sweetly hand in hand—the Colt's arms company making the destruction of our race easy and
convenient, our life-insurance citizens paying for
the victims when they pass away, Mr. Batterson
perpetuating their memory with his stately monuments, and our fire-insurance comrades taking
care of their hereafter. I am glad to assist in
welcoming our guest—first, because he is an Englishman, and I owe a heavy debt of hospitality
to certain of his fellow-countrymen; and secondly,
because he is in sympathy with insurance, and has
been the means of making many other men cast
their sympathies in the same direction.

Certainly there is no nobler field for human
effort than the insurance line of business—especially accident insurance. Ever since I have been

249

a director in an accident-insurance company I have felt that I am a better man. Life has seemed more precious. Accidents have assumed a kindlier aspect. Distressing special providences have lost half their horror. I look upon a cripple now with affectionate interest—as an advertisement. I do not seem to care for poetry any more. I do not care for politics—even agriculture does not excite me. But to me now there is a charm about a railway collision that is unspeakable.

There is nothing more beneficent than accident insurance. I have seen an entire family lifted out of poverty and into affluence by the simple boon of a broken leg. I have had people come to me on crutches, with tears in their eyes, to bless this beneficent institution. In all my experience of life, I have seen nothing so seraphic as the look that comes into a freshly mutilated man's face when he feels in his vest pocket with his remaining hand and finds his accident ticket all right. And I have seen nothing so sad as the look that came into another splintered customer's face when he found he couldn't collect on a wooden leg.

I will remark here, by way of advertisement, that that noble charity which we have named the HARTFORD ACCIDENT INSURANCE COMPANY* is an institution which is peculiarly to be depended upon. A man is bound to prosper who gives it his custom. No man can take out a policy in it

* The speaker was a director of the company named.

and not get crippled before the year is out. Now there was one indigent man who had been disappointed so often with other companies that he had grown disheartened, his appetite left him, he ceased to smile—said life was but a weariness. Three weeks ago I got him to insure with us, and now he is the brightest, happiest spirit in this land—has a good steady income and a stylish suit of new bandages every day, and travels around on a shutter.

I will say, in conclusion, that my share of the welcome to our guest is none the less hearty because I talk so much nonsense, and I know that I can say the same for the rest of the speakers.

OSTEOPATHY

On February 27, 1901, Mr. Clemens appeared before the Assembly Committee in Albany, New York, in favor of the Seymour bill legalizing the practice of osteopathy.

MR. CHAIRMAN AND GENTLEMEN,—Dr. Van Fleet is the gentleman who gave me the character. I have heard my character discussed a thousand times before you were born, sir, and shown the iniquities in it, and you did not get more than half of them.

I was touched and distressed when they brought that part of a child in here, and proved that you cannot take a child to pieces in that way. What remarkable names those diseases have! It makes me envious of the man that has them all. I have had many diseases, and am thankful for all I have had.

One of the gentlemen spoke of the knowledge of something else found in Sweden, a treatment which I took. It is, I suppose, a kindred thing. There is apparently no great difference between them. I was a year and a half in London and Sweden, in the hands of that grand old man, Mr. Kildren.

OSTEOPATHY

I cannot call him a doctor, for he has not the authority to give a certificate if a patient should die, but fortunately they don't.

The State stands as a mighty Gibraltar clothed with power. It stands between me and my body, and tells me what kind of a doctor I must employ. When my soul is sick unlimited spiritual liberty is given me by the State. Now then, it doesn't seem logical that the State shall depart from this great policy, the health of the soul, and change about and take the other position in the matter of smaller consequence—the health of the body.

The Bell bill limitations would drive the osteopaths out of the State. Oh, dear me! when you drive somebody out of the State you create the same condition as prevailed in the Garden of Eden. You want the thing that you can't have. I didn't care much about the osteopaths, but as soon as I found they were going to drive them out I got in a state of uneasiness, and I can't sleep nights now.

I know how Adam felt in the Garden of Eden about the prohibited apple. Adam didn't want the apple till he found out he couldn't have it, just as he would have wanted osteopathy if he couldn't have it.

Whose property is my body? Probably mine. I so regard it. If I experiment with it, who must be answerable? I, not the State. If I choose injudiciously, does the State die? Oh no.

I was the subject of my mother's experiment. She was wise. She made experiments cautiously. She didn't pick out just any child in the flock. No, she chose judiciously. She chose one she could spare, and she couldn't spare the others. I was the choice child of the flock, so I had to take all of the experiments.

In 1844 Kneipp filled the world with the wonder of the water cure. Mother wanted to try it, but on sober second thought she put me through. A bucket of ice-water was poured over to see the effect. Then I was rubbed down with flannels, a sheet was dipped in the water, and I was put to bed. I perspired so much that mother put a life-preserver to bed with me.

But this had nothing but a spiritual effect on me, and I didn't care for that. When they took off the sheet it was yellow from the output of my conscience, the exudation of sin. It purified me spiritually, and it remains until this day.

I have experimented with osteopathy and allopathy. I took a chance at the latter for old times' sake, for, three times, when a boy, mother's new methods got me so near death's door she had to call in the family physician to pull me out.

The physicians think they are moved by regard for the best interests of the public. Isn't there a little touch of self-interest back of it all? It seems to me there is, and I don't claim to have all the virtues—only nine or ten of them.

OSTEOPATHY

I was born in the "Banner State," and by "Banner State" I mean Missouri. Osteopathy was born in the same State, and both of us are getting along reasonably well. At a time during my younger days my attention was attracted to a picture of a house which bore the inscription, "Christ Disputing with the Doctors."

I could attach no other meaning to it than that Christ was actually quarrelling with the doctors. So I asked an old slave, who was a sort of a herb doctor in a small way—unlicensed, of course—what the meaning of the picture was. "What has he done?" I asked. And the colored man replied: "Humph, he ain't got no license."

WATER-SUPPLY

Mr. Clemens visited Albany on February 27 and 28, 1901. The privileges of the floor were granted to him, and he was asked to make a short address to the Senate.

MR. PRESIDENT AND GENTLEMEN,—I do not know how to thank you sufficiently for this high honor which you are conferring upon me. I have for the second time now enjoyed this kind of prodigal hospitality—in the other House yesterday, to-day in this one. I am a modest man, and diffident about appearing before legislative bodies, and yet utterly and entirely appreciative of a courtesy like this when it is extended to me, and I thank you very much for it.

If I had the privilege, which unfortunately I have not got, of suggesting things to the legislators in my individual capacity, I would so enjoy the opportunity that I would not charge anything for it at all. I would do that without a salary. I would give them the benefit of my wisdom and experience in legislative bodies, and if I could have had the privilege for a few minutes of giving advice to the other House I should have liked to, but of course I could not undertake it, as they did not ask me to do it—but if they had only asked me!

Now that the House is considering a measure which is to furnish a water-supply to the city of New York, why, permit me to say I live in New York myself. I know all about its ways, its desires, and its residents, and—if I had the privilege—I should have urged them not to weary themselves over a measure like that to furnish water to the city of New York, for we never drink it.

But I will not venture to advise this body, as I only venture to advise bodies who are not present.

MISTAKEN IDENTITY

ADDRESS AT THE ANNUAL "LADIES' DAY," PAPYRUS CLUB, BOSTON

LADIES AND GENTLEMEN,—I am perfectly astonished — a-s-t-o-n-i-s-h-e-d — ladies and gentlemen—astonished at the way history repeats itself. I find myself situated at this moment exactly and precisely as I was once before, years ago, to a jot, to a tittle—to a very hair. There isn't a shade of difference. It is the most astonishing coincidence that ever—but wait. I will tell you the former instance, and then you will see it for yourself. Years ago I arrived one day at Salamanca, New York, eastward bound; must change cars there and take the sleeper train. There were crowds of people there, and they were swarming into the long sleeper train and packing it full, and it was a perfect purgatory of dust and confusion and gritting of teeth and soft, sweet, and low profanity. I asked the young man in the ticket-office if I could have a sleeping-section, and he answered "No," with a snarl that shrivelled me up like burned leather. I went off, smarting under this insult to my dignity, and

258

asked another local official, supplicatingly, if I couldn't have some poor little corner somewhere in a sleeping-car; but he cut me short with a venomous "No, you can't; every corner is full. Now, don't bother me any more"; and he turned his back and walked off. My dignity was in a state now which cannot be described. I was so ruffled that—well, I said to my companion, "If these people knew who I am they—" But my companion cut me short there—"Don't talk such folly," he said; "if they did know who you are, do you suppose it would help your high-mightiness to a vacancy in a train which has no vacancies in it?"

This did not improve my condition any to speak of, but just then I observed that the colored porter of a sleeping-car had his eye on me. I saw his dark countenance light up. He whispered to the uniformed conductor, punctuating with nods and jerks toward me, and straightway this conductor came forward, oozing politeness from every pore.

"Can I be of any service to you?" he asked. "Will you have a place in the sleeper?"

"Yes," I said, "and much oblige me, too. Give me anything—anything will answer."

"We have nothing left but the big family stateroom," he continued, "with two berths and a couple of arm-chairs in it, but it is entirely at your disposal. Here, Tom, take these satchels aboard!"

Then he touched his hat and we and the colored Tom moved along. I was bursting to drop just one little remark to my companion, but I held in and waited. Tom made us comfortable in that sumptuous great apartment, and then said, with many bows and a perfect affluence of smiles:

"Now, is dey anything you want, sah? Case you kin have jes' anything you wants. It don't make no difference what it is."

"Can I have some hot water and a tumbler at nine to-night—blazing hot?" I asked. "You know about the right temperature for a hot Scotch punch?"

"Yes, sah, dat you kin; you kin pen on it; I'll get it myself."

"Good! Now, that lamp is hung too high. Can I have a big coach candle fixed up just at the head of my bed, so that I can read comfortably?"

"Yes, sah, you kin; I'll fix her up myself, an' I'll fix her so she'll burn all night. Yes, sah; an' you can jes' call for anything you want, and dish yer whole railroad 'll be turned wrong end up an' inside out for to get it for you. Dat's so." And he disappeared.

Well, I tilted my head back, hooked my thumbs in my armholes, smiled a smile on my companion, and said, gently:

"Well, what do you say now?"

My companion was not in the humor to respond, and didn't. The next moment that smiling black face was thrust in at the crack of the door, and this speech followed:

"Laws bless you, sah, I knowed you in a minute. I told de conductah so. Laws! I knowed you de minute I sot eyes on you."

"Is that so, my boy?" (Handing him a quadruple fee.) "Who am I?"

"Jenuel McClellan," and he disappeared again.

My companion said, vinegarishly, "Well, well! what do you say now?" Right there comes in the marvellous coincidence I mentioned a while ago—*viz.*, I was speechless, and that is my condition now. Perceive it?

18

CATS AND CANDY

The following address was delivered at a social meeting of literary men in New York in 1874:

WHEN I was fourteen I was living with my parents, who were very poor—and correspondently honest. We had a youth living with us by the name of Jim Wolfe. He was an excellent fellow, seventeen years old, and very diffident. He and I slept together — virtuously; and one bitter winter's night a cousin Mary—she's married now and gone—gave what they call a candy-pulling in those days in the West, and they took the saucers of hot candy outside of the house into the snow, under a sort of old bower that came from the eaves—it was a sort of an ell then, all covered with vines—to cool this hot candy in the snow, and they were all sitting there. In the mean time we were gone to bed. We were not invited to attend this party; we were too young.

The young ladies and gentlemen were assembled there, and Jim and I were in bed. There was about four inches of snow on the roof of this ell, and our windows looked out on it, and it was frozen hard. A couple of tom-cats—it is possible one might have been of the opposite sex—were assembled on the chimney in the middle of this ell, and they were growling at a fearful rate, and switching their tails about and going on, and we couldn't sleep at all.

Finally Jim said, "For two cents I'd go out and snake them cats off that chimney." So I said, "Of course you would." He said, "Well, I would; I have a mighty good notion to do it." Says I, "Of course you have; certainly you have, you have a great notion to do it." I hoped he might try it, but I was afraid he wouldn't.

Finally I did get his ambition up, and he raised the window and climbed out on the icy roof, with nothing on but his socks and a very short shirt. He went climbing along on all fours on the roof toward the chimney where the cats were. In the mean time these young ladies and gentlemen were enjoying themselves down under the eaves, and when Jim got almost to that chimney he made a pass at the cats, and his heels flew up and he shot down and crashed through those vines, and lit in the midst of the ladies and gentlemen, and sat down in those hot saucers of candy.

There was a stampede, of course, and he came up-stairs dropping pieces of chinaware and candy all the way up, and when he got up there—now anybody in the world would have gone into profanity or something calculated to relieve the mind, but he didn't; he scraped the candy off his legs, nursed his blisters a little, and said, "I could have ketched them cats if I had had on a good ready."

OBITUARY POETRY

ADDRESS AT THE ACTORS' FUND FAIR, PHILADEL-
PHIA, in 1895

LADIES AND GENTLEMEN, — The — er —
this—er—welcome occasion gives me an—
er—opportunity to make an—er—explanation
that I have long desired to deliver myself of. I
rise to the highest honors before a Philadelphia
audience. In the course of my checkered career
I have, on divers occasions, been charged—er—
maliciously with a more or less serious offence.
It is in reply to one of the more—er—important
of these that I wish to speak. More than once
I have been accused of writing obituary poetry
in the Philadelphia *Ledger*.

I wish right here to deny that dreadful assertion. I will admit that once, when a compositor
in the *Ledger* establishment, I did set up some of
that poetry, but for a worse offence than that no
indictment can be found against me. I did not
write that poetry—at least, not all of it.

CIGARS AND TOBACCO

MY friends for some years now have remarked that I am an inveterate consumer of tobacco. That is true, but my habits with regard to tobacco have changed. I have no doubt that you will say, when I have explained to you what my present purpose is, that my taste has deteriorated, but I do not so regard it.

Whenever I held a smoking-party at my house, I found that my guests had always just taken the pledge.

Let me tell you briefly the history of my personal relation to tobacco. It began, I think, when I was a lad, and took the form of a quid, which I became expert in tucking under my tongue. Afterward I learned the delights of the pipe, and I suppose there was no other youngster of my age who could more deftly cut plug tobacco so as to make it available for pipe-smoking.

Well, time ran on, and there came a time when I was able to gratify one of my youthful ambitions—I could buy the choicest Havana cigars without seriously interfering with my income. I smoked a good many, changing off from the Havana cigars to the pipe in the course of a day's smoking.

At last it occurred to me that something was lacking in the Havana cigar. It did not quite fulfil my youthful anticipations. I experimented. I bought what was called a seed-leaf cigar with a Connecticut wrapper. After a while I became satiated of these, and I searched for something else. The Pittsburg stogy was recommended to me. It certainly had the merit of cheapness, if that be a merit in tobacco, and I experimented with the stogy.

Then, once more, I changed off, so that I might acquire the subtler flavor of the Wheeling toby. Now that palled, and I looked around New York in the hope of finding cigars which would seem to most people vile, but which, I am sure, would be ambrosial to me. I couldn't find any. They put into my hands some of those little things that cost ten cents a box, but they are a delusion.

I said to a friend, "I want to know if you can direct me to an honest tobacco merchant who will tell me what is the worst cigar in the New York market, excepting those made for Chinese consumption—I want real tobacco. If you will do this and I find the man is as good as his word, I will guarantee him a regular market for a fair amount of his cigars."

We found a tobacco dealer who would tell the truth—who, if a cigar was bad, would boldly say so. He produced what he called the very worst cigars he had ever had in his shop. He let me experiment with one then and there. The test was satisfactory.

This was, after all, the real thing. I negotiated for a box of them and took them away with me, so that I might be sure of having them handy when I want them.

I discovered that the "worst cigars," so called, are the best for me, after all.

BILLIARDS

Mr. Clemens attended a billiard tourney on the evening of April 24, 1906, and was called on to tell a story.

THE game of billiards has destroyed my naturally sweet disposition. Once, when I was an underpaid reporter in Virginia City, whenever I wished to play billiards I went out to look for an easy mark. One day a stranger came to town and opened a billiard parlor. I looked him over casually. When he proposed a game, I answered, "All right."

"Just knock the balls around a little so that I can get your gait," he said; and when I had done so, he remarked: "I will be perfectly fair with you. I'll play you left-handed." I felt hurt, for he was cross-eyed, freckled, and had red hair, and I determined to teach him a lesson. He won first shot, ran out, took my half-dollar, and all I got was the opportunity to chalk my cue.

"If you can play like that with your left hand," I said, "I'd like to see you play with your right."

"I can't," he said. "I'm left-handed."

THE UNION RIGHT OR WRONG?

REMINISCENCES OF NEVADA

I CAN assure you, ladies and gentlemen, that Nevada had lively newspapers in those days.

My great competitor among the reporters was Boggs, of the *Union*, an excellent reporter.

Once in three or four months he would get a little intoxicated; but, as a general thing, he was a wary and cautious drinker, although always ready to damp himself a little with the enemy.

He had the advantage of me in one thing: he could get the monthly public-school report and I could not, because the principal hated my sheet —the *Enterprise*.

One snowy night, when the report was due, I started out, sadly wondering how I was to get it.

Presently, a few steps up the almost deserted street, I stumbled on Boggs, and asked him where he was going.

"After the school report."

"I'll go along with you."

"No, sir. I'll excuse you."

"Have it your own way."

A saloon-keeper's boy passed by with a steaming pitcher of hot punch, and Boggs snuffed the fragrance gratefully.

He gazed fondly after the boy, and saw him start up the *Enterprise* stairs.

I said:

"I wish you could help me get that school business, but since you can't, I must run up to the *Union* office and see if I can get a proof of it after it's set up, though I don't begin to suppose I can. Good night."

"Hold on a minute. I don't mind getting the report and sitting around with the boys a little while you copy it, if you're willing to drop down to the principal's with me."

"Now you talk like a human being. Come along."

We ploughed a couple of blocks through the snow, got the report — a short document — and soon copied it in our office.

Meantime, Boggs helped himself to the punch.

I gave the manuscript back to him, and we started back to get an inquest.

At four o'clock in the morning, when we had gone to press and were having a relaxing concert as usual (for some of the printers were good singers and others good performers on the guitar and on that atrocity the accordion), the proprietor of the *Union* strode in and asked if anybody had heard anything of Boggs or the school report.

We stated the case, and all turned out to help hunt for the delinquent.

We found him standing on a table in a saloon, with an old tin lantern in one hand and the school report in the other, haranguing a gang of "corned" miners on the iniquity of squandering the public money on education "when hundreds and hundreds of honest, hard-working men were literally starving for whiskey."

He had been assisting in a regal spree with those parties for hours.

We dragged him away, and put him into bed.

Of course there was no school report in the *Union*, and Boggs held me accountable, though I was innocent of any intention or desire to compass its absence from that paper, and was as sorry as any one that the misfortune had occurred. But we were perfectly friendly.

The day the next school report was due the proprietor of the Tennessee Mine furnished us a buggy, and asked us to go down and write something about the property—a very common request, and one always gladly acceded to when people furnished buggies, for we were as fond of pleasure excursions as other people.

The "mine" was a hole in the ground ninety feet deep, and no way of getting down into it but by holding on to a rope and being lowered with a windlass.

The workmen had just gone off somewhere to dinner.

I was not strong enough to lower Boggs's bulk, so I took an unlighted candle in my teeth, made a loop for my foot in the end of the rope, implored Boggs not to go to sleep or let the windlass get the start of him, and then swung out over the shaft.

I reached the bottom muddy and bruised about the elbows, but safe.

I lit the candle, made an examination of the rock, selected some specimens, and shouted to Boggs to hoist away.

No answer.

Presently a head appeared in the circle of day-light away aloft, and a voice came down:

"Are you all set?"

"All set—hoist away!"

"Are you comfortable?"

"Perfectly."

"Could you wait a little?"

"Oh, certainly—no particular hurry."

"Well—good-bye."

"Why, where are you going?"

"After the school report!"

And he did.

I stayed down there an hour, and surprised the workmen when they hauled up and found a man on the rope instead of a bucket of rock.

I walked home, too—five miles—up-hill.

We had no school report next morning — but the *Union* had.

AN IDEAL FRENCH ADDRESS

EXTRACT FROM "PARIS NOTES," IN "TOM SAWYER ABROAD," ETC.

I AM told that a French sermon is like a French speech—it never names an historical event, but only the date of it; if you are not up in dates, you get left. A French speech is something like this:

"Comrades, citizens, brothers, noble parts of the only sublime and perfect nation, let us not forget that the 21st January cast off our chains; that the 10th August relieved us of the shameful presence of foreign spies; that the 5th September was its own justification before Heaven and humanity; that the 18th Brumaire contained the seeds of its own punishment; that the 14th July was the mighty voice of liberty proclaiming the resurrection, the new day, and inviting the oppressed peoples of the earth to look upon the divine face of France and live; and let us here record our everlasting curse against the man of the 2d December, and declare in thunder tones, the native tones of France, that but for him there had been no 17th March in history, no 12th October, no 19th January, no 22d April, no 16th November, no 30th September, no 2d July, no 14th Feb-

ruary, no 29th June, no 15th August, no 31st May—
that but for him, France, the pure, the grand, the peer-
less, had had a serene and vacant almanac to-day.''

I have heard of one French sermon which closed
in this odd yet eloquent way:

''My hearers, we have sad cause to remember
the man of the 13th January. The results of the
vast crime of the 13th January have been in just
proportion to the magnitude of the act itself.
But for it there had been no 30th November—
sorrowful spectacle! The grisly deed of the 16th
June had not been done but for it, nor had the man
of the 16th June known existence; to it alone the
3d September was due, also the fatal 12th October.
Shall we, then, be grateful for the 13th January,
with its freight of death for you and me and all
that breathe? Yes, my friends, for it gave us
also that which had never come but for it, and it
alone—the blessed 25th December.''

It may be well enough to explain. The man
of the 13th January is Adam; the crime of that
date was the eating of the apple; the sorrowful
spectacle of the 30th November was the expulsion
from Eden; the grisly deed of the 16th June was
the murder of Abel; the act of the 3d September
was the beginning of the journey to the land of
Nod; the 12th day of October, the last mountain-
tops disappeared under the flood. When you go
to church in France, you want to take your
almanac with you—annotated.

STATISTICS

During that period of gloom when domestic bereavement had forced Mr. Clemens and his dear ones to secure the privacy they craved until their wounds should heal, his address was known to only a very few of his closest friends. One old friend in New York, after vain efforts to get his address, wrote him a letter addressed as follows:

MARK TWAIN,
God Knows Where,
Try London.

The letter found him, and Mr. Clemens replied to the letter expressing himself surprised and complimented that the person who was credited with knowing his whereabouts should take so much interest in him, adding: "Had the letter been addressed to the care of the 'other party,' I would naturally have expected to receive it without delay."

His correspondent tried again, and addressed the second letter:

MARK TWAIN,
The Devil Knows Where,
Try London.

This found him also no less promptly.

STATISTICS

On June 9, 1899, he consented to visit the Savage Club, London, on condition that there was to be no publicity and no speech was to be expected from him. The toastmaster, in proposing the health of their guest, said that as a Scotchman, and therefore as a born expert, he thought Mark Twain had little or no claim to the title of humorist. Mr. Clemens had tried to be funny but had failed, and his true rôle in life was statistics; that he was a master of statistics, and loved them for their own sake, and it would be the easiest task he ever undertook if he would try to count all the real jokes he had ever made. While the toastmaster was speaking, the members saw Mr. Clemens's eyes begin to sparkle and his cheeks to flush. He jumped up, and made a characteristic speech.

PERHAPS I am not a humorist, but I am a first-class fool—a simpleton; for up to this moment I have believed Chairman MacAlister to be a decent person whom I could allow to mix up with my friends and relatives. The exhibition he has just made of himself reveals him to be a scoundrel and a knave of the deepest dye. I have been cruelly deceived, and it serves me right for trusting a Scotchman. Yes, I do understand figures, and I can count. I have counted the words in MacAlister's drivel (I certainly cannot call it a speech), and there were exactly three thousand four hundred and thirty - nine. I also carefully counted the lies—there were exactly three thousand four hundred and thirty - nine. Therefore, I leave MacAlister to his fate.

I was sorry to have my name mentioned as one of the great authors, because they have a sad habit of dying off. Chaucer is dead, Spencer is dead, so is Milton, so is Shakespeare, and I am not feeling very well myself.

GALVESTON ORPHAN BAZAAR

ADDRESS AT A FAIR HELD AT THE WALDORF-AS-
TORIA, NEW YORK, IN OCTOBER, 1900,
IN AID OF THE ORPHANS
AT GALVESTON

I EXPECTED that the Governor of Texas would occupy this place first and would speak to you, and in the course of his remarks would drop a text for me to talk from; but with the proverbial obstinacy that is proverbial with governors, they go back on their duties, and he has not come here, and has not furnished me with a text, and I am here without a text. I have no text except what you furnish me with your handsome faces, and— but I won't continue that, for I could go on forever about attractive faces, beautiful dresses, and other things. But, after all, compliments should be in order in a place like this.

I have been in New York two or three days, and have been in a condition of strict diligence night and day, the object of this diligence being to regulate the moral and political situation on this planet—put it on a sound basis—and when you are regulating the conditions of a planet it requires a great deal of talk in a great many kinds of ways, and when you have talked a lot the emptier you get, and get also in a position of corking. When I am situated like that, with nothing to say, I feel as though I were a sort of fraud; I seem to be playing a part, and please consider I am playing a part for want of something better, and this is not unfamiliar to me; I have often done this before.

When I was here about eight years ago I was coming up in a car of the elevated road. Very few people were in that car, and on one end of it there was no one, except on the opposite seat, where sat a man about fifty years old, with a most winning face and an elegant eye—a beautiful eye; and I took him from his dress to be a master mechanic, a man who had a vocation. He had with him a very fine little child of about four or five years. I was watching the affection which existed between those two. I judged he was the grandfather, perhaps. It was really a pretty child, and I was admiring her, and as soon as he saw I was admiring her he began to notice me.

I could see his admiration of me in his eye, and I did what everybody else would do—admired the child four times as much, knowing I would get four times as much of his admiration. Things went on very pleasantly. I was making my way into his heart.

By-and-by, when he almost reached the station

where he was to get off, he got up, crossed over, and he said: "Now I am going to say something to you which I hope you will regard as a compliment." And then he went on to say: "I have never seen Mark Twain, but I have seen a portrait of him, and any friend of mine will tell you that when I have once seen a portrait of a man I place it in my eye and store it away in my memory, and I can tell you now that you look enough like Mark Twain to be his brother. Now," he said, "I hope you take this as a compliment. Yes, you are a very good imitation; but when I come to look closer, you are probably not that man."

I said: "I will be frank with you. In my desire to look like that excellent character I have dressed for the character; I have been playing a part."

He said: "That is all right, that is all right; you look very well on the outside, but when it comes to the inside you are not in it with the original."

So when I come to a place like this with nothing valuable to say I always play a part. But I will say before I sit down that when it comes to saying anything here I will express myself in this way: I am heartily in sympathy with you in your efforts to help those who were sufferers in this calamity, and in your desire to help those who were rendered homeless, and in saying this I wish to impress on you the fact that I am not playing a part.

SAN FRANCISCO EARTHQUAKE

After the address at the Robert Fulton Fund meeting, June 19, 1906, Mr. Clemens talked to the assembled reporters about the San Francisco earthquake.

I HAVEN'T been there since 1868, and that great city of San Francisco has grown up since my day. When I was there she had one hundred and eighteen thousand people, and of this number eighteen thousand were Chinese. I was a reporter on the *Virginia City Enterprise* in Nevada in 1862, and stayed there, I think, about two years, when I went to San Francisco and got a job as a reporter on *The Call*. I was there three or four years.

I remember one day I was walking down Third Street in San Francisco. It was a sleepy, dull Sunday afternoon, and no one was stirring. Suddenly as I looked up the street about three hundred yards the whole side of a house fell out. The street was full of bricks and mortar. At the same time I was knocked against the side of a house, and stood there stunned for a moment.

I thought it was an earthquake. Nobody else had heard anything about it and no one said earthquake to me afterward, but I saw it and I wrote it. Nobody else wrote it, and the house I saw go into the street was the only house in the city that felt it. I've always wondered if it wasn't a little performance gotten up for my especial entertainment by the nether regions.

CHARITY AND ACTORS

ADDRESS AT THE ACTORS' FUND FAIR IN THE METRO-
POLITAN OPERA HOUSE, NEW YORK, MAY 6, 1907

Mr. Clemens, in his white suit, formally declared the fair open. Mr. Daniel Frohman, in introducing Mr. Clemens, said:

"We intend to make this a banner week in the history of the Fund, which takes an interest in every one on the stage, be he actor, singer, dancer, or workman. We have spent more than $40,000 during the past year. Charity covers a multitude of sins, but it also reveals a multitude of virtues. At the opening of the former fair we had the assistance of Edwin Booth and Joseph Jefferson. In their place we have to-day that American institution and apostle of wide humanity—Mark Twain."

AS Mr. Frohman has said, charity reveals a multitude of virtues. This is true, and it is to be proved here before the week is over. Mr. Frohman has told you something of the object and something of the character of the work. He told me he would do this—and he has kept his word! I had expected to hear of it through the newspapers. I wouldn't trust anything between Frohman and the newspapers—except when it's a case of charity!

284

CHARITY AND ACTORS

You should all remember that the actor has been your benefactor many and many a year. When you have been weary and downcast he has lifted your heart out of gloom and given you a fresh impulse. You are all under obligation to him. This is your opportunity to be his benefactor—to help provide for him in his old age and when he suffers from infirmities.

At this fair no one is to be persecuted to buy. If you offer a twenty-dollar bill in payment for a purchase of $1 you will receive $19 in change. There is to be no robbery here. There is to be no creed here—no religion except charity. We want to raise $250,000—and that is a great task to attempt.

The President has set the fair in motion by pressing the button in Washington. Now your good wishes are to be transmuted into cash.

By virtue of the authority in me vested I declare the fair open. I call the ball game. Let the transmuting begin!

RUSSIAN REPUBLIC

The American auxiliary movement to aid the cause of freedom in Russia was launched on the evening of April 11, 1906, at the Club A house, 3 Fifth Avenue, with Mr. Clemens and Maxim Gorky as the principal spokesmen. Mr. Clemens made an introductory address, presenting Mr. Gorky.

IF we can build a Russian republic to give to the persecuted people of the Tsar's domain the same measure of freedom that we enjoy, let us go ahead and do it. We need not discuss the methods by which that purpose is to be attained. Let us hope that fighting will be postponed or averted for a while, but if it must come—

I am most emphatically in sympathy with the movement, now on foot in Russia, to make that country free. I am certain that it will be successful, as it deserves to be. Any such movement should have and deserves our earnest and unanimous co-operation, and such a petition for funds as has been explained by Mr. Hunter, with its just and powerful meaning, should have the utmost support of each and every one of us. Anybody whose ancestors were in this country when we were trying to free ourselves from oppression, must sympathize with those who now are trying to do the same thing in Russia.

The parallel I have just drawn only goes to show that it makes no difference whether the oppression is bitter or not; men with red, warm blood in their veins will not endure it, but will seek to cast it off. If we keep our hearts in this matter Russia will be free.

RUSSIAN SUFFERERS

On December 18, 1905, an entertainment was given at the Casino for the benefit of the Russian sufferers. After the performance Mr. Clemens spoke.

LADIES AND GENTLEMEN, — It seems a sort of cruelty to inflict upon an audience like this our rude English tongue, after we have heard that divine speech flowing in that lucid Gallic tongue.

It has always been a marvel to me—that French language; it has always been a puzzle to me. How beautiful that language is. How expressive it seems to be. How full of grace it is.

And when it comes from lips like those, how eloquent and how liquid it is. And, oh, I am always deceived—I always think I am going to understand it.

Oh, it is such a delight to me, such a delight to me, to meet Madame Bernhardt, and laugh hand to hand and heart to heart with her.

I have seen her play, as we all have, and oh, that is divine; but I have always wanted to know

Madame Bernhardt herself—her fiery self. I have wanted to know that beautiful character.

Why, she is the youngest person I ever saw, except myself—for I always feel young when I come in the presence of young people.

I have a pleasant recollection of an incident so many years ago—when Madame Bernhardt came to Hartford, where I lived, and she was going to play and the tickets were three dollars, and there were two lovely women—a widow and her daughter—neighbors of ours, highly cultivated ladies they were; their tastes were fine and elevated, but they were very poor, and they said: "Well, we must not spend six dollars on a pleasure of the mind, a pleasure of the intellect; we must spend it, if it must go at all, to furnish to somebody bread to eat."

And so they sorrowed over the fact that they had to give up that great pleasure of seeing Madame Bernhardt, but there were two neighbors equally highly cultivated and who could not afford bread, and those good-hearted Joneses sent that six dollars — deprived themselves of it — and sent it to those poor Smiths to buy bread with. And those Smiths took it and bought tickets with it to see Madame Bernhardt.

Oh yes, some people have tastes and intelligence also.

Now, I was going to make a speech—I supposed I was, but I am not. It is late, late; and so

I am going to tell a story; and there is this advantage about a story, anyway, that whatever moral or valuable thing you put into a speech, why, it gets diffused among those involuted sentences and possibly your audience goes away without finding out what that valuable thing was that you were trying to confer upon it; but, dear me, you put the same jewel into a story and it becomes the keystone of that story, and you are bound to get it—it flashes, it flames, it is the jewel in the toad's head—you don't overlook that.

Now, if I am going to talk on such a subject as, for instance, the lost opportunity—oh, the lost opportunity. Anybody in this house who has reached the turn of life—sixty, or seventy, or even fifty, or along there—when he goes back along his history, there he finds it mile-stoned all the way with the lost opportunity, and you know how pathetic that is.

You younger ones cannot know the full pathos that lies in those words—the lost opportunity; but anybody who is old, who has really lived and felt this life, he knows the pathos of the lost opportunity.

Now, I will tell you a story whose moral is that, whose lesson is that, whose lament is that.

I was in a village which is a suburb of New Bedford several years ago—well, New Bedford is a suburb of Fair Haven, or perhaps it is the other way; in any case, it took both of those towns to make a great centre of the great whaling industry of the first half of the nineteenth century, and I was up there at Fair Haven some years ago with a friend of mine.

There was a dedication of a great town-hall, a public building, and we were there in the afternoon. This great building was filled, like this great theatre, with rejoicing villagers, and my friend and I started down the centre aisle. He saw a man standing in that aisle, and he said: "Now, look at that bronzed veteran—at that mahogany-faced man. Now, tell me, do you see anything about that man's face that is emotional? Do you see anything about it that suggests that inside that man anywhere there are fires that can be started? Would you ever imagine that that is a human volcano?"

"Why, no," I said, "I would not. He looks like a wooden Indian in front of a cigar store."

"Very well," said my friend, "I will show you that there is emotion even in that unpromising place. I will just go to that man and I will just mention in the most casual way an incident in his life. That man is getting along toward ninety years old. He is past eighty. I will mention an incident of fifty or sixty years ago. Now, just watch the effect, and it will be so casual that if you don't watch you won't know when I do say that thing—but you just watch the effect."

He went on down there and accosted this antiquity, and made a remark or two. I could not catch up. They were so casual I could not recognize which one it was that touched that bottom, for in an instant that old man was literally in eruption and was filling the whole place with profanity of the most exquisite kind. You never heard such accomplished profanity. I never heard it also delivered with such eloquence.

I never enjoyed profanity as I enjoyed it then —more than if I had been uttering it myself. There is nothing like listening to an artist—all his passions passing away in lava, smoke, thunder, lightning, and earthquake.

Then this friend said to me: "Now, I will tell you about that. About sixty years ago that man was a young fellow of twenty-three, and had just come home from a three years' whaling voyage. He came into that village of his, happy and proud because now, instead of being chief mate, he was going to be master of a whaleship, and he was proud and happy about it.

"Then he found that there had been a kind of a cold frost come upon that town and the whole region roundabout; for while he had been away the Father Mathew temperance excitement had come upon the whole region. Therefore, everybody had taken the pledge; there wasn't anybody for miles and miles around that had not taken the pledge.

"So you can see what a solitude it was to this

young man, who was fond of his grog. And he was just an outcast, because when they found he would not join Father Mathew's Society they ostracized him, and he went about that town three weeks, day and night, in utter loneliness—the only human being in the whole place who ever took grog, and he had to take it privately.

"If you don't know what it is to be ostracized, to be shunned by your fellow-man, may you never know it. Then he recognized that there was something more valuable in this life than grog, and that is the fellowship of your fellow-man. And at last he gave it up, and at nine o'clock one night he went down to the Father Mathew Temperance Society, and with a broken heart he said: 'Put my name down for membership in this society.'

"And then he went away crying, and at earliest dawn the next morning they came for him and routed him out, and they said that new ship of his was ready to sail on a three years' voyage. In a minute he was on board that ship and gone.

"And he said—well, he was not out of sight of that town till he began to repent, but he had made up his mind that he would not take a drink, and so that whole voyage of three years was a three years' agony to that man because he saw all the time the mistake he had made.

"He felt it all through; he had constant reminders of it, because the crew would pass him with their grog, come out on the deck and take it, and there was the torturous smell of it.

"He went through the whole three years of suffering, and at last coming into port it was snowy, it was cold, he was stamping through the snow two feet deep on the deck and longing to get home, and there was his crew torturing him to the last minute with hot grog, but at last he had his reward. He really did get to shore at last, and jumped and ran and bought a jug and rushed to the society's office, and said to the secretary:

"'Take my name off your membership books, and do it right away! I have got a three years' thirst on.'

"And the secretary said: 'It is not necessary. You were blackballed!'"

WATTERSON AND TWAIN AS REBELS

ADDRESS AT THE CELEBRATION OF ABRAHAM LIN-
COLN'S 92D BIRTHDAY ANNIVERSARY, CARNEGIE
HALL, FEBRUARY 11, 1901, TO RAISE FUNDS
FOR THE LINCOLN MEMORIAL UNIVER-
SITY AT CUMBERLAND GAP, TENN.

LADIES AND GENTLEMEN,—The remainder
of my duties as presiding chairman here this
evening are but two—only two. One of them
is easy, and the other difficult. That is to say, I
must introduce the orator, and then keep still and
give him a chance. The name of Henry Watterson
carries with it its own explanation. It is like an
electric light on top of Madison Square Garden;
you touch the button and the light flashes up
out of the darkness. You mention the name of
Henry Watterson, and your minds are at once
illuminated with the splendid radiance of his fame
and achievements. A journalist, a soldier, an
orator, a statesman, a rebel. Yes, he was a rebel;
and, better still, now he is a reconstructed rebel.

It is a curious circumstance, a circumstance
brought about without any collusion or pre-
arrangement, that he and I, both of whom were

295

rebels related by blood to each other, should be brought here together this evening bearing a tribute in our hands and bowing our heads in reverence to that noble soul who for three years we tried to destroy. I don't know as the fact has ever been mentioned before, but it is a fact, nevertheless. Colonel Watterson and I were both rebels, and we are blood relations. I was a second lieutenant in a Confederate company—for a while—oh, I could have stayed on if I had wanted to. I made myself felt, I left tracks all around the country. I could have stayed on, but it was such weather. I never saw such weather to be out-of-doors in, in all my life.

The Colonel commanded a regiment, and did his part, I suppose, to destroy the Union. He did not succeed, yet if he had obeyed me he would have done so. I had a plan, and I fully intended to drive General Grant into the Pacific Ocean—if I could get transportation. I told Colonel Watterson about it. I told him what he had to do. What I wanted him to do was to surround the Eastern army and wait until I came up. But he was insubordinate; he stuck on some quibble of military etiquette about a second lieutenant giving orders to a colonel or something like that. And what was the consequence? The Union was preserved. This is the first time I believe that that secret has ever been revealed.

No one outside of the family circle, I think,

knew it before; but there the facts are. Watterson saved the Union; yes, he saved the Union. And yet there he sits, and not a step has been taken or a movement made toward granting him a pension. That is the way things are done. It is a case where some blushing ought to be done. You ought to blush, and I ought to blush, and he —well, he's a little out of practice now.

ROBERT FULTON FUND

Mr. Clemens had been asked to address the association by Gen. Frederick D. Grant, president. He was offered a fee of $1000, but refused it, saying:

"I shall be glad to do it, but I must stipulate that you keep the $1000, and add it to the Memorial Fund as my contribution to erect a monument in New York to the memory of the man who applied steam to navigation."

At this meeting Mr. Clemens made this formal announcement from the platform:

"This is my last appearance on the paid platform. I shall not retire from the gratis platform until I am buried, and courtesy will compel me to keep still and not disturb the others. Now, since I must, I shall say good-bye. I see many faces in this audience well known to me. They are all my friends, and I feel that those I don't know are my friends, too. I wish to consider that you represent the nation, and that in saying good-bye to you I am saying good-bye to the nation. In the great name of humanity, let me say this final word: I offer an appeal in behalf of that vast, pathetic multitude of fathers, mothers, and helpless little children. They were sheltered and happy two days ago. Now they are wandering, forlorn, hopeless, and homeless, the victims of a great disaster. So I beg of you, I beg of you, to open your hearts and open your purses and remember San Francisco, the smitten city."

I WISH to deliver a historical address. I've been studying the history of—er—a—let me see—a [then he stopped in confusion, and walked over to Gen. Fred D. Grant, who sat at the head of the platform. He leaned over in a whisper, and then returned to the front of the stage and continued]. Oh yes! I've been studying Robert Fulton. I've been studying a biographical sketch of Robert Fulton, the inventor of — er — a — let's see—oh yes, the inventor of the electric telegraph and the Morse sewing - machine. Also, I understand he invented the air — diria — pshaw! I have it at last—the dirigible balloon. Yes, the dirigible— but it is a difficult word, and I don't see why anybody should marry a couple of words like that when they don't want to be married at all and are likely to quarrel with each other all the time. I should put that couple of words under the ban of the United States Supreme Court, under its decision of a few days ago, and take 'em out and drown 'em.

I used to know Fulton. It used to do me good to see him dashing through the town on a wild broncho.

And Fulton was born in—er—a—well, it doesn't

make much difference where he was born, does it? I remember a man who came to interview me once, to get a sketch of my life. I consulted with a friend — a practical man — before he came, to know how I should treat him.

"Whenever you give the interviewer a fact," he said, "give him another fact that will contradict it. Then he'll go away with a jumble that he can't use at all. Be gentle, be sweet, smile like an idiot—just be natural." That's what my friend told me to do, and I did it.

"Where were you born?" asked the interviewer.

"Well—er—a," I began, "I was born in Alabama, or Alaska, or the Sandwich Islands; I don't know where, but right around there somewhere. And you had better put it down before you forget it."

"But you weren't born in all those places," he said.

"Well, I've offered you three places. Take your choice. They're all at the same price."

"How old are you?" he asked.

"I shall be nineteen in June," I said.

"Why, there's such a discrepancy between your age and your looks," he said.

"Oh, that's nothing," I said, "I was born discrepantly."

Then we got to talking about my brother Samuel, and he told me my explanations were confusing.

"I suppose he is dead," I said. "Some said that he was dead and some said that he wasn't."

"Did you bury him without knowing whether he was dead or not?" asked the reporter.

"There was a mystery," said I. "We were twins, and one day when we were two weeks old— that is, he was one week old, and I was one week old—we got mixed up in the bath-tub, and one of us drowned. We never could tell which. One of us had a strawberry birthmark on the back of his hand. There it is on my hand. This is the one that was drowned. There's no doubt about it."

"Where's the mystery?" he said.

"Why, don't you see how stupid it was to bury the wrong twin?" I answered. I didn't explain it any more because he said the explanation confused him. To me it is perfectly plain.

But, to get back to Fulton. I'm going along like an old man I used to know who used to start to tell a story about his grandfather. He had an awfully retentive memory, and he never finished the story, because he switched off into something else. He used to tell about how his grandfather one day went into a pasture, where there was a ram. The old man dropped a silver dime in the grass, and stooped over to pick it up. The ram was observing him, and took the old man's action as an invitation.

Just as he was going to finish about the ram this friend of mine would recall that his grandfather had a niece who had a glass eye. She used to loan that glass eye to another lady friend, who used it when she received company. The eye didn't fit the friend's face, and it was loose. And whenever she winked it would turn over.

Then he got on the subject of accidents, and he would tell a story about how he believed accidents never happened.

"There was an Irishman coming down a ladder with a hod of bricks," he said, "and a Dutchman was standing on the ground below. The Irishman 'fell on the Dutchman and killed him. Accident? Never! If the Dutchman hadn't been there the Irishman would have been killed. Why didn't the Irishman fall on a dog which was next to the Dutchman? Because the dog would have seen him coming."

Then he'd get off from the Dutchman to an uncle named Reginald Wilson. Reginald went into a carpet factory one day, and got twisted into the machinery's belt. He went excursioning around the factory until he was properly distributed and was woven into sixty-nine yards of the best three-ply carpet. His wife bought the carpet, and then she erected a monument to his memory. It read:

ROBERT FULTON FUND

Sacred to the memory
of
sixty-nine yards of the best three-ply carpet
containing the mortal remainders of

REGINALD WILSON

Go thou and do likewise

And so on he would ramble about telling the story of his grandfather until we never were told whether he found the ten-cent piece or whether something else happened.

FULTON DAY, JAMESTOWN

ADDRESS DELIVERED SEPTEMBER 23, 1907

Lieutenant-Governor Ellyson, of Virginia, in introducing Mr. Clemens, said:

"The people have come here to bring a tribute of affectionate recollection for the man who has contributed so much to the progress of the world and the happiness of mankind." As Mr. Clemens came down to the platform the applause became louder and louder, until Mr. Clemens held out his hand for silence. It was a great triumph, and it was almost a minute after the applause ceased before Mr. Clemens could speak. He attempted it once, and when the audience noticed his emotion, it cheered again loudly.

LADIES AND GENTLEMEN,—I am but human, and when you give me a reception like that I am obliged to wait a little while I get my voice. When you appeal to my head, I don't feel it; but when you appeal to my heart, I do feel it.

We are here to celebrate one of the greatest events of American history, and not only in American history, but in the world's history.

Indeed it was—the application of steam by Robert Fulton.

It was a world event—there are not many of

them. It is peculiarly an American event, that is true, but the influence was very broad in effect. We should regard this day as a very great American holiday. We have not many that are exclusively American holidays. We have the Fourth of July, which we regard as an American holiday, but it is nothing of the kind. I am waiting for a dissenting voice. All great efforts that led up to the Fourth of July were made, not by Americans, but by English residents of America, subjects of the King of England.

They fought all the fighting that was done, they shed and spilt all the blood that was spilt, in securing to us the invaluable liberties which are incorporated in the Declaration of Independence; but they were not Americans. They signed the Declaration of Independence; no American's name is signed to that document at all. There never was an American such as you and I are until after the Revolution, when it had all been fought out and liberty secured, after the adoption of the Constitution, and the recognition of the Independence of America by all powers.

While we revere the Fourth of July — and let us always revere it, and the liberties it conferred upon us — yet it was not an American event, a great American day.

It was an American who applied that steam successfully. There are not a great many world events, and we have our full share. The telegraph, telephone, and the application of steam to navigation—these are great American events.

To-day I have been requested, or I have requested myself, not to confine myself to furnishing you with information, but to remind you of things, and to introduce one of the nation's celebrants.

Admiral Harrington here is going to tell you all that I have left untold. I am going to tell you all that I know, and then he will follow up with such rags and remnants as he can find, and tell you what he knows.

No doubt you have heard a great deal about Robert Fulton and the influences that have grown from his invention, but the little steamboat is suffering neglect.

You probably do not know a great deal about that boat. It was the most important steamboat in the world. I was there and saw it. Admiral Harrington was there at the time. It need not surprise you, for he is not as old as he looks. That little boat was interesting in every way. The size of it. The boat was one [consults Admiral], he said ten feet long. The breadth of that boat [consults Admiral], two hundred feet. You see, the first and most important detail is the length, then the breadth, and then the depth; the depth of that boat was [consults again]—the Admiral says it was a flat boat. Then her tonnage—you know nothing about a boat until you know two more things: her speed and her tonnage. We know the speed she made. She made four miles—and sometimes five miles. It was on her initial trip, on August 11, 1807, that she made her initial trip, when she went from [consults Admiral] Jersey City — to Chicago. That's right. She went by way of Albany. Now comes the tonnage of that boat. Tonnage of a boat means the amount of displacement; displacement means the amount of water a vessel can shove in a day. The tonnage of man is estimated by the amount of whiskey he can displace in a day.

Robert Fulton named the *Clermont* in honor of his bride, that is, Clermont was the name of the county-seat.

I feel that it surprises you that I know so much. In my remarks of welcome of Admiral Harrington I am not going to give him compliments. Compliments always embarrass a man. You do not know anything to say. It does not inspire you with words. There is nothing you can say in answer to a compliment. I have been complimented myself a great many times, and they always embarrass me—I always feel that they have not said enough.

The Admiral and myself have held public office, and were associated together a great deal in a friendly way in the time of Pocahontas. That incident where Pocahontas saves the life of Smith from her father, Powhatan's club, was gotten up by the Admiral and myself to advertise James-town.

At that time the Admiral and myself did not have the facilities of advertising that you have.

I have known Admiral Harrington in all kinds of situations—in public service, on the platform, and in the chain-gang now and then—but it was a mistake. A case of mistaken identity. I do not think it is at all a necessity to tell you Admiral Harrington's public history. You know that it is in the histories. I am not here to tell you anything about his public life, but to expose his private life.

I am something of a poet. When the great poet laureate, Tennyson, died, and I found that the place was open, I tried to get it—but I did not get it. Anybody can write the first line of a poem, but it is a very difficult task to make the second line rhyme with the first. When I was down in Australia there were two towns named Johnswood and Par-am. I made this rhyme:

"The people of Johnswood are pious and good;
The people of Par-am they don't care a ——."

I do not want to compliment Admiral Harrington, but as long as such men as he devote their lives to the public service the credit of the country will never cease. I will say that the same high qualities, the same moral and in-

308

tellectual attainments, the same graciousness of manner, of conduct, of observation, and expression have caused Admiral Harrington to be mistaken for me—and I have been mistaken for him.

A mutual compliment can go no further, and I now have the honor and privilege of introducing to you Admiral Harrington.

21

LOTOS CLUB DINNER IN HONOR
OF MARK TWAIN

ADDRESS AT THE FIRST FORMAL DINNER IN THE NEW
CLUB-HOUSE, NOVEMBER 11, 1893

In introducing the guest of the evening, Mr. Lawrence said:

"To-night the old faces appear once more amid new surroundings. The place where last we met about the table has vanished, and to-night we have our first Lotos dinner in a home that is all our own. It is peculiarly fitting that the board should now be spread in honor of one who has been a member of the club for full a score of years, and it is a happy augury for the future that our fellow-member whom we assemble to greet should be the bearer of a most distinguished name in the world of letters; for the Lotos Club is ever at its best when paying homage to genius in literature or in art. Is there a civilized being who has not heard the name of Mark Twain? We knew him long years ago, before he came out of the boundless West, brimful of wit and eloquence, with no reverence for anything, and went abroad to educate the untutored European in the subtleties of the American joke. The world has looked on and applauded while he has broken many images. He has led us in imagination all over the globe. With him as our guide we have traversed alike the Mis-

sissippi and the Sea of Galilee. At his bidding we
have laughed at a thousand absurdities. By a labori-
ous process of reasoning he has convinced us that the
Egyptian mummies are actually dead. He has held
us spellbound upon the plain at the foot of the great
Sphinx, and we have joined him in weeping bitter
tears at the tomb of Adam. To-night we greet him
in the flesh. What name is there in literature that
can be likened to his? Perhaps some of the distinguished gentlemen about this table can tell us,
but I know of none. Himself his only parallel!"

MR. PRESIDENT, GENTLEMEN, AND
FELLOW-MEMBERS OF THE LOTOS
CLUB,—I have seldom in my lifetime listened
to compliments so felicitously phrased or so well
deserved. I return thanks for them from a full
heart and an appreciative spirit, and I will say
this in self-defence: While I am charged with
having no reverence for anything, I wish to say
that I have reverence for the man who can utter
such truths, and I also have a deep reverence
and a sincere one for a club that can do such
justice to me. To be the chief guest of such a
club is something to be envied, and if I read your
countenances rightly I am envied. I am glad
to see this club in such palatial quarters. I remember it twenty years ago when it was housed
in a stable.

Now when I was studying for the ministry
there were two or three things that struck my

attention particularly. At the first banquet mentioned in history that other prodigal son who came back from his travels was invited to stand up and have his say. They were all there, his brethren, David and Goliath, and—er, and if he had had such experience as I have had he would have waited until those other people got through talking. He got up and testified to all his failings. Now if he had waited before telling all about his riotous living until the others had spoken he might not have given himself away as he did, and I think that I would give myself away if I should go on. I think I'd better wait until the others hand in their testimony; then if it is necessary for me to make an explanation, I will get up and explain, and if I cannot do that, I'll deny it happened.

Later in the evening Mr. Clemens made another speech, replying to a fire of short speeches by Charles Dudley Warner, Charles A. Dana, Seth Low, General Porter, and many others, each welcoming the guest of honor.

I don't see that I have a great deal to explain. I got off very well, considering the opportunities that these other fellows had. I don't see that Mr. Low said anything against me, and neither did Mr. Dana. However, I will say that I never heard so many lies told in one evening as were told by Mr. McKelway—and I consider myself very capable; but even in his case, when he got through, I was gratified by finding how much he hadn't found out. By accident he missed the very things that I didn't want to have said, and now, gentlemen, about Americanism.

I have been on the continent of Europe for two and a half years. I have met many Americans there, some sojourning for a short time only, others making protracted stays, and it has been very gratifying to me to find that nearly all preserved their Americanism. I have found they all like to see the Flag fly, and that their hearts rise when they see the Stars and Stripes. I met only one lady who had forgotten the land of her birth and glorified monarchical institutions.

I think it is a great thing to say that in two and a half years I met only one person who had fallen a victim to the shams—I think we may call them shams—of nobilities and of heredities. She was entirely lost in them. After I had listened to her for a long time, I said to her: "At least you must admit that we have one merit. We are not like the Chinese, who refuse to allow their citizens who are tired of the country to leave it. Thank God, we don't!"

COPYRIGHT

With Mr. Howells, Edward Everett Hale, Thomas Nelson Page, and a number of other authors, Mr. Clemens appeared before the committee December 6, 1906. The new Copyright Bill contemplated an author's copyright for the term of his life and for fifty years thereafter, applying also for the benefit of artists, musicians, and others, but the authors did most of the talking. F. D. Millet made a speech for the artists, and John Philip Sousa for the musicians.

Mr. Clemens was the last speaker of the day, and its chief feature. He made a speech, the serious parts of which created a strong impression, and the humorous parts set the Senators and Representatives in roars of laughter.

I HAVE read this bill. At least I have read such portions as I could understand. Nobody but a practised legislator can read the bill and thoroughly understand it, and I am not a practised legislator.

I am interested particularly and especially in the part of the bill which concerns my trade. I like that extension of copyright life to the author's life and fifty years afterward. I think that would satisfy any reasonable author, because it would take care of his children. Let the grandchildren take care of themselves. That would take care of my daughters, and after that I am not particular. I shall then have long been out of this struggle, independent of it, indifferent to it.

It isn't objectionable to me that all the trades and professions in the United States are protected by the bill. I like that. They are all important and worthy, and if we can take care of them under the Copyright law I should like to see it done. I should like to see oyster culture added, and anything else.

I am aware that copyright must have a limit, because that is required by the Constitution of the United States, which sets aside the earlier Constitution, which we call the decalogue. The decalogue says you shall not take away from any man his profit. I don't like to be obliged to use the harsh term. What the decalogue really says is, "Thou shalt not steal," but I am trying to use more polite language.

The laws of England and America do take it away, do select but one class, the people who create the literature of the land. They always talk handsomely about the literature of the land, always what a fine, great, monumental thing a great literature is, and in the midst of their enthusiasm they turn around and do what they can to discourage it.

I know we must have a limit, but forty-two years is too much of a limit. I am quite unable to guess why there should be a limit at all to the possession of the product of a man's labor. There is no limit to real estate.

Doctor Hale has suggested that a man might just as well, after discovering a coal-mine and working it forty-two years, have the Government step in and take it away.

What is the excuse? It is that the author who produced that book has had the profit of it long enough, and therefore the Government takes a profit which does not belong to it and generously gives it to the 88,000,000 of people. But it doesn't do anything of the kind. It merely takes the author's property, takes his children's bread, and gives the publisher double profit. He goes on publishing the book and as many of his confederates as choose to go into the conspiracy do so, and they rear families in affluence.

And they continue the enjoyment of those ill-gotten gains generation after generation forever, for they never die. In a few weeks or months or years I shall be out of it, I hope under a monument. I hope I shall not be entirely forgotten, and I shall subscribe to the monument myself. But I shall not be caring what happens if there are fifty years left of my copyright. My copyright produces annually a good deal more than I can use, but my children can use it. I can get along;

COPYRIGHT

I know a lot of trades. But that goes to my daughters, who can't get along as well as I can because I have carefully raised them as young ladies, who don't know anything and can't do anything. I hope Congress will extend to them the charity which they have failed to get from me.

Why, if a man who is not even mad, but only strenuous—strenuous about race-suicide—should come to me and try to get me to use my large political and ecclesiastical influence to get a bill passed by this Congress limiting families to twenty-two children by one mother, I should try to calm him down. I should reason with him. I should say to him, "Leave it alone. Leave it alone and it will take care of itself. Only one couple a year in the United States can reach that limit. If they have reached that limit let them go right on. Let them have all the liberty they want. In restricting that family to twenty-two children you are merely conferring discomfort and unhappiness on one family per year in a nation of 88,000,000, which is not worth while."

It is the very same with copyright. One author per year produces a book which can outlive the forty-two-year limit; that's all. This nation can't produce two authors a year that can do it; the thing is demonstrably impossible. All that the limited copyright can do is to take the bread out of the mouths of the children of that one author per year.

I made an estimate some years ago, when I appeared before a committee of the House of Lords, that we had published in this country since the Declaration of Independence 220,000 books. They have all gone. They had all perished before they were ten years old. It is only one book in 1000 that can outlive the forty-two-year limit. Therefore why put a limit at all? You might as well limit the family to twenty-two children.

If you recall the Americans in the nineteenth century who wrote books that lived forty-two years you will have to begin with Cooper; you can follow with Washington Irving, Harriet Beecher Stowe, Edgar Allan Poe, and there you have to wait a long time. You come to Emerson, and you have to stand still and look further. You find Howells and T. B. Aldrich, and then your numbers begin to run pretty thin, and you question if you can name twenty persons in the United States who in a whole century have written books that would live forty-two years. Why, you could take them all and put them on one bench there [pointing]. Add the wives and children and you could put the result on two or three more benches.

One hundred persons—that is the little, insignificant crowd whose bread-and-butter is to be taken away for what purpose, for what profit to anybody? You turn these few books into the hands of the pirate and of the legitimate publisher, too, and they get the profit that should have gone to the wife and children.

When I appeared before that committee of the House of Lords the chairman asked me what limit I would propose. I said, "Perpetuity." I could see some resentment in his manner, and he said the idea was illogical, for the reason that it has long ago been decided that there can be no such thing as property in ideas. I said there was property in ideas before Queen Anne's time; they had perpetual copyright. He said, "What is a book? A book is just built from base to roof on ideas, and there can be no property in it."

I said I wished he could mention any kind of property on this planet that had a pecuniary value which was not derived from an idea or ideas. He said real estate. I put a supposititious case, a dozen Englishmen who travel through South Africa and camp out, and eleven of them see nothing at all; they are mentally blind. But there is one in the party who knows what this harbor means and what the lay of the land means. To him it means that some day a railway will go through here, and there on that harbor a great city will spring up. That is his idea. And he has another idea, which is to go and trade his last bottle of Scotch whiskey and his last horse-blanket to the principal chief of that region and buy a piece of land the size of Pennsylvania.

That was the value of an idea that the day would come when the Cape to Cairo Railway would be built.

Every improvement that is put upon the real estate is the result of an idea in somebody's head. The skyscraper is another idea; the railroad is another; the telephone and all those things are merely symbols which represent ideas. An andiron, a wash-tub, is the result of an idea that did not exist before.

So if, as that gentleman said, a book does consist solely of ideas, that is the best argument in the world that it is property, and should not be under any limitation at all. We don't ask for that. Fifty years from now we shall ask for it.

I hope the bill will pass without any deleterious amendments. I do seem to be extraordinarily interested in a whole lot of arts and things that I have got nothing to do with. It is a part of my generous, liberal nature; I can't help it. I feel the same sort of charity to everybody that was manifested by a gentleman who arrived at home at two o'clock in the morning from the club and was feeling so perfectly satisfied with life, so happy, and so comfortable, and there was his house weaving, weaving, weaving around. He watched his chance, and by and by when the steps got in his neighborhood he made a jump and climbed up and got on the portico.

And the house went on weaving and weaving

and weaving, but he watched the door, and when it came around his way he plunged through it. He got to the stairs, and when he went up on all fours the house was so unsteady that he could hardly make his way, but at last he got to the top and raised his foot and put it on the top step. But only the toe hitched on the step, and he rolled down and fetched up on the bottom step, with his arm around the newel-post, and he said: "God pity the poor sailors out at sea on a night like this."

IN· AID OF THE BLIND

ADDRESS AT A PUBLIC MEETING OF THE NEW YORK
ASSOCIATION FOR PROMOTING THE INTERESTS
OF THE BLIND AT THE WALDORF-
ASTORIA, MARCH 29, 1906

IF you detect any awkwardness in my movements and infelicities in my conduct I will offer
the explanation that I never presided at a meeting of any kind before in my life, and that I do
find it out of my line.   I supposed I could do anything anybody else could, but I recognize that
experience helps, and I do feel the lack of that
experience.   I don't feel as graceful and easy as
I ought to be in order to impress an audience.   I
shall not pretend that I know how to umpire a
meeting like this, and I shall just take the humble
place of the Essex band.

There was a great gathering in a small New
England town about twenty-five years ago.   I remember that circumstance because there was
something that happened at that time.   It was a
great occasion.   They gathered in the militia and
orators and everybody from all the towns around.
It was an extraordinary occasion.

IN AID OF THE BLIND

The little local paper threw itself into ecstasies of admiration and tried to do itself proud from beginning to end. It praised the orators, the militia, and all the bands that came from everywhere, and all this in honest country newspaper detail, but the writer ran out of adjectives toward the end. Having exhausted his whole magazine of praise and glorification, he found he still had one band left over. He had to say something about it, and he said: "The Essex band done the best it could."

I am an Essex band on this occasion, and I am going to get through as well as inexperience and good intentions will enable me. I have got all the documents here necessary to instruct you in the objects and intentions of this meeting and also of the association which has called the meeting. But they are too voluminous. I could not pack those statistics into my head, and I had to give it up. I shall have to just reduce all that mass of statistics to a few salient facts. There are too many statistics and figures for me. I never could do anything with figures, never had any talent for mathematics, never accomplished anything in my efforts at that rugged study, and to-day the only mathematics I know is multiplication, and the minute I get away up in that, as soon as I reach nine times seven—

[Mr. Clemens lapsed into deep thought for a moment. He was trying to figure out nine times

323

seven, but it was a hopeless task, and he turned to St. Clair McKelway, who sat near him. Mr. McKelway whispered the answer, and the speaker resumed :]

I've got it now. It's eighty-four. Well, I can get that far all right with a little hesitation. After that I am uncertain, and I can't manage a statistic.

" This association for the "—

[Mr. Clemens was in another dilemma. Again he was obliged to turn to Mr. McKelway.]

Oh yes, for promoting the interests of the blind. It's a long name. If I could I would write it out for you and let you take it home and study it, but I don't know how to spell it. And Mr. Carnegie is down in Virginia somewhere. Well, anyway, the object of that association which has been recently organized, five months ago, in fact, is in the hands of very, very energetic, intelligent, and capable people, and they will push it to success very surely, and all the more surely if you will give them a little of your assistance out of your pockets.

The intention, the purpose, is to search out all the blind and find work for them to do so that they may earn their own bread. Now it is dismal enough to be blind—it is dreary, dreary life at best, but it can be largely ameliorated by finding something for these poor blind people to do with their hands. The time passes so heavily that it is never day or night with them, it is always night, and when they have to sit with folded hands and with nothing to do to amuse or entertain or employ their minds, it is drearier and drearier.

And then the knowledge they have that they must subsist on charity, and so often reluctant charity, it would renew their lives if they could have something to do with their hands and pass their time and at the same time earn their bread, and know the sweetness of the bread which is the result of the labor of one's own hands. They need that cheer and pleasure. It is the only way you can turn their night into day, to give them happy hearts, the only thing you can put in the place of the blessed sun. That you can do in the way I speak of.

Blind people generally who have seen the light know what it is to miss the light. Those who have gone blind since they were twenty years old —their lives are unendingly dreary. But they can be taught to use their hands and to employ themselves at a great many industries. That association from which this draws its birth in Cambridge, Massachusetts, has taught its blind to make many things. They make them better than most people, and more honest than people who have the use of their eyes. The goods they make are readily salable. People like them. And so they are supporting themselves, and it is a matter of cheer, cheer. They pass their time now not too irksomely as they formerly did.

What this association needs and wants is $15,-000. The figures are set down, and what the money is for, and there is no graft in it or I would not be here. And they hope to beguile that out of your pockets, and you will find affixed to the programme an opportunity, that little blank which you will fill out and promise so much money now or to-morrow or some time. Then, there is another opportunity which is still better, and that is that you shall subscribe an annual sum.

I have invented a good many useful things in my time, but never anything better than that of getting money out of people who don't want to part with it. It is always for good objects, of course. This is the plan: When you call upon a person to contribute to a great and good object, and you think he should furnish about $1000, he disappoints you as like as not. Much the best way to work him to supply that thousand dollars is to split it into parts and contribute, say a hundred dollars a year, or fifty, or whatever the sum may be. Let him contribute ten or twenty a year. He doesn't feel that, but he does feel it when you call upon him to contribute a large amount. When you get used to it you would rather contribute than borrow money.

I tried it in Helen Keller's case. Mr. Hutton wrote me in 1896 or 1897 when I was in London and said: "The gentleman who has been so liberal in taking care of Helen Keller has died without making provision for her in his will, and now they don't know what to do." They were proposing to raise a fund, and he thought $50,000 enough to furnish an income of $2400 or $2500 a year for the support of that wonderful girl and her wonderful teacher, Miss Sullivan, now Mrs. Macy. I wrote to Mr. Hutton and said: "Go on, get up your fund. It will be slow, but if you want quick work, I propose this system," the system I speak of, of asking people to contribute such and such a sum from year to year and drop out whenever they please, and he would find there wouldn't be any difficulty, people wouldn't feel the burden of it. And he wrote back saying he had raised the $2400 a year indefinitely by that system in a single afternoon. We would like to do something just like that to-night. We will take as many checks as you care to give. You can leave your donations in the big room outside.

I knew once what it was to be blind. I shall never forget that experience. I have been as blind as anybody ever was for three or four hours, and the sufferings that I endured and the mishaps and the accidents that are burning in my memory make my sympathy rise when I feel for the blind and always shall feel. I once went to Heidelberg on an excursion. I took a clergyman along with me, the Rev. Joseph Twichell, of

Hartford, who is still among the living despite that fact. I always travel with clergymen when I can. It is better for them, it is better for me. And any preacher who goes out with me in stormy weather and without a lightning rod is a good one. The Reverend Twichell is one of those people filled with patience and endurance, two good ingredients for a man travelling with me, so we got along very well together. In that old town they have not altered a house nor built one in 1500 years. We went to the inn and they placed Twichell and me in a most colossal bedroom, the largest I ever saw or heard of. It was as big as this room.

I didn't take much notice of the place. I didn't really get my bearings. I noticed Twichell got a German bed about two feet wide, the kind in which you've got to lie on your edge, because there isn't room to lie on your back, and he was way down south in that big room, and I was way up north at the other end of it, with a regular Saraha in between.

We went to bed. Twichell went to sleep, but then he had his conscience loaded and it was easy for him to get to sleep. I couldn't get to sleep. It was one of those torturing kinds of lovely summer nights when you hear various kinds of noises now and then. A mouse away off in the southwest. You throw things at the mouse. That encourages the mouse. But I couldn't stand it, and about two o'clock I got up and thought I would give it up and go out in the square where there was one of those tinkling fountains, and sit on its brink and dream, full of romance.

I got out of bed, and I ought to have lit a candle, but I didn't think of it until it was too late. It was the darkest place that ever was. There has never been darkness any thicker than that. It just lay in cakes.

I thought that before dressing I would accumulate my clothes. I pawed around in the dark and found everything packed together on the floor except one sock. I couldn't get on the track of that sock. It might have occurred to me that maybe it was in the wash. But I didn't think of that. I went excursioning on my hands and knees. Presently I thought, "I am never going to find it; I'll go back to bed again." That is what I tried to do during the next three hours. I had lost the bearings of that bed. I was going in the wrong direction all the time. By-and-by I came in collision with a chair and that encouraged me.

It seemed to me, as far as I could recollect, there was only a chair here and there and yonder, five or six of them scattered over this territory, and I thought maybe after I found that chair I might find the next one. Well, I did. And I found another and another and another. I kept going around on my hands and knees, having

329

those sudden collisions, and finally when I banged into another chair I almost lost my temper. And I raised up, garbed as I was, not for public exhibition, right in front of a mirror fifteen or sixteen feet high.

I hadn't noticed the mirror; didn't know it was there. And when I saw myself in the mirror I was frightened out of my wits. I don't allow any ghosts to bite me, and I took up a chair and smashed at it. A million pieces. Then I reflected. That's the way I always do, and it's unprofitable unless a man has had much experience that way and has clear judgment. And I had judgment, and I would have had to pay for that mirror if I hadn't recollected to say it was Twichell who broke it.

Then I got down on my hands and knees and went on another exploring expedition.

As far as I could remember there were six chairs in that Oklahoma, and one table, a great big heavy table, not a good table to hit with your head when rushing madly along. In the course of time I collided with thirty-five chairs and tables enough to stock that dining-room out there. It was a hospital for decayed furniture, and it was in a worse condition when I got through with it. I went on and on, and at last got to a place where I could feel my way up, and there was a shelf. I knew that wasn't in the middle of the room. Up to that time I was afraid I had gotten out of the city.

330

I was very careful and pawed along that shelf, and there was a pitcher of water about a foot high, and it was at the head of Twichell's bed, but I didn't know it. I felt that pitcher going and I grabbed at it, but it didn't help any and came right down in Twichell's face and nearly drowned him. But it woke him up. I was grateful to have company on any terms. He lit a match, and there I was, way down south when I ought to have been back up yonder. My bed was out of sight it was so far away. You needed a telescope to find it. Twichell comforted me and I scrubbed him off and we got sociable.

But that night wasn't wasted. I had my pedometer on my leg. Twichell and I were in a pedometer match. Twichell had longer legs than I. The only way I could keep up was to wear my pedometer to bed. I always walk in my sleep, and on this occasion I gained sixteen miles on him. After all, I never found that sock. I never have seen it from that day to this. But that adventure taught me what it is to be blind. That was one of the most serious occasions of my whole life, yet I never can speak of it without somebody thinking it isn't serious. You try it and see how serious it is to be as the blind are and I was that night.

[Mr. Clemens read several letters of regret. He then introduced Joseph H. Choate, saying:]

It is now my privilege to present to you Mr.

331

Choate. I don't have to really introduce him. I
don't have to praise him, or to flatter him. I
could say truly that in the forty-seven years
I have been familiarly acquainted with him he
has always been the handsomest man America has
ever produced. And I hope and believe he will
hold the belt forty-five years more. He has
served his country ably, faithfully, and brilliantly.
He stands at the summit, at the very top in the
esteem and regard of his countrymen, and if I
could say one word which would lift him any
higher in his countrymen's esteem and affection,
I would say that word whether it was true or not.

DR. MARK TWAIN, FARMEOPATH

ADDRESS AT THE ANNUAL DINNER OF THE NEW YORK
POST-GRADUATE MEDICAL SCHOOL AND HOS-
PITAL, JANUARY 21, 1909

*The president, Dr. George N. Miller, in introducing
Mr. Clemens, referred to his late experience with
burglars.*

GENTLEMEN AND DOCTORS,—I am glad
to be among my own kind to-night. I was
once a sharpshooter, but now I practise a much
higher and equally as deadly a profession. It
wasn't so very long ago that I became a member
of your cult, and for the time I've been in the
business my record is one that can't be scoffed at.

As to the burglars, I am perfectly familiar with
these people. I have always had a good deal to
do with burglars—not officially, but through
their attentions to me. I never suffered anything at the hands of a burglar. They have in-
vaded my house time and time again. They
never got anything. Then those people who
burglarized our house in September—we got back
the plated ware they took off, we jailed them, and

I have been sorry ever since. They did us a great service—they scared off all the servants in the place.

I consider the Children's Theatre, of which I am president, and the Post-Graduate Medical School as the two greatest institutions in the country. This school, in bringing its twenty thousand physicians from all parts of the country, bringing them up to date, and sending them back with renewed confidence, has surely saved hundreds of thousands of lives which otherwise would have been lost.

I have been practising now for seven months. When I settled on my farm in Connecticut in June I found the community very thinly settled —and since I have been engaged in practice it has become more thinly settled still. This gratifies me, as indicating that I am making an impression on my community. I suppose it is the same with all of you.

I have always felt that I ought to do something for you, and so I organized a Redding (Connecticut) branch of the Post-Graduate School. I am only a country farmer up there, but I am doing the best I can.

Of course, the practice of medicine and surgery in a remote country district has its disadvantages, but in my case I am happy in a division of responsibility. I practise in conjunction with a horse-doctor, a sexton, and an undertaker. The combination is air-tight, and once a man is stricken in our district escape is impossible for him.

These four of us—three in the regular profession and the fourth an undertaker—are all good men. There is Bill Ferguson, the Redding undertaker. Bill is there in every respect. He is a little lukewarm on general practice, and writes his name with a rubber stamp. Like my old Southern friend, he is one of the finest planters anywhere.

Then there is Jim Ruggles, the horse-doctor. Ruggles is one of the best men I have got. He also is not much on general medicine, but he is a fine horse-doctor. Ferguson doesn't make any money off him.

You see, the combination started this way. When I got up to Redding and had become a doctor, I looked around to see what my chances were for aiding in the great work. The first thing I did was to determine what manner of doctor I was to be. Being a Connecticut farmer, I naturally consulted my farmacopia, and at once decided to become a farmeopath.

Then I got circulating about, and got in touch with Ferguson and Ruggles. Ferguson joined readily in my ideas, but Ruggles kept saying that, while it was all right for an undertaker to get aboard, he couldn't see where it helped horses.

Well, we started to find out what was the trouble with the community, and it didn't take

335

long to find out that there was just one disease, and that was race-suicide. And driving about the country-side I was told by my fellow-farmers that it was the only rational human and valuable disease. But it is cutting into our profits so that we'll either have to stop it or we'll have to move.

We've had some funny experiences up there in Redding. Not long ago a fellow came along with a rolling gait and a distressed face. We asked him what was the matter. We always hold consultations on every case, as there isn't business enough for four. He said he didn't know, but that he was a sailor, and perhaps that might help us to give a diagnosis. We treated him for that, and I never saw a man die more peacefully.

That same afternoon my dog Tige treed an African gentleman. We chained up the dog, and then the gentleman came down and said he had appendicitis. We asked him if he wanted to be cut open, and he said yes, that he'd like to know if there was anything in it. So we cut him open and found nothing in him but darkness. So we diagnosed his case as infidelity, because he was dark inside. Tige is a very clever dog, and aids us greatly.

The other day a patient came to me and inquired if I was old Doctor Clemens—

As a practitioner I have given a great deal of my attention to Bright's disease. I have made some rules for treating it that may be valuable. Listen:

Rule 1. When approaching the bedside of one whom an all-wise President—I mean an all-wise Providence—well, anyway, it's the same thing—has seen fit to afflict with disease—well, the rule is simple, even if it is old-fashioned.

Rule 2. I've forgotten just what it is, but—

Rule 3. This is always indispensable: Bleed your patient.

MISSOURI UNIVERSITY SPEECH

ADDRESS DELIVERED JUNE 4, 1902, AT COLUMBIA, MO.

When the name of Samuel L. Clemens was called the humorist stepped forward, put his hand to his hair, and apparently hesitated. There was a dead silence for a moment. Suddenly the entire audience rose and stood in silence. Some one began to spell out the word Missouri with an interval between the letters. All joined in. Then the house again became silent. Mr. Clemens broke the spell:

AS you are all standing [he drawled in his characteristic voice], I guess, I suppose I had better stand too.

[Then came a laugh and loud cries for a speech. As the great humorist spoke of his recent visit to Hannibal, his old home, his voice trembled.]

You cannot know what a strain it was on my emotions [he said]. In fact, when I found myself shaking hands with persons I had not seen for fifty years and looking into wrinkled faces that were so young and joyous when I last saw them, I experienced emotions that I had never expected, and did not know were in me. I was profoundly moved and saddened to think that this was the

338

last time, perhaps, that I would ever behold those kind old faces and dear old scenes of childhood.

[The humorist then changed to a lighter mood, and for a time the audience was in a continual roar of laughter. He was particularly amused at the eulogy on himself read by Gardiner Lathrop in conferring the degree.] He has a fine opportunity to distinguish himself [said Mr. Clemens] by telling the truth about me.

I have seen it stated in print that as a boy I had been guilty of stealing peaches, apples, and watermelons. I read a story to this effect very closely not long ago, and I was convinced of one thing, which was that the man who wrote it was of the opinion that it was wrong to steal, and that I had not acted right in doing so. I wish now, however, to make an honest statement, which is that I do not believe, in all my checkered career, I stole a ton of peaches.

One night I stole—I mean I removed—a watermelon from a wagon while the owner was attending to another customer. I crawled off to a secluded spot, where I found that it was green. It was the greenest melon in the Mississippi Valley. Then I began to reflect. I began to be sorry. I wondered what George Washington would have done had he been in my place. I thought a long time, and then suddenly felt that strange feeling which comes to a man with a good resolution, and took up that watermelon and took it back to its

339

owner. I handed him the watermelon and told him to reform. He took my lecture much to heart, and, when he gave me a good one in place of the green melon, I forgave him.

I told him that I would still be a customer of his, and that I cherished no ill-feeling because of the incident—that would remain green in my memory.

BUSINESS

The alumni of Eastman College gave their annual banquet, March 30, 1901, at the Y. M. C. A. Building. Mr. James G. Cannon, of the Fourth National Bank, made the first speech of the evening, after which Mr. Clemens was introduced by Mr. Bailey as the personal friend of Tom Sawyer, who was one of the types of successful business men.

MR. CANNON has furnished me with texts enough to last as slow a speaker as myself all the rest of the night. I took exception to the introducing of Mr. Cannon as a great financier, as if he were the only great financier present. I am a financier. But my methods are not the same as Mr. Cannon's.

I cannot say that I have turned out the great business man that I thought I was when I began life. But I am comparatively young yet, and may learn. I am rather inclined to believe that what troubled me was that I got the big-head early in the game. I want to explain to you a few points of difference between the principles of business as I see them and those that Mr. Cannon believes in.

23 341

He says that the primary rule of business success is loyalty to your employer. That's all right—as a theory. What is the matter with loyalty to yourself? As nearly as I can understand Mr. Cannon's methods, there is one great drawback to them. He wants you to work a great deal. Diligence is a good thing, but taking things easy is much more—restful. My idea is that the employer should be the busy man, and the employee the idle one. The employer should be the worried man, and the employee the happy one. And why not? He gets the salary. My plan is to get another man to do the work for me. In that there's more repose. What I want is repose first, last, and all the time.

Mr. Cannon says that there are three cardinal rules of business success; they are diligence, honesty, and truthfulness. Well, diligence is all right. Let it go as a theory. Honesty is the best policy—when there is money in it. But truthfulness is one of the most dangerous—why, this man is misleading you.

I had an experience to-day with my wife which illustrates this. I was acknowledging a belated invitation to another dinner for this evening, which seemed to have been sent about ten days ago. It only reached me this morning. I was mortified at the discourtesy into which I had been brought by this delay, and wondered what was being thought of me by my hosts. As I had accepted your invitation, of course I had to send regrets to my other friends.

When I started to write this note my wife came up and stood looking over my shoulder. Women always want to know what is going on. Said she: "Should not that read in the third person?" I conceded that it should, put aside what I was writing, and commenced over again. That seemed to satisfy her, and so she sat down and let me proceed. I then—finished my first note—and so sent what I intended. I never could have done this if I had let my wife know the truth about it. Here is what I wrote:

To THE OHIO SOCIETY,—I have at this moment received a most kind invitation (eleven days old) from Mr. Southard, president; and a like one (ten days old) from Mr. Bryant, president of the Press Club. I thank the society cordially for the compliment of these invitations, although I am booked elsewhere and cannot come.

But, oh, I should like to know the name of the Lightning Express by which they were forwarded; for I owe a friend a dozen chickens, and I believe it will be cheaper to send eggs instead, and let them develop on the road.

Sincerely yours, MARK TWAIN.

I want to tell you of some of my experiences in business, and then I will be in a position to lay down one general rule for the guidance of those who want to succeed in business. My first effort was about twenty-five years ago. I took hold of an invention—I don't know now what it was all about, but some one came to me and told me it was a good thing, and that there was lots of money in it. He persuaded me to invest $15,000, and I lived up to my beliefs by engaging a man to develop it. To make a long story short, I sunk $40,000 in it.

Then I took up the publication of a book. I called in a publisher and said to him: "I want you to publish this book along lines which I shall lay down. I am the employer, and you are the employee. I am going to show them some new kinks in the publishing business. And I want you to draw on me for money as you go along," which he did. He drew on me for $56,000. Then I asked him to take the book and call it off. But he refused to do that.

My next venture was with a machine for doing something or other. I knew less about that than I did about the invention. But I sunk $170,000 in the business, and I can't for the life of me recollect what it was the machine was to do.

I was still undismayed. You see, one of the strong points about my business life was that I never gave up. I undertook to publish General Grant's book, and made $140,000 in six months. My axiom is, to succeed in business: avoid my example.

CARNEGIE THE BENEFACTOR

At the dinner given in honor of Andrew Carnegie by the Lotos Club, March 17, 1909, Mr. Clemens appeared in a white suit from head to feet. He wore a white double-breasted coat, white trousers, and white shoes. The only relief was a big black cigar, which he confidentially informed the company was not from his usual stack bought at $3 per barrel.

THE State of Missouri has for its coat of arms a barrel-head with two Missourians, one on each side of it, and mark the motto—"United We Stand, Divided We Fall." Mr. Carnegie, this evening, has suffered from compliments. It is interesting to hear what people will say about a man. Why, at the banquet given by this club in my honor, Mr. Carnegie had the inspiration for which the club is now honoring him. If Dunfermline contributed so much to the United States in contributing Mr. Carnegie, what would have happened if all Scotland had turned out? These Dunfermline folk have acquired advantages in coming to America.

Doctor McKelway paid the top compliment, the cumulation, when he said of Mr. Carnegie:

"There is a man who wants to pay more taxes than he is charged." Richard Watson Gilder did very well for a poet. He advertised his magazine. He spoke of hiring Mr. Carnegie—the next thing he will be trying to hire me.

If I undertook to pay compliments I would do it stronger than any others have done it, for what Mr. Carnegie wants are strong compliments. Now, the other side of seventy, I have preserved, as my chiefest virtue, modesty.

ON POETRY, VERACITY, AND SUICIDE

Address at a Dinner of the Manhattan Dickens Fellowship, New York City, February 7, 1906

This dinner was in commemoration of the ninety-fourth anniversary of the birth of Charles Dickens. On another occasion Mr. Clemens told the same story with variations and a different conclusion to the University Settlement Society.

I ALWAYS had taken an interest in young people who wanted to become poets. I remember I was particularly interested in one budding poet when I was a reporter. His name was Butter.

One day he came to me and said, disconsolately, that he was going to commit suicide—he was tired of life, not being able to express his thoughts in poetic form. Butter asked me what I thought of the idea.

I said I would; that it was a good idea. "You can do me a friendly turn. You go off in a private place and do it there, and I'll get it all. You do it, and I'll do as much for you some time."

At first he determined to drown himself. Drowning is so nice and clean, and writes up so well in a newspaper.

But things ne'er do go smoothly in weddings, suicides, or courtships. Only there at the edge of the water, where Butter was to end himself, lay a life-preserver—a big round canvas one, which would float after the scrap-iron was soaked out of it.

Butter wouldn't kill himself with the life-preserver in sight, and so I had an idea. I took it to a pawnshop, and soaked it for a revolver. The pawnbroker didn't think much of the exchange, but when I explained the situation he acquiesced. We went up on top of a high building, and this is what happened to the poet:

He put the revolver to his forehead and blew a tunnel straight through his head. The tunnel was about the size of your finger. You could look right through it. The job was complete; there was nothing in it.

Well, after that that man never could write prose, but he could write poetry. He could write it after he had blown his brains out. There is lots of that talent all over the country, but the trouble is they don't develop it.

I am suffering now from the fact that I, who have told the truth a good many times in my life, have lately received more letters than anybody else urging me to lead a righteous life. I have more friends who want to see me develop on a high level than anybody else.

POETRY, VERACITY, SUICIDE

Young John D. Rockefeller, two weeks ago, taught his Bible class all about veracity, and why it was better that everybody should always keep a plentiful supply on hand. Some of the letters I have received suggest that I ought to attend his class and learn, too. Why, I know Mr. Rockefeller, and he is a good fellow. He is competent in many ways to teach a Bible class, but when it comes to veracity he is only thirty-five years old. I'm seventy years old. I have been familiar with veracity twice as long as he.

And the story about George Washington and his little hatchet has also been suggested to me in these letters—in a fugitive way, as if I needed some of George Washington and his hatchet in my constitution. Why, dear me, they overlook the real point in that story. The point is not the one that is usually suggested, and you can readily see that.

The point is not that George said to his father, "Yes, father, I cut down the cheery-tree; I can't tell a lie," but that the little boy—only seven years old—should have his sagacity developed under such circumstances. He was a boy wise beyond his years. His conduct then was a prophecy of later years. Yes, I think he was the most remarkable man the country ever produced—up to my time, anyway.

Now then, little George realized that circumstantial evidence was against him. He knew

that his father would know from the size of the
chips that no full-grown hatchet cut that tree
down, and that no man would have haggled it so.
He knew that his father would send around the
plantation and inquire for a small boy with a
hatchet, and he had the wisdom to come out and
confess it. Now, the idea that his father was
overjoyed when he told little George that he
would rather have him cut down a thousand
cheery-trees than tell a lie is all nonsense. What
did he really mean? Why, that he was absolutely
astonished that he had a son who had the chance
to tell a lie and didn't.

I admire old George—if that was his name—for
his discernment. He knew when he said that his
son couldn't tell a lie that he was stretching it a
good deal. He wouldn't have to go to John D.
Rockefeller's Bible class to find that out. The
way the old George Washington story goes down
it doesn't do anybody any good. It only discourages people who can tell a lie.

WELCOME HOME

ADDRESS AT THE DINNER IN HIS HONOR AT THE
LOTOS CLUB, NOVEMBER 10, 1900

*In August, 1895, just before sailing for Australia,
Mr. Clemens issued the following statement:*

" It has been reported that I sacrificed, for the benefit of the creditors, the property of the publishing firm
whose financial backer I was, and that I am now
lecturing for my own benefit.

" This is an error. I intend the lectures, as well as
the property, for the creditors. The law recognizes
no mortgage on a man's brains, and a merchant who
has given up all he has may take advantage of the
laws of insolvency and may start free again for himself. But I am not a business man, and honor is a
harder master than the law. It cannot compromise
for less than one hundred cents on a dollar, and its
debts are never outlawed.

" I had a two-thirds interest in the publishing firm
whose capital I furnished. If the firm had prospered
I would have expected to collect two-thirds of the
profits. As it is, I expect to pay all the debts. My
partner has no resources, and I do not look for assistance to my wife, whose contributions in cash
from her own means have nearly equalled the claims
of all the creditors combined. She has taken nothing;

351

on the contrary, she has helped and intends to help
me to satisfy the obligations due to the rest of the
creditors.

" It is my intention to ask my creditors to accept
that as a legal discharge, and trust to my honor to
pay the other fifty per cent. as fast as I can earn it.
From my reception thus far on my lecturing tour, I
am confident that if I live I can pay off the last debt
within four years.

" After which, at the age of sixty-four, I can make
a fresh and unincumbered start in life. I am going
to Australia, India, and South Africa, and next year
I hope to make a tour of the great cities of the
United States."

I THANK you all out of my heart for this
fraternal welcome, and it seems almost too
fine, almost too magnificent, for a humble Missourian such as I am, far from his native haunts
on the banks of the Mississippi; yet my modesty
is in a degree fortified by observing that I am not
the only Missourian who has been honored here
to-night, for I see at this very table—here is a
Missourian [indicating Mr. McKelway], and there
is a Missourian [indicating Mr. Depew], and there
is another Missourian—and Hendrix and Clemens;
and last but not least, the greatest Missourian of
them all—here he sits—Tom Reed, who has always concealed his birth till now. And since I
have been away I know what has been happening
in his case: he has deserted politics, and now is
leading a creditable life. He has reformed, and

God prosper him; and I judge, by a remark which he made up-stairs awhile ago, that he had found a new business that is utterly suited to his make and constitution, and all he is doing now is that he is around raising the average of personal beauty.

But I am grateful to the president for the kind words which he has said of me, and it is not for me to say whether these praises were deserved or not. I prefer to accept them just as they stand, without concerning myself with the statistics upon which they have been built, but only with that large matter, that essential matter, the good-fellowship, the kindliness, the magnanimity, and generosity that prompted their utterance. Well, many things have happened since I sat here before, and now that I think of it, the president's reference to the debts which were left by the bankrupt firm of Charles L. Webster & Co. gives me an opportunity to say a word which I very much wish to say, not for myself, but for ninety-five men and women whom I shall always hold in high esteem and in pleasant remembrance—the creditors of that firm. They treated me well; they treated me handsomely. There were ninety-six of them, and by not a finger's weight did ninety-five of them add to the burden of that time for me. Ninety-five out of the ninety-six— they didn't indicate by any word or sign that they were anxious about their money. They treated me well, and I shall not forget it; I could not forget it if I wanted to. Many of them said, "Don't you worry, don't you hurry"; that's what they said. Why, if I could have that kind of creditors always, and that experience, I would recognize it as a personal loss to be out of debt. I owe those ninety-five creditors a debt of homage, and I pay it now in such measure as one may pay so fine a debt in mere words. Yes, they said that very thing. I was not personally acquainted with ten of them, and yet they said, "Don't you worry, and don't you hurry." I know that phrase by heart, and if all the other music should perish out of the world it would still sing to me. I appreciate that; I am glad to say this word; people say so much about me, and they forget those creditors. They were handsomer than I was—or Tom Reed.

Oh, you have been doing many things in this time that I have been absent; you have done lots of things, some that are well worth remembering, too. Now, we have fought a righteous war since I have gone, and that is rare in history—a righteous war is so rare that it is almost unknown in history; but by the grace of that war we set Cuba free, and we joined her to those three or four nations that exist on this earth; and we started out to set those poor Filipinos free, too, and why, why, why that most righteous purpose of ours has apparently miscarried I suppose I never shall know.

But we have made a most creditable record in China in these days—our sound and level-headed administration has made a most creditable record over there, and there are some of the Powers that cannot say that by any means. The Yellow Terror is threatening this world to-day. It is looming vast and ominous on that distant horizon. I do not know what is going to be the result of that Yellow Terror, but our government has had no hand in evoking it, and let's be happy in that and proud of it.

We have nursed free silver, we watched by its cradle; we have done the best we could to raise that child, but those pestiferous Republicans have —well, they keep giving it the measles every chance they get, and we never shall raise that child. Well, that's no matter—there's plenty of other things to do, and we must think of something else. Well, we have tried a President four years, criticised him and found fault with him the whole time, and turned around a day or two ago with votes enough to spare to elect another. O consistency! consistency! thy name—I don't know what thy name is—Thompson will do—any name will do—but you see there is the fact, there is the consistency. Then we have tried for governor an illustrious Rough Rider, and we liked him so much in that great office that now we have made him Vice-President—not in order that that office shall give him distinction, but that he may confer distinction upon that office. And it's needed, too—it's needed. And now, for a while anyway, we shall not be stammering and embarrassed when a stranger asks us, "What is the name of the Vice-President?" This one is known; this one is pretty well known, pretty widely known, and in some quarters favorably. I am not accustomed to dealing in these fulsome compliments, and I am probably overdoing it a little; but—well, my old affectionate admiration for Governor Roosevelt has probably betrayed me into the complimentary excess; but I know him, and you know him; and if you give him rope enough—I mean if—oh yes, he will justify that compliment; leave it just as it is. And now we have put in his place Mr. Odell, another Rough Rider, I suppose; all the fat things go to that profession now. Why, I could have been a Rough Rider myself if I had known that this political Klondike was going to open up, and I would have been a Rough Rider if I could have gone to war on an automobile— but not on a horse! No, I know the horse too well; I have known the horse in war and in peace, and there is no place where a horse is comfortable. The horse has too many caprices, and he is too much given to initiative. He invents too many new ideas. No, I don't want anything to do with a horse.

And then we have taken Chauncey Depew out of a useful and active life and made him a Senator

—embalmed him, corked him up. And I am not grieving. That man has said many a true thing about me in his time, and I always said something would happen to him. Look at that [pointing to Mr. Depew] gilded mummy! He has made my life a sorrow to me at many a banquet on both sides of the ocean, and now he has got it. Perish the hand that pulls that cork!

All these things have happened, all these things have come to pass, while I have been away, and it just shows how little a Mugwump can be missed in a cold, unfeeling world, even when he is the last one that is left—a GRAND OLD PARTY all by himself. And there is another thing that has happened, perhaps the most imposing event of them all: the institution called the Daughters of the Crown—the Daughters of the Royal Crown —has established itself and gone into business. Now, there's an American idea for you; there's an idea born of God knows what kind of specialized insanity, but not softening of the brain—you cannot soften a thing that doesn't exist—the Daughters of the Royal Crown! Nobody eligible but American descendants of Charles II. Dear me, how the fancy product of that old harem still holds out!

Well, I am truly glad to foregather with you again, and partake of the bread and salt of this hospitable house once more. Seven years ago, when I was your guest here, when I was old and despondent, you gave me the grip and the word that lift a man up and make him glad to be alive; and now I come back from my exile young again, fresh and alive, and ready to begin life once more, and your welcome puts the finishing touch upon my restored youth and makes it real to me, and not a gracious dream that must vanish with the morning. I thank you.

AN UNDELIVERED SPEECH

The steamship St. Paul *was to have been launched from Cramp's shipyard in Philadelphia on March 25, 1895. After the launching a luncheon was to nave been given, at which Mr. Clemens was to make a speech. Just before the final word was given a reporter asked Mr. Clemens for a copy of his speech to be delivered at the luncheon. To facilitate the work of the reporter he loaned him a typewritten copy of the speech. It happened, however, that when the blocks were knocked away the big ship refused to budge, and no amount of labor could move her an inch. She had stuck fast upon the ways. As a result, the launching was postponed for a week or two; but in the mean time Mr. Clemens had gone to Europe. Years after a reporter called on Mr. Clemens and submitted the manuscript of the speech, which was as follows:*

DAY after to-morrow I sail for England in a ship of this line, the *Paris*. It will be my fourteenth crossing in three years and a half. Therefore, my presence here, as you see, is quite natural, quite commercial. I am interested in ships. They interest me more now than hotels do. When a new ship is launched I feel a desire to go and see if she will be good quarters for me to live in, particularly if she belongs to this line, for it is by this line that I have done most of my ferrying.

People wonder why I go so much. Well, I go partly for my health, partly to familiarize myself with the road. I have gone over the same road so many times now that I know all the whales that belong along the route, and latterly it is an embarrassment to me to meet them, for they do not look glad to see me, but annoyed, and they seem to say: "Here is this old derelict again."

Earlier in life this would have pained me and made me ashamed, but I am older now, and when I am behaving myself, and doing right, I do not care for a whale's opinion about me. When we are young we generally estimate an opinion by the size of the person that holds it, but later we find that that is an uncertain rule, for we realize that there are times when a hornet's opinion disturbs us more than an emperor's.

I do not mean that I care nothing at all for a whale's opinion, for that would be going to too great a length. Of course, it is better to have the good opinion of a whale than his disapproval; but my position is that if you cannot have a whale's good opinion, except at some sacrifice of principle or personal dignity, it is better to try to live without it. That is my idea about whales.

Yes, I have gone over that same route so often that I know my way without a compass, just by the waves. I know all the large waves and a good many of the small ones. Also the sunsets. I know every sunset and where it belongs just by its color. Necessarily, then, I do not make the passage now for scenery. That is all gone by.

What I prize most is safety, and in the second place swift transit and handiness. These are best furnished by the American line, whose watertight compartments have no passage through them, no doors to be left open, and consequently no way for water to get from one of them to another in time of collision. If you nullify the peril which collisions threaten you with, you nullify the only very serious peril which attends voyages in the great liners of our day, and makes voyaging safer than staying at home.

When the *Paris* was half-torn to pieces some years ago, enough of the Atlantic ebbed and flowed through one end of her, during her long agony, to sink the fleets of the world if distributed among them; but she floated in perfect safety, and no life was lost. In time of collision the rock of Gibraltar is not safer than the *Paris* and other great ships of this line. This seems to be the only great line in the world that takes a passenger from metropolis to metropolis without the intervention of tugs and barges or bridges—takes him through without breaking bulk, so to speak.

On the English side he lands at a dock; on the dock a special train is waiting; in an hour and three-quarters he is in London. Nothing could be handier. If your journey were from a sand-pit on our side to a lighthouse on the other, you could make it quicker by other lines, but that is not the case. The journey is from the city of New York to the city of London, and no line can do that journey quicker than this one, nor anywhere near as conveniently and handily. And when the passenger lands on our side he lands on the American side of the river, not in the provinces. As a very learned man said on the last voyage (he is head quartermaster of the New York land garboard streak of the middle watch): "When we land a passenger on the American side there's nothing betwix him and his hotel but hell and the hackman."

I am glad, with you and the nation, to welcome the new ship. She is another pride, another consolation, for a great country whose mighty fleets have all vanished, and which has almost forgotten what it is to fly its flag to sea. I am not sure as to which St. Paul she is named for. Some think it is the one that is on the upper Mississippi, but the head quartermaster told me it was the one that killed Goliath. But it is not important. No matter which it is, let us give her hearty welcome and godspeed.

SIXTY-SEVENTH BIRTHDAY

At the Metropolitan Club, New York,
November 28, 1902

*Address at a dinner given in honor of Mr. Clemens
by Colonel Harvey, President of Harper & Brothers.*

I THINK I ought to be allowed to talk as long as
I want to, for the reason that I have can-
celled all my winter's engagements of every kind,
for good and sufficient reasons, and am making
no new engagements for this winter, and, therefore, this is the only chance I shall have to dis-
embowel my skull for a year—close the mouth in
that portrait for a year. I want to offer thanks
and homage to the chairman for this innovation
which he has introduced here, which is an improvement, as I consider it, on the old-fashioned
style of conducting occasions like this. That was
bad—that was a bad, bad, bad arrangement.
Under that old custom the chairman got up and
made a speech, he introduced the prisoner at the
bar, and covered him all over with compliments,
nothing but compliments, not a thing but compliments, never a slur, and sat down and left that

man to get up and talk without a text. You cannot talk on compliments; that is not a text. No modest person, and I was born one, can talk on compliments. A man gets up and is filled to the eyes with happy emotions, but his tongue is tied; he has nothing to say; he is in the condition of Doctor Rice's friend who came home drunk and explained it to his wife, and his wife said to him, "John, when you have drunk all the whiskey you want, you ought to ask for sarsaparilla." He said, "Yes, but when I have drunk all the whiskey I want I can't say sarsaparilla." And so I think it is much better to leave a man unmolested until the testimony and pleadings are all in. Otherwise he is dumb—he is at the sarsaparilla stage.

Before I get to the higgledy-piggledy point, as Mr. Howells suggested I do, I want to thank you, gentlemen, for this very high honor you are doing me, and I am quite competent to estimate it at its value. I see around me captains of all the illustrious industries, most distinguished men; there are more than fifty here, and I believe I know thirty-nine of them well. I could probably borrow money from—from the others, anyway. It is a proud thing to me, indeed, to see such a distinguished company gather here on such an occasion as this, when there is no foreign prince to be fêted—when you have come here not to do honor to hereditary privilege and ancient lineage, but to do reverence to mere moral excellence and elemental veracity—and, dear me, how old it seems to make me! I look around me and I see three or four persons I have known so many, many years. I have known Mr. Secretary Hay—John Hay, as the nation and the rest of his friends love to call him—I have known John Hay and Tom Reed and the Reverend Twichell close upon thirty-six years. Close upon thirty-six years I have known those venerable men. I have known Mr. Howells nearly thirty-four years, and I knew Chauncey Depew before he could walk straight, and before he learned to tell the truth. Twenty-seven years ago I heard him make the most noble and eloquent and beautiful speech that has ever fallen from even his capable lips. Tom Reed said that my principal defect was inaccuracy of statement. Well, suppose that that is true. What's the use of telling the truth all the time? I never tell the truth about Tom Reed—but that is his defect, truth; he speaks the truth always. Tom Reed has a good heart, and he has a good intellect, but he hasn't any judgment. Why, when Tom Reed was invited to lecture to the Ladies' Society for the Procreation or Procrastination, or something, of morals, I don't know what it was—advancement, I suppose, of pure morals—he had the immortal indiscretion to begin by saying that some of us can't be optimists, but by judiciously utilizing the opportunities that Providence puts in our way we can all be bigamists. You perceive his limitations. Anything he has in his mind he states, if he thinks it is true. Well, that was true, but that was no place to say it—so they fired him out.

A lot of accounts have been settled here to-night for me; I have held grudges against some of these people, but they have all been wiped out by the very handsome compliments that have been paid me. Even Wayne MacVeagh—I have had a grudge against him many years. The first time I saw Wayne MacVeagh was at a private dinner-party at Charles A. Dana's, and when I got there he was clattering along, and I tried to get a word in here and there; but you know what Wayne MacVeagh is when he is started, and I could not get in five words to his one—or one word to his five. I struggled along and struggled along, and—well, I wanted to tell and I was trying to tell a dream I had had the night before, and it was a remarkable dream, a dream worth people's while to listen to, a dream recounting Sam Jones the revivalist's reception in heaven. I was on a train, and was approaching the celestial way-station— I had a through ticket—and I noticed a man sitting alongside of me asleep, and he had his ticket in his hat. He was the remains of the Archbishop of Canterbury; I recognized him by his photograph. I had nothing against him, so I took his ticket and let him have mine. He didn't object—he wasn't in a condition to object—and

366

presently when the train stopped at the heavenly station—well, I got off, and he went on by request —but there they all were, the angels, you know, millions of them, every one with a torch; they had arranged for a torch-light procession; they were expecting the Archbishop, and when I got off they started to raise a shout, but it didn't materialize. I don't know whether they were disappointed. I suppose they had a lot of superstitious ideas about the Archbishop and what he should look like, and I didn't fill the bill, and I was trying to explain to Saint Peter, and was doing it in the German tongue, because I didn't want to be too explicit. Well, I found it was no use, I couldn't get along, for Wayne MacVeagh was occupying the whole place, and I said to Mr. Dana, "What is the matter with that man? Who is that man with the long tongue? What's the trouble with him, that long, lank cadaver, old oil-derrick out of a job—who is that?" "Well, now," Mr. Dana said, "you don't want to meddle with him; you had better keep quiet; just keep quiet, because that's a bad man. Talk! He was born to talk. Don't let him get out with you; he'll skin you." I said, "I have been skinned, skinned, and skinned for years, there is nothing left." He said, "Oh, you'll find there is; that man is the very seed and inspiration of that proverb which says, 'No matter how close you skin an onion, a clever man can always peel it again.'" Well, I reflected and

I quieted down. That would never occur to Tom Reed. He's got no discretion. Well, MacVeagh is just the same man; he hasn't changed a bit in all those years; he has been peeling Mr. Mitchell lately. That's the kind of man he is.

Mr. Howells—that poem of his is admirable; that's the way to treat a person. Howells has a peculiar gift for seeing the merits of people, and he has always exhibited them in my favor. Howells has never written anything about me that I couldn't read six or seven times a day; he is always just and always fair; he has written more appreciatively of me than any one in this world, and published it in the *North American Review*. He did me the justice to say that my intentions—he italicized that—that my intentions were always good, that I wounded people's conventions rather than their convictions. Now, I wouldn't want anything handsomer than that said of me. I would rather wait, with anything harsh I might have to say, till the convictions become conventions. Bangs has traced me all the way down. He can't find that honest man, but I will look for him in the looking-glass when I get home. It was intimated by the Colonel that it is New England that makes New York and builds up this country and makes it great, overlooking the fact that there's a lot of people here who came from elsewhere, like John Hay from away out West, and Howells from Ohio, and St.

SIXTY-SEVENTH BIRTHDAY

Clair McKelway and me from Missouri, and we are doing what we can to build up New York a little—elevate it. Why, when I was living in that village of Hannibal, Missouri, on the banks of the Mississippi, and Hay up in the town of Warsaw, also on the banks of the Mississippi River— it is an emotional bit of the Mississippi, and when it is low water you have to climb up to it on a ladder, and when it floods you have to hunt for it with a deep-sea lead—but it is a great and beautiful country. In that old time it was a paradise for simplicity—it was a simple, simple life, cheap but comfortable, and full of sweetness, and there was nothing of this rage of modern civilization there at all. It was a delectable land. I went out there last June, and I met in that town of Hannibal a schoolmate of mine, John Briggs, whom I had not seen for more than fifty years. I tell you, that was a meeting! That pal whom I had known as a little boy long ago, and knew now as a stately man three or four inches over six feet and browned by exposure to many climes, he was back there to see that old place again. We spent a whole afternoon going about here and there and yonder, and hunting up the scenes and talking of the crimes which we had committed so long ago. It was a heartbreaking delight, full of pathos, laughter, and tears, all mixed together; and we called the roll of the boys and girls that we picnicked and sweethearted with so many years ago, and there were hardly half a dozen of them left; the rest were in their graves; and we went up there on the summit of that hill, a treasured place in my memory, the summit of Holiday's Hill, and looked out again over that magnificent panorama of the Mississippi River, sweeping along league after league, a level green paradise on one side, and retreating capes and promontories as far as you could see on the other, fading away in the soft, rich lights of the remote distance. I recognized then that I was seeing now the most enchanting river view the planet could furnish. I never knew it when I was a boy; it took an educated eye that had travelled over the globe to know and appreciate it; and John said, "Can you point out the place where Bear Creek used to be before the railroad came?" I said, "Yes, it ran along yonder." "And can you point out the swimming-hole?" "Yes, out there." And he said, "Can you point out the place where we stole the skiff?" Well, I didn't know which one he meant. Such a wilderness of events had intervened since that day, more than fifty years ago, it took me more than five minutes to call back that little incident, and then I did call it back; it was a white skiff, and we painted it red to allay suspicion. And the saddest, saddest man came along—a stranger he was —and he looked that red skiff over so pathetically, and he said: "Well, if it weren't for the complexion I'd know whose skiff that was." He said it in that pleading way, you know, that appeals for sympathy and suggestion; we were full of sympathy for him, but we weren't in any condition to offer suggestions. I can see him yet as he turned away with that same sad look on his face and vanished out of history forever. I wonder what became of that man. I know what became of the skiff. Well, it was a beautiful life, a lovely life. There was no crime. Merely little things like pillaging orchards and watermelon-patches and breaking the Sabbath—we didn't break the Sabbath often enough to signify—once a week perhaps. But we were good boys, good Presbyterian boys, all Presbyterian boys, and loyal and all that; anyway, we were good Presbyterian boys when the weather was doubtful; when it was fair, we did wander a little from the fold.

Look at John Hay and me. There we were in obscurity, and look where we are now. Consider the ladder which he has climbed, the illustrious vocations he has served—and vocations is the right word; he has in all those vocations acquitted himself with high credit and honor to his country and to the mother that bore him. Scholar, soldier, diplomat, poet, historian—now, see where we are. He is Secretary of State and I am a gentleman. It could not happen in any other country. Our institutions give men the positions that of right belong to them through merit; all you men have won your places, not by heredities, and not by family influence or extraneous help, but only by the natural gifts God gave you at your birth, made effective by your own energies; this is the country to live in.

Now, there is one invisible guest here. A part of me is present; the larger part, the better part, is yonder at her home; that is my wife, and she has a good many personal friends here, and I think it won't distress any one of them to know that, although she is going to be confined to that bed for many months to come from that nervous prostration, there is not any danger and she is coming along very well—and I think it quite appropriate that I should speak of her. I knew her for the first time just in the same year that I first knew John Hay and Tom Reed and Mr. Twichell—thirty-six years ago—and she has been the best friend I have ever had, and that is saying a good deal; she has reared me—she and Twichell together—and what I am I owe to them. Twichell —why, it is such a pleasure to look upon Twichell's face! For five-and-twenty years I was under the Rev. Mr. Twichell's tuition, I was in his pastorate, occupying a pew in his church, and held him in due reverence. That man is full of all the graces that go to make a person companionable and be- loved; and wherever Twichell goes to start a church the people flock there to buy the land; they find real estate goes up all around the spot, and the envious and the thoughtful always try to get Twichell to move to their neighborhood and start a church; and wherever you see him go you can go and buy land there with confidence, feeling sure that there will be a double price for you before very long. I am not saying this to flatter Mr. Twichell; it is the fact. Many and many a time I have attended the annual sale in his church, and bought up all the pews on a margin—and it would have been better for me spiritually and financially if I had stayed under his wing.

I have tried to do good in this world, and it is marvellous in how many different ways I have done good, and it is comfortable to reflect—now, there's Mr. Rogers—just out of the affection I bear that man many a time I have given him points in finance that he had never thought of— and if he could lay aside envy, prejudice, and superstition, and utilize those ideas in his business, it would make a difference in his bank account.

Well, I like the poetry. I like all the speeches and the poetry, too. I liked Doctor Van Dyke's poem. I wish I could return thanks in proper measure to you, gentlemen, who have spoken and violated your feelings to pay me compliments; some were merited and some you overlooked, it is true; and Colonel Harvey did slander every one of you, and put things into my mouth that I never said, never thought of at all.

And now, my wife and I, out of our single heart, return you our deepest and most grateful thanks, and—yesterday was her birthday.

TO THE WHITEFRIARS

ADDRESS AT THE DINNER GIVEN BY THE WHITE-
FRIARS CLUB IN HONOR OF MR. CLEMENS,
LONDON, JUNE 20, 1899

*The Whitefriars Club was founded by Dr. Samuel
Johnson, and Mr. Clemens was made an honorary
member in 1874. The members are representative of
literary and journalistic London. The toast of "Our
Guest" was proposed by Louis F. Austin, of the* Illustrated London News, *and in the course of some humorous remarks he referred to the vow and to the imagi-
nary woes of the "Friars," as the members of the club
style themselves.*

MR. CHAIRMAN AND BRETHREN OF THE
VOW—in whatever the vow is; for although
I have been a member of this club for five-and-
twenty years, I don't know any more about what
that vow is than Mr. Austin seems to. But whatever the vow is, I don't care what it is. I have
made a thousand vows.

There is no pleasure comparable to making a
vow in the presence of one who appreciates that
vow, in the presence of men who honor and ap-

preciate you for making the vow, and men who admire you for making the vow.

There is only one pleasure higher than that, and that is to get outside and break the vow. A vow is always a pledge of some kind or other for the protection of your own morals and principles or somebody else's, and generally, by the irony of fate, it is for the protection of your own morals.

Hence we have pledges that make us eschew tobacco or wine, and while you are taking the pledge there is a holy influence about that makes you feel you are reformed, and that you can never be so happy again in this world until—you get outside and take a drink.

I had forgotten that I was a member of this club — it is so long ago. But now I remember that I was here five-and-twenty years ago, and that I was then at a dinner of the Whitefriars Club, and it was in those old days when you had just made two great finds. All London was talking about nothing else than that they had found Livingstone, and that the lost Sir Roger Tichborne had been found—and they were trying him for it.

And at the dinner, Chairman —— (I do not know who he was) — failed to come to time. The gentleman who had been appointed to pay me the customary compliments and to introduce me forgot the compliments, and did not know what they were.

And George Augustus Sala came in at the last moment, just when I was about to go without compliments altogether. And that man was a gifted man. They just called on him instantaneously, while he was going to sit down, to introduce the stranger, and Sala made one of those marvellous speeches which he was capable of making. I think no man talked so fast as Sala did. One did not need wine while he was making a speech. The rapidity of his utterance made a man drunk in a minute. An incomparable speech was that, an impromptu speech, and an impromptu speech is a seldom thing, and he did it so well.

He went into the whole history of the United States, and made it entirely new to me. He filled it with episodes and incidents that Washington never heard of, and he did it so convincingly that although I knew none of it had happened, from that day to this I do not know any history but Sala's.

I do not know anything so sad as a dinner where you are going to get up and say something by-and-by, and you do not know what it is. You sit and wonder and wonder what the gentleman is going to say who is going to introduce you. You know that if he says something severe, that if he will deride you, or traduce you, or do anything of that kind, he will furnish you with a text, because anybody can get up and talk against that.

Anybody can get up and straighten out his character. But when a gentleman gets up and merely tells the truth about you, what can you do?

Mr. Austin has done well. He has supplied so many texts that I will have to drop out a lot of them, and that is about as difficult as when you do not have any text at all. Now, he made a beautiful and smooth speech without any difficulty at all, and I could have done that if I had gone on with the schooling with which I began. I see here a gentleman on my left who was my master in the art of oratory more than twenty-five years ago.

When I look upon the inspiring face of Mr. Depew, it carries me a long way back. An old and valued friend of mine is he, and I saw his career as it came along, and it has reached pretty well up to now, when he, by another miscarriage of justice, is a United States Senator. But those were delightful days when I was taking lessons in oratory.

My other master—the Ambassador—is not here yet. Under those two gentlemen I learned to make after-dinner speeches, and it was charming.

You know the New England dinner is the great occasion on the other side of the water. It is held every year to celebrate the landing of the Pilgrims. Those Pilgrims were a lot of people who were not needed in England, and you know

378

they had great rivalry, and they were persuaded to go elsewhere, and they chartered a ship called *Mayflower* and set sail, and I have heard it said that they pumped the Atlantic Ocean through that ship sixteen times.

They fell in over there with the Dutch from Rotterdam, Amsterdam, and a lot of other places with profane names, and it is from that gang that Mr. Depew is descended.

On the other hand, Mr. Choate is descended from those Puritans who landed on a bitter night in December. Every year those people used to meet at a great banquet in New York, and those masters of mind in oratory had to make speeches. It was Doctor Depew's business to get up there and apologize for the Dutch, and Mr. Choate had to get up later and explain the crimes of the Puritans, and grand, beautiful times we used to have.

It is curious that after that long lapse of time I meet the Whitefriars again, some looking as young and fresh as in the old days, others showing a certain amount of wear and tear, and here, after all this time, I find one of the masters of oratory and the others named in the list.

And here we three meet again as exiles on one pretext or another, and you will notice that while we are absent there is a pleasing tranquillity in America—a building up of public confidence. We are doing the best we can for our country. I think we have spent our lives in serving our country, and we never serve it to greater advantage than when we get out of it.

But impromptu speaking—that is what I was trying to learn. That is a difficult thing. I used to do it in this way. I used to begin about a week ahead, and write out my impromptu speech and get it by heart. Then I brought it to the New England dinner printed on a piece of paper in my pocket, so that I could pass it to the reporters all cut and dried, and in order to do an impromptu speech as it should be done you have to indicate the places for pauses and hesitations. I put them all in it. And then you want the applause in the right places.

When I got to the place where it should come in, if it did not come in I did not care, but I had it marked in the paper. And these masters of mind used to wonder why it was my speech came out in the morning in the first person, while theirs went through the butchery of synopsis.

I do that kind of speech (I mean an offhand speech), and do it well, and make no mistake in such a way to deceive the audience completely and make that audience believe it is an impromptu speech—that is art.

I was frightened out of it at last by an experience of Doctor Hayes. He was a sort of Nansen of that day. He had been to the North

Pole, and it made him celebrated. He had even seen the polar bear climb the pole.

He had made one of those magnificent voyages such as Nansen made, and in those days when a man did anything which greatly distinguished him for the moment he had to come on to the lecture platform and tell all about it.

Doctor Hayes was a great, magnificent creature like Nansen, superbly built. He was to appear in Boston. He wrote his lecture out, and it was his purpose to read it from manuscript; but in an evil hour he concluded that it would be a good thing to preface it with something rather handsome, poetical, and beautiful that he could get off by heart and deliver as if it were the thought of the moment.

He had not had my experience, and could not do that. He came on the platform, held his manuscript down, and began with a beautiful piece of oratory. He spoke something like this:

"When a lonely human being, a pigmy in the midst of the architecture of nature, stands solitary on those icy waters and looks abroad to the horizon and sees mighty castles and temples of eternal ice raising up their pinnacles tipped by the pencil of the departing sun—"

Here a man came across the platform and touched him on the shoulder, and said: "One minute." And then to the audience:

"Is Mrs. John Smith in the house? Her husband has slipped on the ice and broken his leg."

And you could see the Mrs. John Smiths get up everywhere and drift out of the house, and it made great gaps everywhere. Then Doctor Hayes began again: "When a lonely man, a pigmy in the architecture—" The janitor came in again and shouted: "It is not Mrs. John Smith! It is Mrs. John Jones!"

Then all the Mrs. Jones got up and left. Once more the speaker started, and was in the midst of the sentence when he was interrupted again, and the result was that the lecture was not delivered. But the lecturer interviewed the janitor afterward in a private room, and of the fragments of the janitor they took "twelve basketsful."

Now, I don't want to sit down just in this way. I have been talking with so much levity that I have said no serious thing, and you are really no better or wiser, although Robert Buchanan has suggested that I am a person who deals in wisdom. I have said nothing which would make you better than when you came here.

I should be sorry to sit down without having said one serious word which you can carry home and relate to your children and the old people who are not able to get away.

And this is just a little maxim which has saved me from many a difficulty and many a disaster, and in times of tribulation and uncertainty has come to my rescue, as it shall to yours if you observe it as I do day and night.

I always use it in an emergency, and you can take it home as a legacy from me, and it is: "When in doubt, tell the truth."

THE ASCOT GOLD CUP

The news of Mr. Clemens's arrival in England in June, 1907, was announced in the papers with big headlines. Immediately following the announcement was the news—also with big headlines—that the Ascot Gold Cup had been stolen the same day. The combination, MARK TWAIN ARRIVES—ASCOT CUP STOLEN, amused the public. The Lord Mayor of London gave a banquet at the Mansion House in honor of Mr. Clemens.

I DO assure you that I am not so dishonest as I look. I have been so busy trying to rehabilitate my honor about that Ascot Cup that I have had no time to prepare a speech.

I was not so honest in former days as I am now, but I have always been reasonably honest. Well, you know how a man is influenced by his surroundings. Once upon a time I went to a public meeting where the oratory of a charitable worker so worked on my feelings that, in common with others, I would have dropped something substantial in the hat—if it had come round at that moment.

The speaker had the power of putting those

vivid pictures before one. We were all affected. That was the moment for the hat. I would have put two hundred dollars in. Before he had finished I could have put in four hundred dollars. I felt I could have filled up a blank check—with somebody else's name—and dropped it in.

Well, now, another speaker got up, and in fifteen minutes damped my spirit; and during the speech of the third speaker all my enthusiasm went away. When at last the hat came round I dropped in ten cents—and took out twenty-five.

I came over here to get the honorary degree from Oxford, and I would have encompassed the seven seas for an honor like that — the greatest honor that has ever fallen to my share. I am grateful to Oxford for conferring that honor upon me, and I am sure my country appreciates it, because first and foremost it is an honor to my country.

And now I am going home again across the sea. I am in spirit young but in the flesh old, so that it is unlikely that when I go away I shall ever see England again. But I shall go with the recollection of the generous and kindly welcome I have had.

I suppose I must say "Good-bye." I say it not with my lips only, but from the heart.

THE SAVAGE CLUB DINNER

A portrait of Mr. Clemens, signed by all the members of the club attending the dinner, was presented to him, July 6, 1907, and in submitting the toast " The Health of Mark Twain" Mr. J. Scott Stokes recalled the fact that he had read parts of Doctor Clemens's works to Harold Frederic during Frederic's last illness.

MR. CHAIRMAN AND FELLOW-SAVAGES, —I am very glad indeed to have that portrait. I think it is the best one that I have ever had, and there have been opportunities before to get a good photograph. I have sat to photographers twenty-two times to-day. Those sittings added to those that have preceded them since I have been in Europe—if we average at that rate—must have numbered one hundred to two hundred sittings. Out of all those there ought to be some good photographs. This is the best I have had, and I am glad to have your honored names on it. I did not know Harold Frederic personally, but I have heard a great deal about him, and nothing that was not pleasant and nothing except such things as lead a man to honor another man and to love him. I consider that it is a misfortune of mine that I have never had the luck to meet him, and if any book of mine read to him in his last hours made those hours easier for him and more comfortable, I am very glad and proud of that. I call to mind such a case many years ago of an English authoress, well known in her day, who wrote such beautiful child tales, touching and lovely in every possible way. In a little biographical sketch of her I found that her last hours were spent partly in reading a book of mine, until she was no longer able to read. That has always remained in my mind, and I have always cherished it as one of the good things of my life. I had read what she had written, and had loved her for what she had done.

Stanley apparently carried a book of mine feloniously away to Africa, and I have not a doubt that it had a noble and uplifting influence there in the wilds of Africa—because on his previous journeys he never carried anything to read except Shakespeare and the Bible. I did not know of that circumstance. I did not know that he had carried a book of mine. I only noticed that when he came back he was a reformed man. I knew Stanley very well in those old days. Stanley was the first man who ever reported a lecture of mine, and that was in St. Louis. When I was down there the next time to give the same lecture I was told to give them something fresh, as they had read that in the papers. I met

Stanley here when he came back from that first expedition of his which closed with the finding of Livingstone. You remember how he would break out at the meetings of the British Association, and find fault with what people said, because Stanley had notions of his own, and could not contain them. They had to come out or break him up—and so he would go round and address geographical societies. He was always on the warpath in those days, and people always had to have Stanley contradicting their geography for them and improving it. But he always came back and sat drinking beer with me in the hotel up to two in the morning, and he was then one of the most civilized human beings that ever was.

I saw in a newspaper this evening a reference to an interview which appeared in one of the papers the other day, in which the interviewer said that I characterized Mr. Birrell's speech the other day at the Pilgrims' Club as "bully." Now, if you will excuse me, I never use slang to an interviewer or anybody else. That distresses me. Whatever I said about Mr. Birrell's speech was said in English, as good English as anybody uses. If I could not describe Mr. Birrell's delightful speech without using slang I would not describe it at all. I would close my mouth and keep it closed, much as it would discomfort me.

Now that comes of interviewing a man in the first person, which is an altogether wrong way to interview him. It is entirely wrong because none of you, I, or anybody else, could interview a man —could listen to a man talking any length of time and then go off and reproduce that talk in the first person. It can't be done. What results is merely that the interviewer gives the substance of what is said and puts it in his own language and puts it in your mouth. It will always be either better language than you use or worse, and in my case it is always worse. I have a great respect for the English language. I am one of its supporters, its promoters, its elevators. I don't degrade it. A slip of the tongue would be the most that you would get from me. I have always tried hard and faithfully to improve my English and never to degrade it. I always try to use the best English to describe what I think and what I feel, or what I don't feel and what I don't think.

I am not one of those who in expressing opinions confine themselves to facts. I don't know anything that mars good literature so completely as too much truth. Facts contain a deal of poetry, but you can't use too many of them without damaging your literature. I love all literature, and as long as I am a doctor of literature—I have suggested to you for twenty years I have been diligently trying to improve my own literature, and now, by virtue of the University of Oxford, I mean to doctor everybody else's.

26   389

Now I think I ought to apologize for my clothes. At home I venture things that I am not permitted by my family to venture in foreign parts. I was instructed before I left home and ordered to refrain from white clothes in England. I meant to keep that command fair and clean, and I would have done it if I had been in the habit of obeying instructions, but I can't invent a new process in life right away. I have not had white clothes on since I crossed the ocean until now.

In these three or four weeks I have grown so tired of gray and black that you have earned my gratitude in permitting me to come as I have. I wear white clothes in the depth of winter in my home, but I don't go out in the streets in them. I don't go out to attract too much attention. I like to attract some, and always I would like to be dressed so that I may be more conspicuous than anybody else.

If I had been an ancient Briton, I would not have contented myself with blue paint, but I would have bankrupted the rainbow. I so enjoy gay clothes in which women clothe themselves that it always grieves me when I go to the opera to see that, while women look like a flower-bed, the men are a few gray stumps among them in their black evening dress. These are two or three reasons why I wish to wear white clothes. When I find myself in assemblies like this, with everybody in black clothes, I know I possess something that is superior to everybody else's. Clothes are never clean. You don't know whether they are clean or not, because you can't see.

Here or anywhere you must scour your head every two or three days or it is full of grit. Your clothes must collect just as much dirt as your hair. If you wear white clothes you are clean, and your cleaning bill gets so heavy that you have to take care. I am proud to say that I can wear a white suit of clothes without a blemish for three days. If you need any further instruction in the matter of clothes I shall be glad to give it to you. I hope I have convinced some of you that it is just as well to wear white clothes as any other kind. I do not want to boast. I only want to make you understand that you are not clean.

As to age, the fact that I am nearly seventy-two years old does not clearly indicate how old I am, because part of every day—it is with me as with you—you try to describe your age, and you cannot do it. Sometimes you are only fifteen; sometimes you are twenty-five. It is very seldom in a day that I am seventy-two years old. I am older now sometimes than I was when I used to rob orchards; a thing which I would not do to-day — if the orchards were watched. I am so glad to be here to-night. I am so glad to renew with the Savages that now ancient time when I first sat with a company of this club in London in 1872. That is a long time ago. But I did stay with the Savages a night in London long ago, and as I had come into a very strange land, and was with friends, as I could see, that has always remained in my mind as a peculiarly blessed evening, since it brought me into contact with men of my own kind and my own feelings.

I am glad to be here, and to see you all again, because it is very likely that I shall not see you again. It is easier than I thought to come across the Atlantic. I have been received, as you know, in the most delightfully generous way in England ever since I came here. It keeps me choked up all the time. Everybody is so generous, and they do seem to give you such a hearty welcome. Nobody in the world can appreciate it higher than I do. It did not wait till I got to London, but when I came ashore at Tilbury the stevedores on the dock raised the first welcome—a good and hearty welcome from the men who do the heavy labor in the world, and save you and me having to do it. They are the men who with their hands build empires and make them prosper. It is because of them that the others are wealthy and can live in luxury. They received me with a "Hurrah!" that went to my heart. They are the men that build civilization, and without them no civilization can be built. So I came first to the authors and creators of civilization, and I blessedly end this happy meeting with the Savages who destroy it.

GENERAL MILES AND THE DOG

Mr. Clemens was the guest of honor at a dinner given by the Pleiades Club at the Hotel Brevoort, December 22, 1907. The toastmaster introduced the guest of the evening with a high tribute to his place in American literature, saying that he was dear to the hearts of all Americans.

IT is hard work to make a speech when you have listened to compliments from the powers in authority. A compliment is a hard text to preach to. When the chairman introduces me as a person of merit, and when he says pleasant things about me, I always feel like answering simply that what he says is true; that it is all right; that, as far as I am concerned, the things he said can stand as they are. But you always have to say something, and that is what frightens me.

I remember out in Sydney once having to respond to some complimentary toast, and my one desire was to turn in my tracks like any other worm—and run for it. I was remembering that occasion at a later date when I had to introduce a speaker. Hoping, then, to spur his speech by putting him, in joke, on the defensive, I accused him in my introduction of everything I thought it impossible for him to have committed. When I finished there was an awful calm. I had been telling his life history by mistake.

One must keep up one's character. Earn a character first if you can, and if you can't, then assume one. From the code of morals I have been following and revising and revising for seventy-two years I remember one detail. All my life I have been honest—comparatively honest. I could never use money I had not made honestly —I could only lend it.

Last spring I met General Miles again, and he commented on the fact that we had known each other thirty years. He said it was strange that we had not met years before, when we had both been in Washington. At that point I changed the subject, and I changed it with art. But the facts are these:

I was then under contract for my *Innocents Abroad*, but did not have a cent to live on while I wrote it. So I went to Washington to do a little journalism. There I met an equally poor friend, William Davidson, who had not a single vice, unless you call it a vice in a Scot to love Scotch. Together we devised the first and original newspaper syndicate, selling two letters a week to twelve newspapers and getting $1 a letter. That $24 a week would have been enough for us—if we had not had to support the jug.

GENERAL MILES AND THE DOG

But there was a day when we felt that we must have $3 right away—$3 at once. That was how I met the General. It doesn't matter now what we wanted so much money at one time for, but that Scot and I did occasionally want it. The Scot sent me out one day to get it. He had a great belief in Providence, that Scottish friend of mine. He said: "The Lord will provide."

I had given up trying to find the money lying about, and was in a hotel lobby in despair, when I saw a beautiful unfriended dog. The dog saw me, too, and at once we became acquainted. Then General Miles came in, admired the dog, and asked me to price it. I priced it at $3. He offered me an opportunity to reconsider the value of the beautiful animal, but I refused to take more than Providence knew I needed. The General carried the dog to his room.

Then came in a sweet little middle-aged man, who at once began looking around the lobby.

"Did you lose a dog?" I asked. He said he had.

"I think I could find it," I volunteered, "for a small sum."

"'How much?'" he asked. And I told him $3.

He urged me to accept more, but I did not wish to outdo Providence. Then I went to the General's room and asked for the dog back. He was very angry, and wanted to know why I had sold him a dog that did not belong to me.

"That's a singular question to ask me, sir," I replied. "Didn't you ask me to sell him? You started it." And he let me have him. I gave him back his $3 and returned the dog, collect, to its owner. That second $3 I carried home to the Scot, and we enjoyed it, but the first $3, the money I got from the General, I would have had to lend.

The General seemed not to remember my part in that adventure, and I never had the heart to tell him about it.

WHEN IN DOUBT, TELL THE TRUTH

Mark Twain's speech at the dinner of the "Freund-schaft Society," March 9, 1906, had as a basis the words of introduction used by Toastmaster Frank, who, referring to Pudd'nhead Wilson, *used the phrase, "When in doubt, tell the truth."*

MR. CHAIRMAN, MR. PUTZEL, AND GEN-TLEMEN OF THE FREUNDSCHAFT,— That maxim I did invent, but never expected it to be applied to me. I did say, "When you are in doubt," but when I am in doubt myself I use more sagacity.

Mr. Grout suggested that if I have anything to say against Mr. Putzel, or any criticism of his career or his character, I am the last person to come out on account of that maxim and tell the truth. That is altogether a mistake.

I do think it is right for other people to be virtuous so that they can be happy hereafter, but if I knew every impropriety that even Mr. Putzel has committed in his life, I would not mention one of them. My judgment has been maturing for seventy years, and I have got to that point where I know better than that.

Mr. Putzel stands related to me in a very tender way (through the tax office), and it does not behoove me to say anything which could by any possibility militate against that condition of things.

Now, that word—taxes, taxes, taxes! I have heard it to-night. I have heard it all night. I wish somebody would change that subject; that is a very sore subject to me.

I was so relieved when Judge Leventritt did find something that was not taxable—when he said that the commissioner could not tax your patience. And that comforted me. We've got so much taxation. I don't know of a single foreign product that enters this country untaxed except the answer to prayer.

On an occasion like this the proprieties require that you merely pay compliments to the guest of the occasion, and I am merely here to pay compliments to the guest of the occasion, not to criticise him in any way, and I can say only complimentary things to him.

When I went down to the tax office some time ago, for the first time in New York, I saw Mr. Putzel sitting in the "Seat of Perjury." I recognized him right away. I warmed to him on the spot. I didn't know that I had ever seen him before, but just as soon as I saw him I recognized him. I had met him twenty-five years before, and at that time had achieved a knowledge of his abilities and something more than that.

WHEN IN DOUBT, TELL THE TRUTH

I thought: "Now, this is the man whom I saw twenty-five years ago." On that occasion I not only went free at his hands, but carried off something more than that. I hoped it would happen again.

It was twenty-five years ago when I saw a young clerk in Putnam's book-store. I went in there and asked for George Haven Putnam, and handed him my card, and then the young man said Mr. Putnam was busy and I couldn't see him. Well, I had merely called in a social way, and so it didn't matter.

I was going out when I saw a great big, fat, interesting-looking book lying there, and I took it up. It was an account of the invasion of England in the fourteenth century by the Preaching Friar, and it interested me.

I asked him the price of it, and he said four dollars.

"Well," I said, "what discount do you allow to publishers?"

He said: "Forty per cent. off."

I said: "All right, I am a publisher."

He put down the figure, forty per cent. off, on a card.

Then I said: "What discount do you allow to authors?"

He said: "Forty per cent. off."

"Well," I said, "set me down as an author."

"Now," said I, "what discount do you allow to the clergy?"

He said: "Forty per cent. off."

I said to him that I was only on the road, and that I was studying for the ministry. I asked him wouldn't he knock off twenty per cent. for that. He set down the figure, and he never smiled once.

I was working off these humorous brilliancies on him and getting no return—not a scintillation in his eye, not a spark of recognition of what I was doing there. I was almost in despair.

I thought I might try him once more, so I said: "Now, I am also a member of the human race. Will you let me have the ten per cent. off for that?" He set it down, and never smiled.

Well, I gave it up. I said: "There is my card with my address on it, but I have not any money with me. Will you please send the bill to Hartford?" I took up the book and was going away.

He said: "Wait a minute. There is forty cents coming to you."

When I met him in the tax office I thought maybe I could make something again, but I could not. But I had not any idea I could when I came, and as it turned out I did get off entirely free.

I put up my hand and made a statement. It gave me a good deal of pain to do that. I was not used to it. I was born and reared in the higher circles of Missouri, and there we don't do such things—didn't in my time, but we have got that little matter settled—got a sort of tax levied on me.

Then he touched me. Yes, he touched me this time, because he cried—cried! He was moved to tears to see that I, a virtuous person only a year before, after immersion for one year—during one year in the New York morals—had no more conscience than a millionaire.

THE DAY WE CELEBRATE

I NOTICED in Ambassador Choate's speech that he said: "You may be Americans or Englishmen, but you cannot be both at the same time." You responded by applause.

Consider the effect of a short residence here. I find the Ambassador rises first to speak to a toast, followed by a Senator, and I come third. What a subtle tribute that to monarchial influence of the country when you place rank above respectability!

I was born modest, and if I had not been things like this would force it upon me. I understand it quite well. I am here to see that between them they do justice to the day we celebrate, and in case they do not I must do it myself. But I notice they have considered this day merely from one side—its sentimental, patriotic, poetic side. But it has another side. It has a commercial, a business side that needs reforming. It has a historical side.

THE DAY WE CELEBRATE

I do not say "an" historical side, because I am speaking the American language. I do not see why our cousins should continue to say "an" hospital, "an" historical fact, "an" horse. It seems to me the Congress of Women, now in session, should look to it. I think "an" is having a little too much to do with it. It comes of habit, which accounts for many things.

Yesterday, for example, I was at a luncheon party. At the end of the party a great dignitary of the English Established Church went away half an hour before anybody else and carried off my hat. Now, that was an innocent act on his part. He went out first, and of course had the choice of hats. As a rule I try to get out first myself. But I hold that it was an innocent, unconscious act, due, perhaps, to heredity. He was thinking about ecclesiastical matters, and when a man is in that condition of mind he will take anybody's hat. The result was that the whole afternoon I was under the influence of his clerical hat and could not tell a lie. Of course, he was hard at it.

It is a compliment to both of us. His hat fitted me exactly; my hat fitted him exactly. So I judge I was born to rise to high dignity in the Church some how or other, but I do not know what he was born for. That is an illustration of the influence of habit, and it is perceptible here when they say "an" hospital, "an" European, "an" historical.

The business aspects of the Fourth of July is not perfect as it stands. See what it costs us every year with loss of life, the crippling of thousands with its fireworks, and the burning down of property. It is not only sacred to patriotism and universal freedom, but to the surgeon, the undertaker, the insurance offices—and they are working it for all it is worth.

I am pleased to see that we have a cessation of war for the time. This coming from me, a soldier, you will appreciate. I was a soldier in the Southern war for two weeks, and when gentlemen get up to speak of the great deeds our army and navy have recently done, why, it goes all through me and fires up the old war spirit. I had in my first engagement three horses shot under me. The next ones went over my head, the next hit me in the back. Then I retired to meet an engagement.

I thank you, gentlemen, for making even a slight reference to the war profession, in which I distinguished myself, short as my career was.

INDEPENDENCE DAY

The American Society in London gave a banquet, July 4, 1907, at the Hotel Cecil. Ambassador Choate called on Mr. Clemens to respond to the toast "The Day We Celebrate."

MR. CHAIRMAN, MY LORD, AND GEN- TLEMEN,—Once more it happens, as it has happened so often since I arrived in England a week or two ago, that instead of celebrating the Fourth of July properly as has been indicated, I have to first take care of my personal character.

Sir Mortimer Durand still remains unconvinced. Well, I tried to convince these people from the beginning that I did not take the Ascot Cup; and as I have failed to convince anybody that I did not take the cup, I might as well confess I did take it and be done with it. I don't see why this uncharitable feeling should follow me everywhere, and why I should have that crime thrown up to me on all occasions. The tears that I have wept over it ought to have created a different feeling than this—and, besides, I don't think it is very right or fair that, considering England has

27 405

been trying to take a cup of ours for forty years—
I don't see why they should take so much trouble
when I tried to go into the business myself.

Sir Mortimer Durand, too, has had trouble
from going to a dinner here, and he has told you
what he suffered in consequence. But what did
he suffer? He only missed his train and one
night of discomfort, and he remembers it to this
day. Oh! if you could only think what I have
suffered from a similar circumstance. Two or
three years ago, in New York, with that Society
there which is made up of people from all British
Colonies, and from Great Britain generally, who
were educated in British colleges and British
schools, I was there to respond to a toast of some
kind or other, and I did then what I have been in
the habit of doing, from a selfish motive, for a
long time, and that is, I got myself placed No. 3
in the list of speakers—then you get home early.

I had to go five miles up-river, and had to catch
a particular train or not get there. But see the
magnanimity which is born in me, which I have
cultivated all my life. A very famous and very
great British clergyman came to me presently,
and he said: "I am away down in the list; I have
got to catch a certain train this Saturday night;
if I don't catch that train I shall be carried beyond midnight and break the Sabbath. Won't
you change places with me?" I said: "Certainly
I will." I did it at once. Now, see what happened.

INDEPENDENCE DAY

Talk about Sir Mortimer Durand's sufferings for a single night! I have suffered ever since because I saved that gentleman from breaking the Sabbath—yes, saved him. I took his place, but I lost my train, and it was I who broke the Sabbath. Up to that time I never had broken the Sabbath in my life, and from that day to this I never have kept it.

Oh! I am learning much here to-night. I find I didn't know anything about the American Society—that is, I didn't know its chief virtue. I didn't know its chief virtue until his Excellency our Ambassador revealed it—I may say, exposed it. I was intending to go home on the 13th of this month, but I look upon that in a different light now. I am going to stay here until the American Society pays my passage.

Our Ambassador has spoken of our Fourth of July and the noise it makes. We have got a double Fourth of July—a daylight Fourth and a midnight Fourth. During the day in America, as our Ambassador has indicated, we keep the Fourth of July properly in a reverent spirit. We devote it to teaching our children patriotic things —reverence for the Declaration of Independence. We honor the day all through the daylight hours, and when night comes we dishonor it. Presently — before long — they are getting nearly ready to begin now—on the Atlantic coast, when night shuts down, that pandemonium will begin, and there will be noise, and noise, and noise—all night long—and there will be more than noise— there will be people crippled, there will be people killed, there will be people who will lose their eyes, and all through that permission which we give to irresponsible boys to play with firearms and fire-crackers, and all sorts of dangerous things. We turn that Fourth of July, alas! over to rowdies to drink and get drunk and make the night hideous, and we cripple and kill more people than you would imagine.

We probably began to celebrate our Fourth-of-July night in that way one hundred and twenty-five years ago, and on every Fourth-of-July night since these horrors have grown and grown, until now, in our five thousand towns of America, somebody gets killed or crippled on every Fourth-of-July night, besides those cases of sick persons whom we never hear of, who die as the result of the noise or the shock. They cripple and kill more people on the Fourth of July in America than they kill and cripple in our wars nowadays, and there are no pensions for these folk. And, too, we burn houses. Really we destroy more property on every Fourth-of-July night than the whole of the United States was worth one hundred and twenty-five years ago. Really our Fourth of July is our day of mourning, our day of sorrow. Fifty thousand people who have lost friends, or who have had friends crippled, receive that

INDEPENDENCE DAY

Fourth of July, when it comes, as a day of mourning for the losses they have sustained in their families.

I have suffered in that way myself. I have had relatives killed in that way. One was in Chicago years ago—an uncle of mine, just as good an uncle as I have ever had, and I had lots of them—yes, uncles to burn, uncles to spare. This poor uncle, full of patriotism, opened his mouth to hurrah, and a rocket went down his throat. Before that man could ask for a drink of water to quench that thing, it blew up and scattered him all over the forty-five States, and—really, now, this is true—I know about it myself—twenty-four hours after that it was raining buttons, recognizable as his, on the Atlantic seaboard. A person cannot have a disaster like that and be entirely cheerful the rest of his life. I had another uncle, on an entirely different Fourth of July, who was blown up that way, and really it trimmed him as it would a tree. He had hardly a limb left on him anywhere. All we have left now is an expurgated edition of that uncle. But never mind about these things; they are merely passing matters. Don't let me make you sad.

Sir Mortimer Durand said that you, the English people, gave up your colonies over there—got tired of them—and did it with reluctance. Now I wish you just to consider that he was right about that, and that he had his reasons for saying that England did not look upon our Revolution as a foreign war, but as a civil war fought by Englishmen.

Our Fourth of July which we honor so much, and which we love so much, and which we take so much pride in, is an English institution, not an American one, and it comes of a great ancestry. The first Fourth of July in that noble genealogy dates back seven centuries lacking eight years. That is the day of the Great Charter—the Magna Charta—which was born at Runnymede in the next to the last year of King John, and portions of the liberties secured thus by those hardy Barons from that reluctant King John are a part of our Declaration of Independence, of our Fourth of July, of our American liberties. And the second of those Fourths of July was not born until four centuries later, in Charles the First's time, in the Bill of Rights, and that is ours, that is part of our liberties. The next one was still English, in New England, where they established that principle which remains with us to this day, and will continue to remain with us—no taxation without representation. That is always going to stand, and that the English Colonies in New England gave us.

The Fourth of July, and the one which you are celebrating now, born in Philadelphia on the 4th of July, 1776—that is English, too. It is not American. Those were English colonists, sub-

410

jects of King George III., Englishmen at heart, who protested against the oppressions of the Home Government. Though they proposed to cure those oppressions and remove them, still remaining under the Crown, they were not intending a revolution. The revolution was brought about by circumstances which they could not control. The Declaration of Independence was written by a British subject, every name signed to it was the name of a British subject. There was not the name of a single American attached to the Declaration of Independence—in fact, there was not an American in the country in that day except the Indians out on the plains. They were Englishmen, all Englishmen—Americans did not begin until seven years later, when that Fourth of July had become seven years old, and then the American Republic was established. Since then there have been Americans. So you see what we owe to England in the matter of liberties.

We have, however, one Fourth of July which is absolutely our own, and that is that great proclamation issued forty years ago by that great American to whom Sir Mortimer Durand paid that just and beautiful tribute—Abraham Lincoln. Lincoln's proclamation, which not only set the black slaves free, but set the white man free also. The owner was set free from the burden and offence, that sad condition of things where he was in so many instances a master and owner of slaves when he did not want to be. That proclamation set them all free. But even in this matter England suggested it, for England had set her slaves free thirty years before, and we followed her example. We always followed her example, whether it was good or bad.

And it was an English judge that issued that other great proclamation, and established that great principle that, when a slave, let him belong to whom he may, and let him come whence he may, sets his foot upon English soil, his fetters by that act fall away and he is a free man before the world. We followed the example of 1833, and we freed our slaves as I have said.

It is true, then, that all our Fourths of July, and we have five of them, England gave to us, except that one that I have mentioned—the Emancipation Proclamation, and, lest we forget, let us all remember that we owe these things to England. Let us be able to say to Old England, this great-hearted, venerable old mother of the race, you gave us our Fourths of July that we love and that we honor and revere, you gave us the Declaration of Independence, which is the Charter of our rights, you, the venerable Mother of Liberties, the Protector of Anglo-Saxon Freedom—you gave us these things, and we do most honestly thank you for them.

AMERICANS AND THE ENGLISH

ADDRESS AT A GATHERING OF AMERICANS IN
LONDON, JULY 4, 1872

MR. CHAIRMAN AND LADIES AND GEN-
TLEMEN,—I thank you for the compliment
which has just been tendered me, and to show
my appreciation of it I will not afflict you with
many words. It is pleasant to celebrate in this
peaceful way, upon this old mother soil, the
anniversary of an experiment which was born of
war with this same land so long ago, and wrought
out to a successful issue by the devotion of our
ancestors. It has taken nearly a hundred years
to bring the English and Americans into kindly
and mutually appreciative relations, but I believe it has been accomplished at last. It was a
great step when the two last misunderstandings
were settled by arbitration instead of cannon.
It is another great step when England adopts
our sewing-machines without claiming the invention—as usual. It was another when they
imported one of our sleeping-cars the other day.
And it warmed my heart more than I can tell,

yesterday, when I witnessed the spectacle of an Englishman ordering an American sherry cobbler of his own free will and accord—and not only that but with a great brain and a level head reminding the barkeeper not to forget the strawberries. With a common origin, a common language, a common literature, a common religion, and—common drinks, what is longer needful to the cementing of the two nations together in a permanent bond of brotherhood?

This is an age of progress, and ours is a progressive land. A great and glorious land, too—a land which has developed a Washington, a Franklin, a Wm. M. Tweed, a Longfellow, a Motley, a Jay Gould, a Samuel C. Pomeroy, a recent Congress which has never had its equal (in some respects), and a United States Army which conquered sixty Indians in eight months by tiring them out—which is much better than uncivilized slaughter, God knows. We have a criminal jury system which is superior to any in the world; and its efficiency is only marred by the difficulty of finding twelve men every day who don't know anything and can't read. And I may observe that we have an insanity plea that would have saved Cain. I think I can say, and say with pride, that we have some legislatures that bring higher prices than any in the world.

I refer with effusion to our railway system, which consents to let us live, though it might do the opposite, being our owners. It only destroyed three thousand and seventy lives last year by collisions, and twenty-seven thousand two hundred and sixty by running over heedless and unnecessary people at crossings. The companies seriously regretted the killing of these thirty thousand people, and went so far as to pay for some of them—voluntarily, of course, for the meanest of us would not claim that we possess a court treacherous enough to enforce a law against a railway company. But, thank Heaven, the railway companies are generally disposed to do the right and kindly thing without compulsion. I know of an instance which greatly touched me at the time. After an accident the company sent home the remains of a dear distant old relative of mine in a basket, with the remark, "Please state what figure you hold him at—and return the basket." Now there couldn't be anything friendlier than that.

But I must not stand here and brag all night. However, you won't mind a body bragging a little about his country on the Fourth of July. It is a fair and legitimate time to fly the eagle. I will say only one more word of brag—and a hopeful one. It is this. We have a form of government which gives each man a fair chance and no favor. With us no individual is born with a right to look down upon his neighbor and hold him in contempt. Let such of us as are not dukes find

our consolation in that. And we may find hope
for the future in the fact that as unhappy as is
the condition of our political morality to-day,
England has risen up out of a far fouler since the
days when Charles I. ennobled courtesans and all
political place was a matter of bargain and sale.
There is hope for us yet.*

---

* At least the above is the speech which I was *going* to
make, but our minister, General Schenck, presided, and after
the blessing, got up and made a great, long, inconceivably dull
harangue, and wound up by saying that inasmuch as speech-
making did not seem to exhilarate the guests much, all
further oratory would be dispensed with during the evening,
and we could just sit and talk privately to our elbow-neighbors
and have a good, sociable time. It is known that in consequence of that remark forty-four perfected speeches died in
the womb. The depression, the gloom, the solemnity that
reigned over the banquet from that time forth will be a lasting memory with many that were there. By that one thought-
less remark General Schenck lost forty-four of the best
friends he had in England. More than one said that night:
"And this is the sort of person that is sent to represent us
in a great sister empire!"

ABOUT LONDON

Address at a Dinner Given by the Savage Club,
London, September 28, 1872.

Reported by Moncure D. Conway in the Cincinnati
Commercial.

IT affords me sincere pleasure to meet this distinguished club, a club which has extended its hospitalities and its cordial welcome to so many of my countrymen. I hope [and here the speaker's voice became low and fluttering] you will excuse these clothes. I am going to the theatre; that will explain these clothes. I have other clothes than these. Judging human nature by what I have seen of it, I suppose that the customary thing for a stranger to do when he stands here is to make a pun on the name of this club, under the impression, of course, that he is the first man that that idea has occurred to. It is a credit to our human nature, not a blemish upon it; for it shows that underlying all our depravity (and God knows and you know we are depraved enough) and all our sophistication, and untarnished by them, there is a sweet germ of innocence and simplicity still. When a stranger says to me, with a glow of inspiration in his eye, some gentle, innocuous little thing about "Twain and one flesh," and all that sort of thing, I don't try to crush that man into the earth—no. I feel like saying: "Let me take you by the hand, sir; let me embrace you; I have not heard that pun for weeks." We will deal in palpable puns. We will call parties named King "Your Majesty," and we will say to the Smiths that we think we have heard that name before somewhere. Such is human nature. We cannot alter this. It is God that made us so for some good and wise purpose. Let us not repine. But though I may seem strange, may seem eccentric, I mean to refrain from punning upon the name of this club, though I could make a very good one if *I* had time to think about it—a week.

I cannot express to you what entire enjoyment I find in this first visit to this prodigious metropolis of yours. Its wonders seem to me to be limitless. I go about as in a dream—as in a realm of enchantment—where many things are rare and beautiful, and all things are strange and marvellous. Hour after hour I stand — I stand spellbound, as it were—and gaze upon the statuary in Leicester Square. [Leicester Square being a horrible chaos, with the relic of an equestrian statue in the centre, the king being headless and limbless, and the horse in little better condition.]

418

I visit the mortuary effigies of noble old Henry
VIII., and Judge Jeffreys, and the preserved go-
rilla, and try to make up my mind which of my
ancestors I admire the most. I go to that matchless Hyde Park and drive all around it, and then
I start to enter it at the Marble Arch—and—am
induced to "change my mind." [Cabs are not permitted in Hyde Park — nothing less aristocratic
than a private carriage.] It is a great benefac-
tion—is Hyde Park. There, in his hansom cab,
the invalid can go — the poor, sad child of misfortune—and insert his nose between the railings,
and breathe the pure, health-giving air of the
country and of heaven. And if he is a swell invalid, who isn't obliged to depend upon parks for
his country air, he can drive inside—if he owns
his vehicle. I drive round and round Hyde Park,
and the more I see of the edges of it the more
grateful I am that the margin is extensive.

And I have been to the Zoological Gardens.
What a wonderul place that is! I never have
seen such a curious and interesting variety of wild
animals in any garden before—except "Mabille."
I never believed before there were so many different kinds of animals in the world as you can
find there — and I don't believe it yet. I have
been to the British Museum. I would advise
you to drop in there some time when you have
nothing to do for — five minutes — if you have
never been there. It seems to me the noblest

monument that this nation has yet erected to her greatness. I say to her, our greatness—as a nation. True, she has built other monuments, and stately ones, as well; but these she has uplifted in honor of two or three colossal demigods who have stalked across the world's stage, destroying tyrants and delivering nations, and whose prodigies will still live in the memories of men ages after their monuments shall have crumbled to dust—I refer to the Wellington and Nelson monuments, and—the Albert memorial. [Sarcasm. The Albert memorial is the finest monument in the world, and celebrates the existence of as commonplace a person as good luck ever lifted out of obscurity.]

The library at the British Museum I find particularly astounding. I have read there hours together, and hardly made an impression on it. I revere that library. It is the author's friend. I don't care how mean a book is, it always takes one copy. [A copy of every book printed in Great Britain must by law be sent to the British Museum, a law much complained of by publishers.] And then every day that author goes there to gaze at that book, and is encouraged to go on in the good work. And what a touching sight it is of a Saturday afternoon to see the poor, careworn clergymen gathered together in that vast reading - room cabbaging sermons for Sunday. You will pardon my referring to these things.

ABOUT LONDON

Everything in this monster city interests me, and I cannot keep from talking, even at the risk of being instructive. People here seem always to express distances by parables. To a stranger it is just a little confusing to be so parabolic — so to speak. I collar a citizen, and I think I am going to get some valuable information out of him. I ask him how far it is to Birmingham, and he says it is twenty-one shillings and six-pence. Now we know that doesn't help a man who is trying to learn. I find myself down-town somewhere, and I want to get some sort of idea where I am—being usually lost when alone—and I stop a citizen and say: "How far is it to Charing Cross?" "Shilling fare in a cab," and off he goes. I suppose if I were to ask a Londoner how far it is from the sublime to the ridiculous, he would try to express it in coin. But I am trespassing upon your time with these geological statistics and historical reflections. I will not longer keep you from your orgies. 'Tis a real pleasure for me to be here, and I thank you for it. The name of the Savage Club is associated in my mind with the kindly interest and the friendly offices which you lavished upon an old friend of mine who came among you a stranger, and you opened your English hearts to him and gave him welcome and a home—Artemus Ward. Asking that you will join me, I give you his memory.

28

PRINCETON

Mr. Clemens spent several days in May, 1901, in Princeton, New Jersey, as the guest of Lawrence Hutton. He gave a reading one evening before a large audience composed of university students and professors. Before the reading Mr. Clemens said:

I FEEL exceedingly surreptitious in coming down here without a1 announcement of any kind. I do not want to see any advertisements around, for the reason that I'm not a lecturer any longer. I reformed long ago, and I break over and commit this sin only just one time this year—and that is moderate, I think, for a person of my disposition. It is not my purpose to lecture any more as long as I live. I never intend to stand up on a platform any more—unless by the request of a sheriff or something like that.

THE ST. LOUIS HARBOR-BOAT
"MARK TWAIN"

The Countess de Rochambeau christened the St. Louis harbor-boat Mark Twain *in honor of Mr. Clemens, June 6, 1902. Just before the luncheon he acted as pilot.*

"Lower away lead!" boomed out the voice of the pilot.

"Mark twain, quarter five and one-half—six feet!" replied the leadsman below.

"You are all dead safe as long as I have the wheel— but this is my last time at the wheel."

At the luncheon Mr. Clemens made a short address.

FIRST of all, no—second of all—I wish to offer my thanks for the honor done me by naming this last rose of summer of the Mississippi Valley for me, this boat which represents a perished interest, which I fortified long ago, but did not save its life. And, in the first place, I wish to thank the Countess de Rochambeau for the honor she has done me in presiding at this christening.

I believe that it is peculiarly appropriate that I should be allowed the privilege of joining my voice with the general voice of St. Louis and Missouri in welcoming to the Mississippi Valley and this part of the continent these illustrious visitors from France.

When La Salle came down this river a century and a quarter ago there was nothing on its banks but savages. He opened up this great river, and by his simple act was gathered in this great Louisiana territory. I would have done it myself for half the money.

SEVENTIETH BIRTHDAY

Address at a Dinner Given by Colonel George
Harvey at Delmonico's, December 5, 1905,
to Celebrate the Seventieth Anniversary of Mr. Clemens' Birth

Mr. Howells introduced Mr. Clemens:

"Now, ladies and gentlemen, and Colonel Harvey, I
will try not to be greedy on your behalf in wishing the
health of our honored and, in view of his great age,
our revered guest. I will not say, 'Oh King, live
forever!' but 'Oh King, live as long as you like!'"
[Amid great applause and waving of napkins all rise
and drink to Mark Twain.]

WELL, if I made that joke, it is the best one
I ever made, and it is in the prettiest language, too. I never can get quite to that height.
But I appreciate that joke, and I shall remember
it—and I shall use it when occasion requires.

I have had a great many birthdays in my time.
I remember the first one very well, and I always
think of it with indignation; everything was so
crude, unæsthetic, primeval. Nothing like this at
all. No proper appreciative preparation made;
nothing really ready. Now, for a person born with

high and delicate instincts—why, even the cradle wasn't whitewashed—nothing ready at all. I hadn't any hair, I hadn't any teeth, I hadn't any clothes, I had to go to my first banquet just like that. Well, everybody came swarming in. It was the merest little bit of a village—hardly that, just a little hamlet, in the backwoods of Missouri, where nothing ever happened, and the people were all interested, and they all came; they looked me over to see if there was anything fresh in my line. Why, nothing ever happened in that village—I— why, I was the only thing that had really happened there for months and months and months; and although I say it myself that shouldn't, I came the nearest to being a real event that had happened in that village in more than two years. Well, those people came, they came with that curiosity which is so provincial, with that frankness which also is so provincial, and they examined me all around and gave their opinion. Nobody asked them, and I shouldn't have minded if anybody had paid me a compliment, but nobody did. Their opinions were all just green with prejudice, and I feel those opinions to this day. Well, I stood that as long as—well, you know I was born courteous, and I stood it to the limit. I stood it an hour, and then the worm turned. I was the worm; it was my turn to turn, and I turned. I knew very well the strength of my position; I knew that I was the only spotlessly pure and innocent person

in that whole town, and I came out and said so.
And they could not say a word. It was so true.
They blushed; they were embarrassed. Well, that
was the first after-dinner speech I ever made. I
think it was after dinner.

It's a long stretch between that first birthday
speech and this one. That was my cradle-song,
and this is my swan-song, I suppose. I am used
to swan-songs; I have sung them several times.

This is my seventieth birthday, and I wonder
if you all rise to the size of that proposition, realiz-
ing all the significance of that phrase, seventieth
birthday.

The seventieth birthday! It is the time of life
when you arrive at a new and awful dignity; when
you may throw aside the decent reserves which
have oppressed you for a generation and stand unafraid and unabashed upon your seven-terraced
summit and look down and teach—unrebuked.
You can tell the world how you got there. It is
what they all do. You shall never get tired of
telling by what delicate arts and deep moralities
you climbed up to that great place. You will explain the process and dwell on the particulars with
senile rapture. I have been anxious to explain
my own system this long time, and now at last I
have the right.

I have achieved my seventy years in the usual
way: by sticking strictly to a scheme of life which
would kill anybody else. It sounds like an exag-

geration, but that is really the common rule for attaining to old age. When we examine the programme of any of these garrulous old people we always find that the habits which have preserved them would have decayed us; that the way of life which enabled them to live upon the property of their heirs so long, as Mr. Choate says, would have put us out of commission ahead of time. I will offer here, as a sound maxim, this: That we can't reach old age by another man's road.

I will now teach, offering my way of life to whomsoever desires to commit suicide by the scheme which has enabled me to beat the doctor and the hangman for seventy years. Some of the details may sound untrue, but they are not. I am not here to deceive; I am here to teach.

We have no permanent habits until we are forty. Then they begin to harden, presently they petrify, then business begins. Since forty I have been regular about going to bed and getting up—and that is one of the main things. I have made it a rule to go to bed when there wasn't anybody left to sit up with; and I have made it a rule to get up when I had to. This has resulted in an unswerving regularity of irregularity. It has saved me sound, but it would injure another person.

In the matter of diet—which is another main thing—I have been persistently strict in sticking to the things which didn't agree with me until one or the other of us got the best of it. Until lately I got the best of it myself. But last spring I stopped frolicking with mince-pie after midnight; up to then I had always believed it wasn't loaded. For thirty years I have taken coffee and bread at eight in the morning, and no bite nor sup until seven-thirty in the evening. Eleven hours. That is all right for me, and is wholesome, because I have never had a headache in my life, but headachy people would not reach seventy comfortably by that road, and they would be foolish to try it. And I wish to urge upon you this—which I think is wisdom—that if you find you can't make seventy by any but an uncomfortable road, don't you go. When they take off the Pullman and retire you to the rancid smoker, put on your things, count your checks, and get out at the first way station where there's a cemetery.

I have made it a rule never to smoke more than one cigar at a time. I have no other restriction as regards smoking. I do not know just when I began to smoke, I only know that it was in my father's lifetime, and that I was discreet. He passed from this life early in 1847, when I was a shade past eleven; ever since then I have smoked publicly. As an example to others, and not that I care for moderation myself, it has always been my rule never to smoke when asleep, and never to refrain when awake. It is a good rule. I mean, for me; but some of you know quite well that it wouldn't answer for everybody that's trying to get to be seventy.

I smoke in bed until I have to go to sleep; I wake up in the night, sometimes once, sometimes twice, sometimes three times, and I never waste any of these opportunities to smoke. This habit is so old and dear and precious to me that I would feel as you, sir, would feel if you should lose the only moral you've got—meaning the chairman— if you've got one: I am making no charges. I will grant, here, that I have stopped smoking now and then, for a few months at a time, but it was not on principle, it was only to show off; it was to pulverize those critics who said I was a slave to my habits and couldn't break my bonds.

To-day it is all of sixty years since I began to smoke the limit. I have never bought cigars with life-belts around them. I early found that those were too expensive for me. I have always bought cheap cigars — reasonably cheap, at any rate. Sixty years ago they cost me four dollars a barrel, but my taste has improved, latterly, and I pay seven now. Six or seven. Seven, I think. Yes, it's seven. But that includes the barrel. I often have smoking-parties at my house; but the people that come have always just taken the pledge. I wonder why that is?

As for drinking, I have no rule about that. When the others drink I like to help; otherwise I remain dry, by habit and preference. This dryness does not hurt me, but it could easily hurt you, because you are different. You let it alone.

Since I was seven years old I have seldom taken a dose of medicine, and have still seldomer needed one. But up to seven I lived exclusively on allopathic medicines. Not that I needed them, for I don't think I did; it was for economy; my father took a drug-store for a debt, and it made cod-liver oil cheaper than the other breakfast foods. We had nine barrels of it, and it lasted me seven years. Then I was weaned. The rest of the family had to get along with rhubarb and ipecac and such things, because I was the pet. I was the first Standard Oil Trust. I had it all. By the time the drugstore was exhausted my health was established, and there has never been much the matter with me since. But you know very well it would be foolish for the average child to start for seventy on that basis. It happened to be just the thing for me, but that was merely an accident; it couldn't happen again in a century.

I have never taken any exercise, except sleeping and resting, and I never intend to take any. Exercise is loathsome. And it cannot be any benefit when you are tired; and I was always tired. But let another person try my way, and see where he will come out.

I desire now to repeat and emphasize that maxim: We can't reach old age by another man's

431

road. My habits protect my life, but they would assassinate you.

I have lived a severely moral life. But it would be a mistake for other people to try that, or for me to recommend it. Very few would succeed: you have to have a perfectly colossal stock of morals; and you can't get them on a margin; you have to have the whole thing, and put them in your box. Morals are an acquirement—like music, like a foreign language, like piety, poker, paralysis—no man is born with them. I wasn't myself, I started poor. I hadn't a single moral. There is hardly a man in this house that is poorer than I was then. Yes, I started like that—the world before me, not a moral in the slot. Not even an insurance moral. I can remember the first one I ever got. I can remember the landscape, the weather, the—I can remember how everything looked. It was an old moral, an old second-hand moral, all out of repair, and didn't fit, anyway. But if you are careful with a thing like that, and keep it in a dry place, and save it for processions, and Chautauquas, and World's Fairs, and so on, and disinfect it now and then, and give it a fresh coat of whitewash once in a while, you will be surprised to see how well she will last and how long she will keep sweet, or at least inoffensive. When I got that mouldy old moral, she had stopped growing, because she hadn't any exercise; but I worked her hard, I worked her Sundays and all. Under this cultivation she waxed in might and stature beyond belief, and served me well and was my pride and joy for sixty-three years; then she got to associating with insurance presidents, and lost flesh and character, and was a sorrow to look at and no longer competent for business. She was a great loss to me. Yet not all loss. I sold her—ah, pathetic skeleton, as she was—I sold her to Leopold, the pirate King of Belgium; he sold her to our Metropolitan Museum, and it was very glad to get her, for without a rag on, she stands 57 feet long and 16 feet high, and they think she's a brontosaur. Well, she looks it. They believe it will take nineteen geological periods to breed her match.

Morals are of inestimable value, for every man is born crammed with sin microbes, and the only thing that can extirpate these sin microbes is morals. Now you take a sterilized Christian—I mean, you take *the* sterilized Christian, for there's only one. Dear sir, I wish you wouldn't look at me like that.

Threescore years and ten!

It is the Scriptural statute of limitations. After that, you owe no active duties; for you the strenuous life is over. You are a time-expired man, to use Kipling's military phrase: You have served your term, well or less well, and you are mustered out. You are become an honorary member of the republic, you are emancipated, compulsions are not for you, nor any bugle-call but "lights out." You pay the time-worn duty bills if you choose, or decline if you prefer—and without prejudice—for they are not legally collectable.

The previous-engagement plea, which in forty years has cost you so many twinges, you can lay aside forever; on this side of the grave you will never need it again. If you shrink at thought of night, and winter, and the late home-coming from the banquet and the lights and the laughter through the deserted streets—a desolation which would not remind you now, as for a generation it did, that your friends are sleeping, and you must creep in a-tiptoe and not disturb them, but would only remind you that you need not tiptoe, you can never disturb them more—if you shrink at thought of these things, you need only reply, "Your invitation honors me, and pleases me because you still keep me in your remembrance, but I am seventy; seventy, and would nestle in the chimney-corner, and smoke my pipe, and read my book, and take my rest, wishing you well in all affection, and that when you in your return shall arrive at pier No. 70 you may step aboard your waiting ship with a reconciled spirit, and lay your course toward the sinking sun with a contented heart.

THE END

AFTERWORD

David Barrow

ublished in 1910, in the summer after Mark Twain's death, the first edition of his collected speeches exploited the immediate intensification of public interest in a departed national favorite. In some ways this eclectic compilation, spanning more than forty years, is an appropriate last word, for in its sheer variety it represents the decades-long phenomenon that was Mark Twain better than any single extended work could hope to do. It also sets in prominent place those contributions most likely to be nudged out of the popular memory of successive generations by his role as novelist and travel writer. The speeches highlight the Twain of the intimate banquet room, the charity event, the birthday celebration, and the local or national "occasion." Along with the hundreds of obituaries and personal tributes that flooded newspapers and magazines immediately after his death, *Mark Twain's Speeches* contributed to the consolidation of a public personality that overflowed the constraints of purely literary fame.

Mark Twain was throughout his professional life as much a speaker as a writer, and there was a synergy between these two careers that may account in part for the uniqueness of his written expressions. His episodic style, his eagerness to amuse as much as instruct, and his near perfect sense of timing owed much, no doubt, to the pleasure and discipline of performing live. Compared to the millions who had read something by Mark Twain by the time of his death, the many thousands who had heard him speak made up a select group, yet it is part of Mark Twain's legend that the voices of the man and his characters somehow emerged unmediated from his writings. When he died, many thought the voice of an old friend had been silenced.

The record shows that Twain, as a speaker, had indeed been a friend to many people. While the lectures he delivered on tour were moneymaking propositions, providing a substantial addition to his writing income over the course of his career, speeches such as the ones gathered here were part of the basic fabric of his public life. To be asked to speak at a banquet before a distinguished audience was an honor, not an offer of employment. Speaking before a clubroom full of congenial companions was a pleasure. Although he could not always accept invitations from every charitable organization, civic club, or political cause he was in sympathy with, Twain did consider it his duty to do so frequently. Sometimes his expenses were covered by a sponsor, but there is no evidence that he regularly accepted payment for these services. In his later years, Twain eschewed the practice of talking for money altogether, savoring both the freedom this gave him to speak his mind and the force of dignity it gave to his opinions. He could afford at that stage of his life, as few are able to do at any stage, to speak as one beyond the cares of money and reputation — to speak, as it were, as a kind of public friend.

No wonder, then, that many who had never heard a word directly from Mark Twain's mouth felt something personal in his passing. Reviews of *Mark Twain's Speeches*, following closely on the great tide of public mourning attending his death, often reflected this sense of personal loss. A reviewer for the *New York Times* took the occasion to sound one more elegiac note:

> It is the ludicrous, not the ridiculous, that he depicts nine times in ten. He laughs, and makes others laugh, with the victim of the moment, not at him, so that in a certain circle it was rather a privilege, a kind of honor, to be selected by him as the protagonist of one of his sparkling attacks. Now that he is dead and we shall never again hear that strange, penetrating, sympathetic voice or catch the confident gleams from beneath his bushy eyebrows, or share in the wild mirth he kindled in such varying company, it is good to have this record. To many it will be precious; to none, coming upon it anew, or coming back to it, will it bring pain.[1]

In other reviews, however, there is an air of calculated reserve, possibly intended to contrast with the outpouring of unqualified praise that had filled newspaper and magazine columns during the previous few months. Perhaps these reviews signal as well the first attempts to gain some critical distance on a figure who had played a dominant role on the public stage for nearly forty years. A reviewer for the *Independent*, who claimed to prefer the photograph of Twain on the frontispiece to anything else in the volume, ended his brief notice on this strident note: "It is a question whether he who delivered them [the speeches] would have favored their publication; or publishing, would have acted wisely."[2] H. B. Smith of the *Bookman* complained that "Mark Twain's curiously inconsecutive manner of expressing himself, a familiar and delightful quality in his humorous writings, goes so far in his speeches that some of them are unintelligible," and added that "some of the serious speeches are as dull and ponderous as any that could well be devised for occasions of public somnolence."[3] Other reviewers were not so critical, but seemed anxious nevertheless to commend the collection as something "to take up lightly in a leisure moment — not an hour — and as lightly to drop."[4] In this, however, they did nothing more than follow the lead of Twain's own preface, borrowed from the English edition of *Mark Twain's Sketches*, which warned the reader against overindulging in the verbal equivalent of candy.[5]

Another common theme was the reviewers' concern that the speeches, stripped of their original context and frozen in type, misrepresented Twain. The writer for the *New York Times* saw evidence in the printed speeches to support William Dean Howells' assertion in the introduction that Twain was a highly prepared rather than spontaneous speaker, but argued:

> To the *reader* [italics mine] the impression thus made is not wholly pleasant. There seems to be vital incongruity in a pre-digested and accurately compounded joke and still more in a series of jokes leading up to a climax. When the thing is heard and the speaker is seen it may come off supremely well. It certainly did in every case recalled by the present writer. . . .

Possibly it is the recollection of such talk that makes the collected speeches seem a little unfair to the author of them, causes them to fall short of the unique and telling effect of which he was known to be capable.[6]

Likewise, the writer for the *Dial* cautioned that a "quiet perusal [of the speeches] may not move the reader to praise them quite so highly as does Mr. Howells, who heard many of them at banquet or other festal occasion."[7]

Again, one wonders if the reviewers were not simply picking up cues that had been left for them. Mark Twain himself often complained about the violence print did to his spoken performances. To Edward Bok, who had sent him a copy of an interview for approval, Twain wrote, "the moment 'talk' is put into print you recognize that it is not what it was when you heard it; you perceive that an immense something has disappeared from it. That is its soul. You have nothing but a dead carcass left on your hands."[8] Twain's physical expression, timing, and inflection were frequently remarked upon by those who saw him speak, but as Fred Lorch observes in his book on Twain's lecture tours, "many newspaper reporters confessed in attempting to describe Mark Twain's platform manner [that] pen and ink were simply inadequate to the task. . . . It was as elusive to define as an aroma."[9] Today, perhaps only Hal Holbrook's masterful stage rendition of Twain affords us an adequate means of gauging the gulf between the Twain of the printed page and the Twain of the banquet hall or lyceum platform. Certainly anyone who has seen Holbrook perform will read the speeches in this book with an improved sense of their original impact.

And the fact remains that Twain's speeches not only come down to us now in the form of written artifacts, but that a great number of his contemporaries, as well, would have had access to them only in their printed form. As Louis Budd notes, "Twain's America could not pass for an oral, face-to-face community. Most of his audience engaged his presence through print or in even less direct ways."[10] Simple distinctions between oral and written performance thus become complicated when we approach the subject of Twain's speeches.

A reporter himself, Twain knew from the earliest phase of his career as a platform lecturer that the words he spoke in public were very likely to appear, even more publicly, in print. He openly resented the verbatim reporting of his paid lectures, which were more or less set pieces, for such accounts sometimes preceded him into towns where he was engaged to speak, stealing his thunder by undermining the spontaneous effect of his words. To the extent that a press report could affect the house receipts or cool his reviews by making him seem stale, Twain felt that his bread and butter was being tampered with by parasitic newspapermen.

Still, Twain generally enjoyed a congenial relationship with the popular press, one that worked to their mutual benefit. Certainly after the success of his first best-seller, *The Innocents Abroad* (1869), he would have come to understand that the toasts, tributes, and occasional pieces he was increasingly called on to deliver before select audiences would often find their way, in part or whole, into the next day's papers — most often to his personal advantage. Indeed, such accounts are the nearest to an original source we have for many of his speeches, and in his own day they provided him with valuable publicity. Thus, while Twain's speeches demanded tailoring to the needs of a specific audience on a specific occasion, he could not escape the fact that he also spoke to a print audience that was certainly larger and more heterogeneous than the one he faced in the flesh on a given afternoon or evening.

The intimacy, then, that played to his strengths as an actor was always something of an illusion, and one that might backfire unpredictably. Because speeches were delivered by invitation, they would have posed a special challenge to Twain's famously overworked conscience, for failure on such an occasion had ramifications for persons other than himself. The tastes of whoever had engaged Twain, and indirectly the tastes of the group itself, were expected to be vindicated by his performance. However, as a humorist and sometime social critic, he was also expected to deliver something more than the standard comforting confirmation of the group's identity, purposes, or aspirations. In short, he was often in the position of having to pull something off without pulling off too much. That he seldom failed is evidenced not only by his usually favorable reviews in the press and in the writings and correspondence of those who saw him speak, but also by the continuing demand for his services, which remained unabated almost until his death. As Budd observes of Twain's speechmaking talents, "Although the biographers' fancy for the colorful stresses his few blunders, he set a superstar's average for hitting his target, whether it was his listeners' sense of humor or their feelings."[11]

It is of note, therefore, that this volume opens with Twain's most famous "failure" as a speechmaker. The wide publicity given shortly after his death to the "Whittier Birthday Speech," then thirty-three years old, may in part be attributed to a desire to dramatize as turbulent an almost uniformly successful public career. The placement by Harper and Brothers of the Whittier speech in such a conspicuous spot coordinated conveniently with Howells' forthcoming account of the incident in the September issue of *Harper's* — part of the series of reminiscences that would become the book *My Mark Twain*, also published by Harper and Brothers in 1910. Twain's own account, reprinted here as "The Story of a Speech," had been published three years earlier in the *North American Review* in a series edited by Frederick A. Duneka, general manager and secretary of Harper and Brothers. Duneka had negotiated in 1903 to make the company the exclusive publisher of Twain's work, and the highlighting of the "Whittier Birthday Speech" may reflect his efforts to make the most of his author's reputation as an iconoclast. Twain developed a somewhat irrational distrust of and dislike for Duneka, but surely he would have managed a smile, one marketing man to another, at this attempt to locate the central drama of his public life in a single coolly received dinner speech.

The prominent positioning of the "Whittier Birthday Speech" may nevertheless be said to illuminate this volume's scholarly value as one of the few "new" primary Twain texts published between 1910 and 1937 that does not bear the editorial imprint or interpretive influence of Twain's protective official biographer and first literary executor, Albert Bigelow Paine. As James Cox has noted, the biographical portrait of Twain that Paine presented to the world "follows taste" and "seeks to mediate between the irreverent Western outlaw Mark Twain and the refined, sensitive Eastern Mark Twain; between the vernacular and treasonous Southern Mark Twain and the moral, loyal Northern Mark Twain."[12] Significantly, in a subsequent Harper's edition of Twain's speeches edited by Paine (1923), the Whittier episode would be moved from its tone-setting spot. Paine further manipulated the chronology of his edition so that an even more audacious speech, "The Babies," appeared to come before rather than after the Whittier debacle. The order suggests a Twain gradually coming into contrite conformity with genteel literary culture — the Twain that Paine cultivated assiduously until his death.

But "The Babies," delivered just two years after the Whittier speech, matched and even surpassed the impertinence of the earlier address. Its closing image of an infant Ulysses S. Grant attempting to put his toe in his mouth was a send-up of the former commander of the Union Army and past president of the United States, and Grant's administration had not been so exemplary as to render the image entirely toothless. Still, by all accounts, the speech was a great success that Grant appeared to enjoy as much as the rest of the guests. No doubt it helped that the toast was delivered at 3:30 a.m. to a group of probably well-lubricated army men. In any event, "The Babies" clearly achieved the edge-skirting success that the "Whittier Birthday Speech" had not.

Justin Kaplan, sensing a connection that Paine perhaps sought to obscure, claims that "The Babies" was for Twain a kind of cultural counterattack against the forces that had earlier rebuffed his lampoon of the Boston elites.

> . . . three or four hours after his performance, in long letters he was writing to Livy in Hartford and Orion in Keokuk, Clemens saw himself as the hero of the banquet, as if he had been borne aloft in triumph after a symbolic tournament in which he had vanquished Grant himself. By making this iron man laugh and cheer with all the others he had, in a sense, destroyed him. And in keeping with a speech which, until its very last sentence, had seemed headed toward catastrophic insult, the images that Clemens used to describe his triumph suggest that on this occasion, as well as on so many others, he thought of his humor as something violent and painful that he did to someone else. "I fetched him! I broke him up utterly!" he wrote to Livy. "The audience *saw* that for once in his life he had been knocked out of his iron serenity." "I knew I could lick him," he told Howells. "I shook him up like dynamite . . . my truths had wracked all the bones of his body apart."[13]

A month after giving "The Babies" speech, Twain did speak humbly and eloquently at a breakfast for Oliver Wendell Holmes ("Unconscious Plagiarism"), striking what for many seemed a final note of apology for his earlier offenses in the Whittier speech. But if it was an apology, it came only after Twain, to his own satisfaction, had publicly redeemed his nerve.

For those seeking to understand the culture in which Twain played such a prominent role, as well as the ways in which that culture shaped his public art, these rhetorical balancing acts represent an unusually valuable resource. Today, we often think of the rich and varied club life of Victorian England and America as a homogeneous mass of tailcoats and top hats, monied smugness and social exclusivity. Certainly Twain did speak more often *of* the working class than to them, and as his speeches honoring the likes of Andrew Carnegie and Henry Huttleston Rogers attest, he moved in the highest circles of Gilded Age power. Nevertheless, in many of the associations that called on Twain, particularly, perhaps, the English ones, there was a Bohemian element that provided some relief from the ubiquitous respectability of Victorian life. It might even be argued that Twain crossed the Atlantic so often in part to re-capture something of the unfettered camaraderie he had enjoyed in his early days as a journalist reporting on the silver frontier of the American West.

The Savage Club in London, for instance, as Paul Fatout notes, was "a co-terie of authors, actors, and bon vivants."[14] Twain appeared there for the first time in 1872, five years after the death of their first American darling, Artemus Ward (Charles Farrar Browne). Overseas, Twain seems to have stepped happily for the most part into Ward's shoes as the token Bohemian spirit of American culture. How far that spirit could go is suggested by a speech, unpublished until the 1950s, entitled "Some Thoughts on the Science of Onanism," which was delivered in Paris to an informal group of artists and writers called the Stomach Club.[15] Much racier than anything Twain deliv-ered for general public consumption, this disquisition on the merits and drawbacks of masturbation bespeaks the freewheeling atmosphere that per-vaded the drawing rooms of many of the "gentlemen's clubs" that Twain fre-quented overseas and highlights the masculine context of so much of Twain's speechmaking.

Paul Fatout observes of the banquets and club meetings Twain addressed that "women were such a rarity at these affairs that if any lady sat among the gentlemen, the papers reported the fact as news," and he further notes that Twain himself "believed that women at a dinner meant failure for a speaker because they were too timid to show their feelings, and their presence made the men timid, too."[16] As if to parry any charge that this exclusiveness was a result of misogyny or bawdy purpose, the etiquette of respectable all-male assemblages often demanded a paean "to woman" in the form of a toast. Two such toasts by Twain, "The Ladies" and "Woman — An Opinion," are included in this volume. Though Twain ends both on a sentimental note, invoking the sacred image of the wife or mother, it is difficult to say whether their generally satirical tone is typical of the genre. The text of "Woman — An Opinion" is particularly interesting for its equivocal references to Lucretia Borgia, the suffragists Lucy Stone and Elizabeth Cady Stanton, and the staunch defender of Women's rights George Francis Train, jokingly included as a woman. When Twain notes that he loves "all the women, irrespective of age or color," and praises woman because "she bears our children — ours as a general thing" (104), he belies, as he often does, the popular myth of his consistent sensitivity to racial and other social issues. Moreover, the sexual content of these words clearly plays at the edge of genteel propriety. Because he was speaking before the banquet of the Washington Correspondents' Club, it is unlikely Twain thought his remarks would not be reported. Indeed they were, two days later, in the *Washington Evening Star*.

"Woman — An Opinion," delivered in January of 1868, predates Twain's serious personal involvement with Olivia Langdon, and it can be instructively contrasted with "The Ladies," which was delivered some five years later (the text is misdated in this edition), after Twain had married and twice become a father. Still a parody of romantic hyperbole, the later speech nevertheless lacks the strong sexual innuendo of the earlier one. The reader may be tempted to trace in these differences the evolution of Twain's public persona from reckless bachelor with prairie dust on his shoes, striving for immediate effect at any price, to responsible insider who was still capable of winking at genteel conventions but had also come to understand his stake in them.

There is, no doubt, some truth in this reasoning, but a careful reading of the speeches shows that Twain continued to test the limits of propriety throughout his career. As late as 1907, he could remind an audience gathered in honor of and including Andrew Carnegie that "simplified spelling is all right, but, like chastity, you can carry it too far" (203).

Despite his reservations about female audiences, Twain regularly made himself available to charitable organizations, reform groups, professional associations, and public institutions that produced mixed or even predominantly female attendance. It is probably not coincidental that such occasions drew out the moralist in Twain, but if he adhered to some extent to the patronizing cultural convention of "instructing the young ladies," he seems at times also to have sensed the humorous potential of this pose and provided a self-effacing subtext. For example, lampooning habits which, save one, were notoriously his own, Twain in his last public speech adjures the girls in his audience not to smoke, drink, or marry — to excess (107).

Twain mildly but consistently supported women's suffrage, and sometimes showed frustration at the movement's repeated failures to gain the ballot for women. For example, "Votes for Women" contains an instructive anecdote illustrating the maxim that "time leads to crime" (102). It must nevertheless be conceded that women *in* Twain's speeches are sometimes the butt of homosocial jokes, or more often are idealized in the person of a Joan of Arc or an Eve as something more, and yet less, than human.

On other social issues, Twain was more aggressive. In his later years, he was an avowed anti-imperialist, and in the speech entitled "China and the Philippines" his introduction of a young Winston Churchill borders on a snub intended to demonstrate Twain's own disapproval of the Boer and Philippine wars. His attacks on the urban political machine in "Tammany and Croker" and "Municipal Corruption" ring with a sincere belief in his own independence from base political self-interest. However, it is easier to see from a distance that Twain was also a mouthpiece in such speeches for conservatives' fears of the urban masses. The effectiveness with which immigrants and the urban poor were organized by savvy ward bosses was cause for concern to many belonging to Twain's economic class, and it is fair to say that he himself had an anti-democratic streak that flared from time to time, if it never came to dominate his thinking completely. Unlike his friend Howells, Twain never plumbed too deeply the systemic economic ills that motivated solidarity and cronyism alike among the lower classes.

To his credit, however, like the anecdotal farmer in the "Public Education Association" speech, Twain favored schools over jails. Moreover, unlike many a politician of today, he did not confuse schools with ideological training camps. In "Education and Citizenship" he makes the distinction clear:

> I agreed when the Mayor said that there was not a man within hearing who did not agree that citizenship should be placed above everything else, even learning.
>
> Have you ever thought about this? Is there a college in the whole country where there is a chair of good citizenship? There is a kind of bad citizenship which is taught in the schools, but no real good citizenship is taught. There are some which teach insane citizenship, bastard citizenship, but that is all. Patriotism! Yes; but patriotism is usually the refuge of the scoundrel. He is the man who talks the loudest. (147)

Late in his life Twain's own education in citizenship had clearly moved beyond the orthodoxies of a nation he had chronicled better than any author before him, and in some respects even beyond the genteel liberalism of the well-to-do class he swam with in pleasant style. Twain's willingness in the above passage to play one piety off another perhaps comes close to revealing the inner workings of his social conscience, which remained active to the end of his life. The sacred might be indispensable to a culture's well being, but it was ever in need of critique and reexamination. By the time of Twain's death, the United States faced multiple threats to its founding ideals. Imperial ambitions abroad, as well as race and class divisions at home, insured that Twain's famous penchant for irreverence was seldom aimless, his pragmatic conscience seldom idle.

In recent years, the prejudice against topical materials as anything but an adjunct to the study of literature has been abandoned, and literature itself has come to be widely seen as that which evidences rather than transcends historically specific contexts. In the light of these changing attitudes, Twain's speeches will no doubt draw even greater scrutiny from cultural historians and critics. Ultimately, however, they may reveal nothing so clearly as that the search for an essential Twain, a Twain existing above or beyond the fray of a varied, shifting, and involutional public discourse, is illusory. As Twain himself remarked, "the fashion in literature changes, and the literary tailors have to change their cuts or go out of business" (194). Ironically, the secret to the lasting interest Twain's speeches have had for readers would seem to rest precisely in their modest claims on posterity. Brief, almost never entirely serious, and yet, as a body, revealing an unquestionably earnest engagement with and affection for a vibrant passage of human history, Mark Twain's speeches set a standard for involvement in one's own time.

NOTES

1. "Mark Twain, Orator," reviews of *Mark Twain's Speeches*, *New York Times* 6 August 1910: 434.

2. Review of *Mark Twain's Speeches*, *Independent* Summer 1, 1910: 484.

3. Review of *Mark Twain's Speeches*, *Bookman* Summer 1910: 78.

4. "Mark Twain, Orator," 434.

5. The reviewer for the London-based *Athenaeum* voiced a dissatisfaction over the editorial planning of the collection that today's reader may well share. He observes:

The discourses skip to and fro, from later years to earlier, and back, in an irritating fashion. On p. 31 Mark Twain replied to a neat speech by Mr. Birrel (June 25th, 1907); but for a reference to the same occasion on July 6th of the same year we have to wait till p. 388. On p. 386 we have a second speech at the Savage Club (1907), and have to wait for the earlier one of 1872 till p. 417. There is a good deal of repetition in various places; we do not think, for instance, that three versions of the stealing of a watermelon were worth giving.

To these complaints we might add that F. A. Nast, who compiled the volume for Harper and Brothers, failed to give any dates at all for some speeches and gave incorrect ones for others. Nast seems to have depended primarily on newspaper accounts for the texts, so most of the errors are probably a result of inaccuracies in the original reports. On occasion, it appears that Nast confused the date on which a speech was reported with the date on which it was given. Following is a list of speeches whose dates were either omitted or incorrectly recorded in the 1910 edition of *Mark Twain's Speeches*. The correct dates are provided from Paul Fatout's *Mark Twain Speaking* (Iowa City: U of Iowa P, 1976).

"Die Schrecken der Deutschen Sprache," October 31, 1897

"German for the Hungarians," March 23, 1899

"Unconscious Plagiarism," December 3, 1879 (it was a breakfast, not a dinner)

"The Weather," December 22, 1876

"The Babies," November 13, 1876

"Our Children and Great Discoveries," April 22, 1886

"Poets as Policemen," March 23, 1901

"The Dress of Civilized Woman," December 22, 1882

"Dress Reform and Copyright," December 7, 1906 (interview)

"Girls," February 10, 1887

"The Ladies," November 1873

"Woman — An Opinion," January 11, 1868

"Advice to Girls," June 9, 1909

"Tammany and Croker," October 17, 1901

"China and the Philippines," December 12, 1900

"Theoretical and Practical Morals," June 29, 1899

"The Dinner to Mr. Choate," November 16, 1901

"On Stanley and Livingstone," October 1872

"Henry M. Stanley," December 9, 1886

"Introducing Nye and Riley," February 28, 1889

"Reading-Room Opening," September 27, 1900

"Literature," May 2, 1900

"The New York Press Club Dinner," November 12, 1900

"Spelling and Pictures," September 19, 1906

"Authors' Club," June 12, 1899

"'Mark Twain's First Appearance,'" September 22, 1906

"Joan of Arc," December 21, 1905

"Accident Insurance — Etc." October 12, 1874

"Mistaken Identity," February 24, 1881

"Cats and Candy," early February, 1872 (an excerpt from a longer speech given at a dinner hosted by the *Aldine*, a typographical journal)

"Obituary Poetry," April 9, 1885

"Galveston Orphan Bazaar," October 17, 1900

"San Francisco Earthquake," April 19, 1906

"Copyright," December 7, 1906

"Dr. Mark Twain, Farmeopath," January 20, 1909

"To the Whitefriars," June 16, 1899

"The Ascot Gold Cup," June 29, 1907

"When in Doubt, Tell the Truth," March 8, 1906

"Americans and the English," July 4, 1873

"About London," September 22, 1872

6. "Mark Twain, Orator," 434.

7. "Mark Twain's Premeditated Impromptus," review of *Mark Twain's Speeches*, *Dial*, Summer 1, 1910: 117.

8. Edward Bok, *The Americanization of Edward Bok* (New York: Scribner's, 1922) 205–6.

9. Fred W. Lorch, *The Trouble Begins at Eight: Mark Twain's Lecture Tours* (Ames: Iowa State UP, 1968) 236.

10. Louis J. Budd, *Our Mark Twain: The Making of His Public Personality* (Philadelphia: U of Pennsylvania P, 1983) 22.

11. Budd, 57.

12. James M. Cox, introduction to *Mark Twain*, by Albert Bigelow Paine, 3 vols. (1912; New York: Chelsea House, 1980) 1:xxii.

13. Justin Kaplan, *Mr. Clemens and Mark Twain* (New York: Simon and Schuster, 1966) 227.

14. Fatout, 71.

15. For the full text of this speech, see Fatout, 125–27.

16. Fatout, xix.

David Barrow

There are several primary collections in addition to the Harper and Brothers 1910 edition of *Mark Twain's Speeches*, among them the revised Harper's edition edited by Albert Bigelow Paine, also titled *Mark Twain's Speeches* (New York, 1923), which overlaps with but does not entirely supersede the 1910 edition. The first edition contains thirty-five speeches not reprinted in the Paine edition, and the Paine edition includes nineteen new selections, as well as Paine's interesting introduction. *Mark Twain Speaking* (Iowa City: U of Iowa P, 1976), edited by Paul Fatout, is the most comprehensive collection of Mark Twain's speeches and lectures and remains the standard scholarly resource. Fatout provides brief but extremely useful introductory paragraphs for most of the speeches and lectures, as well as textual and informational notes that are indispensable to the study of Mark Twain as public performer and speaker. A good selection of speeches has been reprinted in the Library of America's *Mark Twain: Collected Tales, Sketches, Speeches, & Essays* (New York: 1922), edited by Louis J. Budd. The texts of the speeches are usually drawn from Fatout, but Budd's notes in this two-volume work are copious and ought to be consulted by any serious researcher. While no complete texts are found in Robert L. Gale's *Plots and Characters in the Works of Mark Twain* (Hamden, Conn.: Archon Books, 1973), useful synopses of many of the speeches are included.

Despite its faults, Albert Bigelow Paine's three-volume authorized biography of Mark Twain (New York: Harper, 1912) remains essential reading. Justin Kaplan's *Mr. Clemens and Mark Twain* (New York: Simon and Schuster, 1966) provides a supplement and partial corrective to Paine, and it stands on its own as one of the great works of American biography. Unsurpassed as examinations of the political and social contexts that shaped Twain's writings are Louis J. Budd's *Mark Twain: Social Philosopher* (Bloomington: Indiana UP, 1962) and *Our Mark Twain: The Making of His Public Personality* (Philadelphia: U of Pennsylvania P, 1983). Elsewhere, Budd has insightfully suggested that Twain's ability to finesse the fading distinctions between one mode of communication and another, specifically between the spoken and the printed, has a special significance for our own historical moment, in which the meaning of "print" itself has been stretched to the limits by new technologies; see Louis J. Budd, "A 'Talent for Posturing': The Achievement of Mark Twain's Public Personality," in *The Mythologizing of Mark Twain*, ed. Sara deSaussure Davis and Philip D. Beidler (Tuscaloosa: U of Alabama P, 1984) 77–98. *The Mark Twain Encyclopedia* (New York: Garland, 1993), edited by J. R. LeMaster and James D. Wilson, provides an amazing array of information on every aspect of Twain's life and career. Readers will find it an extremely useful guide to personalities, issues, and events alluded to in the speeches.

The first standard-setting model for analysis of a single Twain speech is unquestionably Henry Nash Smith's "'That Hideous Mistake of Poor Clemens's,'" *Harvard Library Bulletin* 9.2 (Spring 1955): 145–80. Smith offers a rhetorical dissection of the "Whittier Birthday Speech" based on an in-depth analysis of its reception. Other recent essays dealing with the importance of individual speeches include David Barrow's "The Bound Apprentice," *Mark Twain Journal* 21.1 (1991): 13–21, which reads the "The Old-Fashioned Printer" against an undelivered speech also written for the occasion of the annual Typothetae dinner, and a chapter from Susan Gillman's *Dark Twins: Imposture and Identity in Mark Twain's America* (Chicago: U of Chicago P, 1989), 181–88, that analyzes Twain's impromptu address to the Washington press, later titled "Dress Reform and Copyright."

Materials dealing not only with Twain's speeches but with all aspects of his speaking career, including his lecture tours, are well recorded in a recent and excellent bibliographic essay that concludes Marlen Boyd Vallin's *Mark Twain: Protagonist for the Popular Culture* (Westport, Conn.: Greenwood Press, 1992). Those seeking a more comprehensive bibliography than that included here should consult Vallin.

A NOTE ON THE TEXT

Robert H. Hirst

This text of *Mark Twain's Speeches, with an Introduction by William Dean Howells* is a photographic facsimile of a copy of the first American edition, all known copies of which are dated 1910 on the title page (*BAL* 3513). The first edition was published posthumously, on June 22, 1910. The original volume reproduced here is in the collection of the Mark Twain House in Hartford, Connecticut (810/C625sp/1910/c. 3).

THE MARK TWAIN HOUSE

The Mark Twain House is a museum and research center dedicated to the study of Mark Twain, his works, and his times. The museum is located in the nineteen-room mansion in Hartford, Connecticut, built for and lived in by Samuel L. Clemens, his wife, and their three children, from 1874 to 1891. The Picturesque Gothic-style residence, with interior design by the firm of Louis Comfort Tiffany and Associated Artists, is one of the premier examples of domestic Victorian architecture in America. Clemens wrote *Adventures of Huckleberry Finn*, *The Adventures of Tom Sawyer*, *A Connecticut Yankee in King Arthur's Court*, *The Prince and the Pauper*, and *Life on the Mississippi* while living in Hartford.

The Mark Twain House is open year-round. In addition to tours of the house, the educational programs of the Mark Twain House include symposia, lectures, and teacher training seminars that focus on the contemporary relevance of Twain's legacy. Past programs have featured discussions of literary censorship with playwright Arthur Miller and writer William Styron; of the power of language with journalist Clarence Page, comedian Dick Gregory, and writer Gloria Naylor; and of the challenges of teaching *Adventures of Huckleberry Finn* amidst charges of racism.

CONTRIBUTORS

David Barrow is assistant professor of English at Northern Illinois University in De Kalb, where he teaches nineteenth-century American literature and critical theory. He received his Ph.D. from Duke University. His publications on Mark Twain include the essays "Ben Coon," "Orality," and "Lecturer" in *The Mark Twain Encyclopedia* (1993); "The Ending of Huckleberry Finn: Mark Twain's Cryptic Lament," in *CCTE Studies* 51 (1986); "The Bound Apprentice," in the *Mark Twain Journal* 29 (1991); and a review of *Mark Twain's Letters, Volume 2* for *Nineteenth Century Prose* 19 (1992). His book *Refigurin' the Vernacular: Mark Twain and the Rhetorics of Print Culture* is under contract with the University of Massachusetts Press.

Shelley Fisher Fishkin, professor of American Studies and English at the University of Texas at Austin, is the author of the award-winning books *Was Huck Black? Mark Twain and African-American Voices* (1993) and *From Fact to Fiction: Journalism and Imaginative Writing in America* (1985). Her most recent book is *Lighting Out for the Territory: Reflections on Mark Twain and American Culture* (1996). She holds a Ph.D. in American Studies from Yale University, has lectured on Mark Twain in Belgium, England, France, Israel, Italy, Mexico, the Netherlands, and Turkey, as well as throughout the United States, and is president-elect of the Mark Twain Circle of America.

Robert H. Hirst is the General Editor of the Mark Twain Project at The Bancroft Library, University of California at Berkeley. Apart from that, he has no other known eccentricities.

As a young actor, *Hal Holbrook* stunned Broadway theatergoers in 1959 with his solo portrayal of Mark Twain at seventy, garnering "the best reviews since *My Fair Lady*," according to the *New York Tribune*, and winning a Tony Award and a special Drama Critics' Circle Award. He has been developing his Twain material ever since, and has continued to perform

Mark Twain Tonight! in America as well as abroad. He also has had a notable career as an actor in motion pictures, including such films as *Magnum Force*, *All the President's Men*, and *The Firm*; in television, receiving five Emmy Awards; and on the stage, in such productions as *The Glass Menagerie*, *Man of La Mancha*, and *King Lear*. He has just completed a national tour as Willy Loman in *Death of a Salesman*. *Mark Twain Tonight!* was published in book form in 1959.

ACKNOWLEDGMENTS

There are a number of people without whom The Oxford Mark Twain would not have happened. I am indebted to Laura Brown, senior vice president and trade publisher, Oxford University Press, for suggesting that I edit an "Oxford Mark Twain," and for being so enthusiastic when I proposed that it take the present form. Her guidance and vision have informed the entire undertaking.

Crucial as well, from the earliest to the final stages, was the help of John Boyer, executive director of the Mark Twain House, who recognized the importance of the project and gave it his wholehearted support.

My father, Milton Fisher, believed in this project from the start and helped nurture it every step of the way, as did my stepmother, Carol Plaine Fisher. Their encouragement and support made it all possible. The memory of my mother, Renée B. Fisher, sustained me throughout.

I am enormously grateful to all the contributors to The Oxford Mark Twain for the effort they put into their essays, and for having been such fine, collegial collaborators. Each came through, just as I'd hoped, with fresh insights and lively prose. It was a privilege and a pleasure to work with them, and I value the friendships that we forged in the process.

In addition to writing his fine afterword, Louis J. Budd provided invaluable advice and support, even going so far as to read each of the essays for accuracy. All of us involved in this project are greatly in his debt. Both his knowledge of Mark Twain's work and his generosity as a colleague are legendary and unsurpassed.

Elizabeth Maguire's commitment to The Oxford Mark Twain during her time as senior editor at Oxford was exemplary. When the project proved to be more ambitious and complicated than any of us had expected, Liz helped make it not only manageable, but fun. Assistant editor Elda Rotor's wonderful help in coordinating all aspects of The Oxford Mark Twain, along with literature editor T. Susan Chang's enthusiastic involvement with the project in its final stages, helped bring it all to fruition.

I am extremely grateful to Joy Johannessen for her astute and sensitive copyediting, and for having been such a pleasure to work with. And I appreciate the conscientiousness and good humor with which Kathy Kuhtz Campbell heroically supervised all aspects of the set's production. Oxford president Edward Barry, vice president and editorial director Helen McInnis, marketing director Amy Roberts, publicity director Susan Rotermund, art director David Tran, trade editorial, design and production manager Adam Bohannon, trade advertising and promotion manager Woody Gilmartin, director of manufacturing Benjamin Lee, and the entire staff at Oxford were as supportive a team as any editor could desire.

The staff of the Mark Twain House provided superb assistance as well. I would like to thank Marianne Curling, curator, Debra Petke, education director, Beverly Zell, curator of photography, Britt Gustafson, assistant director of education, Beth Ann McPherson, assistant curator, and Pam Collins, administrative assistant, for all their generous help, and for allowing us to reproduce books and photographs from the Mark Twain House collection. One could not ask for more congenial or helpful partners in publishing.

G. Thomas Tanselle, vice president of the John Simon Guggenheim Memorial Foundation, and an expert on the history of the book, offered essential advice about how to create as responsible a facsimile edition as possible. I appreciate his very knowledgeable counsel.

I am deeply indebted to Robert H. Hirst, general editor of the Mark Twain Project at The Bancroft Library in Berkeley, for bringing his outstanding knowledge of Twain editions to bear on the selection of the books photographed for the facsimiles, for giving generous assistance all along the way, and for providing his meticulous notes on the text. The set is the richer for his advice. I would also like to express my gratitude to the Mark Twain Project, not only for making texts and photographs from their collection available to us, but also for nurturing Mark Twain studies with a steady infusion of matchless, important publications.

I would like to thank Jeffrey Kaimowitz, curator of the Watkinson Library at Trinity College, Hartford (where the Mark Twain House collection is kept), along with his colleagues Peter Knapp and Alesandra M. Schmidt, for having been instrumental in Robert Hirst's search for first editions that could be safely reproduced. Victor Fischer, Harriet Elinor Smith, and especially Kenneth M. Sanderson, associate editors with the Mark Twain Project, reviewed the note on the text in each volume with cheerful vigilance. Thanks are also due to Mark Twain Project associate editor Michael Frank and administrative assistant Brenda J. Bailey for their help at various stages.

I am grateful to Helen K. Copley for granting permission to publish photographs in the Mark Twain Collection of the James S. Copley Library in La Jolla, California, and to Carol Beales and Ron Vanderhye of the Copley Library for making my research trip to their institution so productive and enjoyable.

Several contributors — David Bradley, Louis J. Budd, Beverly R. David, Robert Hirst, Fred Kaplan, James S. Leonard, Toni Morrison, Lillian S. Robinson, Jeffrey Rubin-Dorsky, Ray Sapirstein, and David L. Smith — were particularly helpful in the early stages of the project, brainstorming about the cast of writers and scholars who could make it work. Others who participated in that process were John Boyer, James Cox, Robert Crunden, Joel Dinerstein, William Goetzmann, Calvin and Maria Johnson, Jim Magnuson, Arnold Rampersad, Siva Vaidhyanathan, Steve and Louise Weinberg, and Richard Yarborough.

Kevin Bochynski, famous among Twain scholars as an "angel" who is gifted at finding methods of making their research run more smoothly, was helpful in more ways than I can count. He did an outstanding job in his official capacity as production consultant to The Oxford Mark Twain, supervising the photography of the facsimiles. I am also grateful to him for having put me in touch via e-mail with Kent Rasmussen, author of the magisterial *Mark Twain A to Z*, who was tremendously helpful as the project proceeded, sharing insights on obscure illustrators and other points, and generously being "on call" for all sorts of unforeseen contingencies.

I am indebted to Siva Vaidhyanathan of the American Studies Program of the University of Texas at Austin for having been such a superb research assistant. It would be hard to imagine The Oxford Mark Twain without the benefit of his insights and energy. A fine scholar and writer in his own right, he was crucial to making this project happen.

Georgia Barnhill, the Andrew W. Mellon Curator of Graphic Arts at the American Antiquarian Society in Worcester, Massachusetts, Tom Staley, director of the Harry Ransom Humanities Research Center at the University of Texas at Austin, and Joan Grant, director of collection services at the Elmer Holmes Bobst Library of New York University, granted us access to their collections and assisted us in the reproduction of several volumes of The Oxford Mark Twain. I would also like to thank Kenneth Craven, Sally Leach, and Richard Oram of the Harry Ransom Humanities Research Center for their help in making HRC materials available, and Jay and John Crowley, of Jay's Publishers Services in Rockland, Massachusetts, for their efforts to photograph the books carefully and attentively.

I would like to express my gratitude for the grant I was awarded by the University Research Institute of the University of Texas at Austin to defray some of the costs of researching The Oxford Mark Twain. I am also grateful to American Studies director Robert Abzug and the University of Texas for the computer that facilitated my work on this project (and to UT systems analyst Steve Alemán, who tried his best to repair the damage when it crashed). Thanks also to American Studies administrative assistant Janice Bradley and graduate coordinator Melanie Livingston for their always generous and thoughtful help.

The Oxford Mark Twain would not have happened without the unstinting, wholehearted support of my husband, Jim Fishkin, who went way beyond the proverbial call of duty more times than I'm sure he cares to remember as he shared me unselfishly with that other man in my life, Mark Twain. I am also grateful to my family — to my sons Joey and Bobby, who cheered me on all along the way, as did Fannie Fishkin, David Fishkin, Gennie Gordon, Mildred Hope Witkin, and Leonard, Gillis, and Moss

Plaine — and to honorary family member Margaret Osborne, who did the same.

My greatest debt is to the man who set all this in motion. Only a figure as rich and complicated as Mark Twain could have sustained such energy and interest on the part of so many people for so long. Never boring, never dull, Mark Twain repays our attention again and again and again. It is a privilege to be able to honor his memory with The Oxford Mark Twain.

Shelley Fisher Fishkin
Austin, Texas
April 1996